THOMAS HORN

WITH CONTRIBUTORS

Lt. Col. Robert Maginnis, Carl Gallups, Derek Gilbert, Althia Anderson, Gary Stearman

SABOTEURS

FROM SHOCKING WIKILEAKS REVELATIONS ABOUT SATANISM IN THE US CAPITOL
TO THE CONNECTION BETWEEN WITCHCRAFT, THE BABYLON WORKING,
SPIRIT COOKING, AND THE FOURTH TURNING GREY CHAMPION. HOW SECRET, DEEP STATE
OCCULTISTS ARE MANIPULATING AMERICAN SOCIETY THROUGH A WASHINGTON-BASED

SHADOW GOVERNMENT

IN QUEST OF THE FINAL WORLD ORDER

DEFENDER

CRANE, MO

SABOTEURS: From Shocking WikiLeaks Revelations About Satanism in the US Capitol to the Connection Between Witchcraft, the Babalon Working, Spirit Cooking, and the Fourth Turning Grey Champion. How Secret, Deep State Occultists Are Manipulating American Society Through a Washington-Based Shadow Government in Quest of the Final World Order

Defender Crane, MO 65633 ©2017 by Thomas Horn.

ISBN: 9780999189429

A CIP catalog record of this book is available from the Library of Congress.

Cover illustration and design by Jeffrey Mardis.

All Scripture quotations from the King James Version; in cases of academic comparison, those instances are noted.

Introduction

By Sharon Gilbert

Lest we forget at least an over the shoulder acknowledgment to the very first radical: from all our legends, mythology and history (and who is to know where mythology leaves off and history begins—or which is which), the very first radical known to man who rebelled against the establishment and did it so effectively that he at least won his own kingdom—Lucifer.
> —SAUL ALINSKY, *Rules for Radicals,*
> *A Practical Primer for Realistic Radicals* (1971)[1]

Sabotage is a form of warfare. Plain and simple. Emerging in the late nineteenth century from within rising unionist organizations, workers were encouraged to force employers to yield to union demands by any means possible. One of the most famous of these early progressives was a man named William Dudley Haywood, a socialist who found the Industrial Workers of the World. The IWW served as a military arm of this new movement, complete with battle plans and political ideals:

> You ask me why the IWW is not patriotic to the United States. If you were a bum without a blanket; if you had left your wife and kids when you went west for a job, and had never located them since; if your job had never kept you long enough in a

place to qualify to vote; if you slept in a lousy, sour bunkhouse, and ate food just as rotten as they could give you and get by with it; if deputy sheriffs shot your cooking cans full of holes and spilled your grub on the ground; if your wages were lowered on you when the bosses thought they had you down…if every person who represented law and order and the nation beat you up, railroaded you to jail, and the good Christian people cheered and told them to go to it, how in hell do you expect a man to be patriotic? This war is a businessman's war and we don't see why we should go out and get shot in order to save the lovely state of affairs that we now enjoy.

—WILLIAM DUDLEY "Big Bill" Haywood,
on IWW neutrality and opposition to World War I

It's obvious from the above quote that Haywood had little good to say about Christians. In fact, he's quoted as saying, "To me [Christianity] was all nonsense based on that profane compilation of fables called the Bible."

Anarchists of the late nineteenth and early twentieth centuries spun rhetorical straw into gleaming, political gold, laying the foundation for the Progressive Party (called Democrats) that we know today. It is an *ordo ab chao* mandate for these saboteurs. Chop down the current world forest of religion, freedom, individual rights, and entrepreneur spirit—and replace it with a rising tower of rotted wood, where all sense of self disappears into the collective mind. It is an exercise in futility, but one that captures the imaginations of many through the promise of Robin Hood: Steal from the rich and give to the poor, a maxim that sounds good on the surface, but which inevitably undermines the pillars of civilization.

Since the election of Donald Trump, these worker bee, unionist saboteurs have sawn and nibbled at the roots of our beautiful forest. Like the "little foxes" of the Song of Solomon, they sneak into our vineyard under cover of darkness and chew upon the life-giving roots, causing the fruit to wither and the leaves to fall.

As Christians, we are called upon to stand against such attacks—to confront the enemy upon the battlefield, clad in armor provided by Christ's redemptive blood and the Holy Spirit. It is a defensive posture, and we are commanded by Paul to stand, again and again and again. The saboteurs, those little foxes, would have us sleeping upon this field of battle, wearing only our socks and a cell phone. The socks are to keep us unaware of our naked, bleeding feet, and the cellphone is to keep us occupied and selfie-obsessed—and *programmed.*

Alinsky and Haywood and all the radical anarchists of this world revel in our naivety, our gullibility to their wiles. They use our own foolishness against us, but transient pleasures inevitably bring endless pain. Even music is a mountain upon which these saboteurs stand, and it's been used—along with all other brands of entertainment (and *infotainment*—one includes many current "mainstream media" outlets in this ever-expanding basket)—to trick us into looking the other way.

There's a popular song, released the very same year that Saul Alinsky published the book that would become the handbook for the forty-fourth presidential administration, *Rules for Radicals*; and the inspired lyrics reveal just what damage the "little foxes" let loose by Haywood and company (along with all their spiritual underwriters) have perpetrated through their anarchy. The song premiered on Don McLean's remarkable freshman album of the same name, *American Pie*.

This may well be the epitaph of America and the Christian church.

> Oh and while the **king** was looking down
> The jester stole his **thorny crown**
> [the crown of thorns worn by Christ]
> The courtroom was adjourned
> No verdict was returned

So come on Jack be nimble, Jack be quick
Jack Flash sat on a candlestick
    [Mick Jagger portrayed himself "Jumpin Jack Flash," but also as "the Devil"]
'Cause fire is **the devil's** only friend

Oh and as I watched him on the stage
My hands were clenched in fists of rage
No angel born in Hell
Could break that Satan's spell
    [nor would these fallen angels want to break it; Christians have been lulled into a complacent slumber by their hellish "music"]

And as the flames climbed high into the night
To **light the sacrificial rite**
I saw **Satan laughing with delight**
The day the music died

And in the streets **the children screamed**
    [our children and grandchildren]
The **lovers cried, and the poets dreamed**
    [lovers should be happy, and poets should write not only dream—a dreaming mind indicates one of inaction]
But **not a word was spoken**
    [Christians must speak up!]
The **church bells all were broken**
    [they summon no one to prayer or to worship; they have been silenced]

And the three men I admire most
The **Father, Son, and the Holy Ghost**

[the Christian church is departing for parts unknown—
unless we put down our cell phones and "suit up," according to
Ephesians 6]
They caught the last train for the coast
The day the music died.
                    —DON MCLEAN, *American Pie*[2] (emphasis added)

While this song was ostensibly written as an homage to Buddy
Holly and the Big Bopper, the language instilled within it by McLean is
much broader in scope. He refers to the Beatles in one stanza, mentioning "Helter Skelter in the summer swelter," and later says, "the sergeants
played a marching tune." These, respectively, are references to a song
on the Beatles' *White Album* ("Helter Skelter," which inspired Charles
Manson, another anarchist, who believed a race war would erupt in the
US within his lifetime), and the *Sergeant Pepper* album, which featured
Aleister Crowley, Carl Jung, Aldous Huxley, and Karl Marx, among
many other influential artists and politicians, on the cover.

Men like Haywood and Alinsky want us to yield the battlefield to
them. In fact, they want us to join them! Here's one of Saul Alinsky's
primary rules:

> The fourth rule is: "Make the enemy live up to their own book of
> rules." You can kill them with this, for they can no more obey their
> own rules than the Christian church can live up to Christianity.[3]

Get that last part? The saboteurs assume, going in, that you and I
are going to sit on our hands. We'll just roll over, pull up our little socks,
and keep on taking selfies.

No longer.

Our world reels with madness most days, bouncing precariously
upon the slender thread contained within a web of lies, but there is
hope. The Christian church must stop looking the other way. We must

refuse to let the "marching band" take the field and pipe their soothing music into our psyches. This book is step one. We'll reveal the identities of the saboteurs. Unmask the little foxes, both human and nonhuman. And we'll reveal the secretive puppetmasters who twirl us about like a marionette.

It's time to cut the strings and start sabotaging the saboteurs.

Beginning now.

chapter one

Meet the Saboteurs

Some of the biggest men in the United States, in the field of commerce and manufacture, are afraid of something. They know that there is a power somewhere so organized, so subtle, so watchful, so interlocked, so complete, so pervasive, that they had better not speak above their breath when they speak in condemnation of it.

—WOODROW WILSON

The real rulers in Washington are invisible and exercise power from behind the scenes.

—US SUPREME COURT JUSTICE FELIX FRANKFURTER

On January 20, 2017, with four of his predecessors listening—George H. W. Bush, Bill Clinton, George W. Bush, and Barack Obama—newly elected US President Donald J. Trump spoke straightforwardly to establishment, bureaucratic, deep state, shadow-government elites in a way nobody had seen or heard before. He made it clear that his agenda had not ended on the campaign trail and that he had gathered on the West front of the Capitol to announce more than the orderly and peaceful transition of power from the Obama administration to his.

"Today's ceremony," he began, "has very special meaning. Because today we are not merely transferring power from one administration to another, or from one party to another—but we are transferring power from Washington, D.C., and giving it back to you, the American people."

Then, with former presidents squirming in their seats, wishing they could be somewhere else, he offered no quarter:

For too long, a small group in our nation's Capital has reaped the rewards of government while the people have borne the cost.

Washington flourished—but the people did not share in its wealth.

Politicians prospered—but the jobs left, and the factories closed.

The establishment protected itself, but not the citizens of our country.

Their victories have not been your victories; their triumphs have not been your triumphs; and while they celebrated in our nation's Capital, there was little to celebrate for struggling families all across our land.

That all changes—starting right here, and right now, because this moment is your moment: it belongs to you.

It belongs to everyone gathered here today and everyone watching all across America.

This is your day. This is your celebration.

And this, the United States of America, is your country.

With that, knowingly or unknowing, Donald J. Trump declared war against very powerful enemies, both ancient and contemporary, both visible and invisible.

To the illumined elite, this inaugural address was a clear salvo that promptly drew a line in the sand.

To a handful of historians and scholars, "the Donald" would soon learn a lesson—pulling the drain plug from the swamp in Washington was going to be much easier said than done.

This is because winning a presidential election has very little to do with how modern Washington's establishment functions.

Every four years, voters choose to elect or reelect a president, who then selects a cabinet and other federal appointees to oversee executive departments such as the Secretaries of Agriculture, Commerce, Defense, Education, Energy, Health and Human Services, Homeland Security, and so on. But "the real government of the United States is not the Congress, not the president, not the courts, not the Constitution, but the federal bureaucracy."[4] This is what some have called the "fourth branch of government," and it daily influences the constitutional three branches of government most voters perceive as functioning to serve we the people (legislative, executive, and judicial).

This bureaucracy, which is immersed in liberal DC culture and ideology, globalist objectives (which view US borders as nationalistic impediments), multinational corporate payouts, and social democracy goals, is monstrous. It is made up of roughly 2.6 million employees, career government personnel, many freelance contractors, the press (an analogy for the Fourth Estate), and special interest groups that increasingly perceive America's Judeo-Christian morality, historical emphasis on rugged individualism, and free-market capitalism as enemies of a socialistic New World Order they aspire to embrace.

Since this ever-growing behemoth called "bureaucracy" was never authorized by the US Constitution in the first place, it represents an unelected force that, for the time being, cannot be unelected and that is free from the rubric of constitutional confines. Every day, this intrinsically and extrinsically connected machine—as part of "the deep state" that includes some, but not all, in intelligence agencies, armed forces, administrative agencies, entrenched unelected career civil servants, and so on—coordinates efforts via its interconnected relationship with international business interests, defense contractors, lobbyists, and "fake news" media conglomerates to peddle unparalleled and tacit influence within state, federal, and foreign-policy corridors without any real regard for democratically elected leadership.

This is why conservative political activist Alan Keyes once described bureaucracies as:

> …inherently antidemocratic. Bureaucrats derive their power from their position in the structure, not from their relations with the people they are supposed to serve. The people are not masters of the bureaucracy, but its clients. They receive its services, but only insofar as they conform to its authority. The bureaucracy is like a computer; it responds only to those who address it in the proper form. In this sense, a bureaucratic government program has a double meaning: The program serves its clients, but it also programs them.[5]

Such power is obviously unbalanced and perfectly poised to be tyrannical and to dictate through its numerous tentacles global collectivist policies and multiculturalism in Washington, which in turn influences foreign policy, the intelligence agencies, the National Security Agency (NSA), think-tanks, and every other key government bureau and para-agency.

Unfortunately, this near-omnipresent bureaucracy is just the beginning of what non-politician Donald J. Trump is up against.

Dateline 2017: The Shadow Government Settles in Two Miles from the White House

When former president Barack Obama, the first-ever president to have a Masonic Inaugural Ball held in his honor, in his final official speech as president said he was "heartened" by anti-Trump protesters taking to the streets in communities around the country and on college campuses where fascist vandalism, violence, riots, and fires were being set to protest Trump's first attempt at an immigration ban, he was sending the first of several clear messages to his army of thirty-thousand-plus agitators. The two-term scheme (January 20, 2009–January 20, 2017) to engineer America away from its Christian and traditional moorings was not over, and no Republican successor was going to change that.

Since then, a lot has happened, and very quickly.

Obama immediately moved across town and set up bunkers just two miles from the White House, where he and his Organizing for Action (OFA) associates and their 250 offices nationwide commenced efforts to effectively function as what some in the Capital Beltway are already calling a "shadow government," third-term, pseudo-presidency. There, "legacies" from Obama era "accomplishments" are being crafted (often against established facts) and spoon-fed to media accomplices while unprecedented efforts to fight, dismiss, and sabotage Trump and his popular "America First" agenda are being funded by a $40-million-dollar (and growing) war chest. Young liberal activists, like Manchurian candidates, have been activated to oppose the new administration at every turn—immigration reform, Obamacare replacement, border security, and more. They are also aided in that effort by the Obama Foundation, whose IRS-approved mission is supposed to be for funding and operating a library to house the former president's official papers for posterity, much like other presidents have done.

But Obama is taking his foundation down "the same controversial—and, by some accounts, illegal—post-presidency path of his predecessor Bill Clinton, according to documents reviewed by The Daily Caller News Foundation's Investigative Group.[6] The foundation's language that caught the eye of Caller's investigators involves not just the building and maintaining of a library, but the diversion of funds for "activities reflecting President Obama's values and priorities throughout his career in public service."

In other words, the nonprofit foundation will serve whatever Obama needs to shadow, obstruct, resist, and subvert the policies and directives of the Trump administration.

And make no mistake, Obama has made this personal. He himself is overseeing the blitzkrieg. The former president has swiftly returned to his early station as a radical Saul Alinsky-style agitation organizer.

Alinsky, the 1960s radical who wrote *Rules for Radicals,* and by whom Obama was guided, once said, "In the beginning, the organizers first job is to create the issues or problems. Creating the problems allows people to feel so frustrated, so defeated, so lost, so futureless in the prevailing system that they are willing to let go of the past and chance the future."[7] This is the playbook the Obama team is using today to create the appearance of "issues and problems" and a general sense of desperation among Millennials so that people will "feel so frustrated, so defeated, so lost, so futureless" that they turn to them for solutions.

According to Alinsky biographer Sanford Horwitt, Obama and his presidential campaign and polity were also significantly influenced by this kind of Alinsky-based radicalism that Obama chose to follow in his footsteps as a Chicago-based community organizer. For three years during the 1980s, "Obama worked for the Developing Communities Project, which was influenced by Alinsky's work, and he [Obama] wrote an essay that was collected in a book memorializing Alinsky."[8] (Of course, Alinsky dedicated his book to "Lucifer," the original radical and inspiration for those who follow his example.)[9]

This is why, at Organizing for Action, it is Obama himself who "is intimately involved in OFA operations and even tweets from the group's account," writes Paul Sperry for the *New York Post.*

In fact, he gave marching orders to OFA foot soldiers following Trump's upset victory [and is] overseeing it all from a shadow White House located within two miles of Trump. It features a mansion, which he's fortifying with construction of a tall brick perimeter, and a nearby taxpayer-funded office with his own chief of staff and press secretary. Michelle Obama will also open an office there, along with the Obama Foundation.[10]

Valerie Jarrett, former senior advisor and close confidante of Obama, has also moved into the 8,200-square-foot, $5.3-million nerve-center mansion to assist Obama in organizing the mounting insurgency against Trump's stated objectives regarding Reagan-like economic policies, government deregulation, and middle-class jobs programs. According to Washington insiders, Obama's goal in this is straightforward—to fuel the "resistance" that will force Trump's resignation or see him impeached. Investigative reporter Matthew Vadum said it this way:

> Former President Obama is waging war against the Trump administration through his generously funded agitation outfit, Organizing for Action, to defend his monumentally destructive record of failure and violent polarization. It is a chilling reminder that the increasingly aggressive, in-your-face Left in this country is on the march.[11]

A new, $80 million, anti-Trump network funded by liberal billionaire George Soros has also joined the effort and is being led by the former members of the now-defunct and notorious Association of Community Organizations for Reform Now (ACORN).

The Center for Popular Democracy Action Fund is the sister organization of the Center for Popular Democracy (CPD), a New York-based nonprofit "that receives the bulk of its funding from George Soros [and] announced at their spring gala Tuesday that they will be heading up the new $80 million anti-Trump network that will span 32 states and have 48 local partners," CNN reported.[12]

Together with other "Trump Derangement Syndrome" sufferers, Soros-funded Obama-era holdovers with axes to grind who are still part of the federal bureaucracy but whose allegiance remains with the forty-fourth president have as part of "the resistance" been selectively leaking classified government information (a federal crime that senior U.S. officials say is endangering American security operations and servicemen)[13] in the hopes of either directly damaging Trump or, at a minimum, producing a false impression that the new president either obstructed justice (by allegedly asking former FBI Director James Comey to stop investigating former National Security Adviser Michael Flynn), colluded with the Russians (supposedly to influence the 2016 election, albeit the newest evidence suggests there really was massive Russian collusion and that it was not Trump but Obama and Hillary working behind the scenes), committed some other unspecified crime, or is simply too inept to run the country (and to be fair, while no evidence exists at this time to support the deceit, demagoguery, and mass hysteria aimed at denigrating Trump, his incessant tweeting and general inability to articulate has not helped alleviate the situation).

And then there are those who say the rabbit hole goes even deeper.

According to several leading analysts, an actual "coup" is afoot to overturn the 2016 election. "A soft coup is underway right here in the United States of America in an attempt to overturn November's election result, and forcibly remove a duly elected president," Sean Hannity of Fox News warned recently.[14] Lou Dobbs, Ben Stein, Gary Bauer, members of the US House of Representatives such as Tom Tancredo, congressmen like Mike Kelly, and others are drawing the same conclusion.

Even ultra-liberal Right Wing Watch of "People for the American Way," who have attacked me personally on their website, and which was formed in 1980 to counter the Christian Right, Republican Party, and Jerry Falwell's Moral Majority, recently quoted pastor E. W. Jackson, who argued on his radio program that a *coup d'etat* (a change of government illegally or by force) is being orchestrated.[15]

"Folks, hold on to your seats, because I really believe that we are witnessing an attempted coup d'état in America. I'm serious about that.

I believe that we are witnessing an attempted coup d'état in America," Jackson said.

According to criminal attorney Robert Barnes, the shadow-man directly responsible for this deep state de facto coup is none other than Barack Obama. [16]

A growing number of Americans, regardless of party affiliation, are aware of the huge extent of anti-Trump media bias (supported by the findings of Harvard Kennedy School academics at the Shorenstein Center on Media, Politics, and Public Policy, who found all ten of the major media outlets in America were negative in as many as 98 percent of their reports on Trump during the first one hundred days of his administration), [17] are already exhausted by the hysterical attacks on and typecasting of every breath Trump makes, and simply want their elected officials to actually govern (imagine that!). However, the extreme left, which controls the media megaphone and who owns a massive swath of establishment RINOs ("Republicans In Name Only") and members of the Democratic party are firmly committed to nothing less than the engineering of a new socialist world order from the chaos and ashes of our formerly great Republic (which speaks to the occult roots and agenda playing out in the United States, which I will deal with later in this work).

Michael Laitman over at *The Jerusalem Post* said it very well:

Neoliberalism, which has destroyed Europe through immigration, and nearly destroyed the US by eliminating its middle class, has been the sole ruling agenda in the US for decades. It serves the interests of the small elite group of magnates who control the American economy, the media, and thereby the government, all the way up to the White House. They determine what is reported and what is not, who is defamed and who is glorified. By controlling the media, they have dominated public discourse, public opinion, and have avoided criticism. This is ingenious, but deadly to society.

Their best interest is not the best interest of the American people. They aspire for world domination…through proxies such as Obama and Clinton.

Every American needs not only to understand these facts, but something else, too. Daniel Webster, the great eighteenth-century orator, statesman, and constitutional lawyer, said:

> I apprehend no danger to our country from a foreign foe. Our destruction, should it come at all, will be from…the inattention of the people to the concerns of their government…. I fear that they may place too implicit a confidence in their public servants, and fail properly to scrutinize their conduct; that in this way they may be made the dupes of designing men, and become the instruments of their own undoing.

With these words, Webster was speaking directly to the vice of this current coup. In other words, I am arguing that what we are witnessing isn't just a calculated effort to bring down the non-establishment's president. It's a scheme against every citizen of free society that values the ability to govern itself. It's a plot—and an ancient one at that—to disrupt momentum aimed at circumventing the entrenched cabal's cross-party, perpetual rule from DC. An outsider named Trump came to Washington's power center "to restore a traditional regime of citizenship, individualism, assimilation, territorial sovereignty, recognized borders, strong defense, deterrence abroad, and free-market capitalism,"[18] and he is not part of the Bohemian club. They will not tolerate that. They are committed to expelling him, and by extension, any effort from you—the grassroots—to liberate yourself, your family, and the nation's future from the ruling class.

This is not a bold statement.

What you see happening in media and on the extreme left right now is more than just the activity of "sore losers." This is the manifest incarnation of a Fourth Reich (the term "Third Reich" was coined by Arthur Moeller van den Bruck as the title of his 1923 book, *Das Dritte Reich.* It was used by the Nazis for propaganda purposes to legitimize their regime as a successor state to the retroactively renamed First Reich (the Holy Roman Empire, 962–1806) and the Second Reich (Imperial Germany, 1871–1918) whose purpose in sabotaging Trump as the duly elected president of the United States is an outright and hostile rejection of the choice voters made on Tuesday, November 8, 2016.

"With the election over, the Democratic Party is now in the hands of the Bernie Sanders-Tom Perez-Keith Ellison-Barack Obama radical left," David Horowitz recently wrote. He continued:

> Abetted by a corrupt media, funded by the anti-American billionaire George Soros, egged on by Obama's corrupt attorney general, Loretta Lynch, and a collusive press, the left has launched vile and violent demonstrations in the streets, rancid witch-hunts in the halls of Congress posing as "confirmation hearings," and treasonous intelligence leaks [through which] Obama and his cohorts have disregarded the Constitution and the law to spy on reporters they do not like, to use the IRS and other government agencies to take down their opponents and undermine the democratic system.[19]

Presidential historian Doug Wead echoed Horowitz's comments in June 2017 on the air with Lou Dobbs, saying he is convinced that "operatives" of the deep state really are attempting a coup d'état of President Trump.[20]

But, as professor Wead also pointed out during that program, this shouldn't come as any real surprise, because America's intelligence agencies, including the CIA, the State Department, and the media have a long history of overthrowing duly elected democratic foreign governments.

Recent examples include Iraq, Iran, the Ukraine, and before that, Vietnam, Egypt, the Phillippines, and other countries where highly skilled American operatives engrained themselves among civilian provocateurs and assisted "popular uprisings."

Obama even admitted the United States' involvement in the Ukrainian crisis and that he "brokered a deal" in support of regime change and transition of power.[21]

With Obama admittedly educated in the tried-and-true policies of coups and coercive propaganda, Wead's analysis to Dobbs that the same decidedly trained apparatus has now been put into motion in our own country to overthrow the duly-elected Republican president holds merit.

The reason to employ such a slow, or "soft," coup (as some have described what we are witnessing) is self-evident—a violent or military overthrow of the American government would not be tolerated by the vast majority of citizens regardless of party, and the enterprising cult behind it would expose too much of their hand and quickly be rejected. We are just too comfortable in modern America to tolerate such a strategy. Thus, working to get the populace to surrender their will through brainwashing over a long period of time is the preferred modus operandi. *(Shucks! It's even entertaining for activists and so-called progressives who believe the mechanisms of the deep state were put in place for the very purpose of enforcing a thoroughly left-wing society on the populace anyway to watch how contemporary society has forgotten the lessons of history and are open to empowering them to repeat the mistakes of the past!)*

And, as bat-wing crazy as some of these enemies of the state are, they are correct in their understanding that lasting political power in industrialized countries is not gained through bloody revolution. Even Karl Marx—who advocated violent overthrows—recognized this when he wrote in his 1848 *Communist Manifesto* how to defeat America from the inside-out. He knew that in this "land of the free and the home of the brave," you would have to change the course of the nation slowly, incrementally, through winning elections and creating laws, using what he called "cultural hegemony" or domination of a culturally diverse society by the ruling class who manipulates the culture of that society—the beliefs, explanations, perceptions, values, and mores—so that their imposed, ruling-class worldview eventually becomes the accepted cultural norm.[22]

If a populace remains conservative in their values, then they will always vote conservatives into places of authority. Thus, according to Marx, the best way to slowly change a developed nation to communistic, is to first win over the populace with liberal or "progressive" ideas—from pop-culture memes to mass media propaganda to infiltrating institutions of higher education with leftist philosophers and so on—and then eventually socialism or communism would take root without the need for violent overthrow.

With that in mind, when I look at what has happened since the 1950s through the Obama-era experiment and Bernie Sanders' "democratic socialism," I gasp at where we may be today. Our forefathers, who gave their lives on the battlefield to defend and protect the American dream, could be rolling over in their graves while the ghost of Karl Marx laughs from somewhere deep inside Cocytus, the Ninth Circle of Hell.

And when I consider how the slow coup playing out before us today could be the manifestation of this decades-long scheme to bring our nation to a tipping point for a new "order out of chaos," and how those efforts at first appear frighteningly successful on our college campuses, I perceive that the contempt of Trump by the ludicrous fringe may be a symptom of a much deeper national malaise.

But then, when I look at how Trump was elected against all odds and despite an unmerciful propaganda machine, I realize that the average American and the values held dear by the majority of them may not be buying into the great lie after all. Like generations of Americans have done before, the grassroots over recent decades may simply have been patient, willing to listen, and weighed options—then, in 2016, they woke up, rose up, and made their decision to reject the demonic conspiracy.

That is what it looks like happened, and this is why the radical left is in a tizzy now. Trump's historic victory appears to be a rejection of their globalist vision by a small but significant majority, a paradigm shift away from Marxism, and they are beside themselves because of it. Trump torpedoing their proletarian plan to use America's resources for the final stages of a worldwide borderless, de-populationist economic order and world government echoes Brexit and perhaps even the final era of socialist-communist philosophies worldwide, which aligns with what Trump said he would work toward if elected.

Another relevant issue here that Trump promised was to reenact the economic policies of Ronald Reagan, which nearly singlehandedly saved the West from its inflationary spiral "that had allowed communist resource-based economies to flourish. After the Berlin Wall fell on November 9, 1989, Russia was forced into a U.S. bailout and China adopted 'Capitalism with Chinese Characteristics.'"[23]

Later in this book, we will examine financial policy as reflected in Trump administration campaign promises, why Wall Street reacts so positively every time it thinks "the Donald" may actually get a chance to expedite a new Reaganomics era, and why free-market competition has historically and consistently outperformed socialist-communist alternatives and delivered commercial trade and industry successes time after time.

But for now, if you've read the anthology, *When Once We Were a Nation* (Defender Publishing, 2017), you already know why I am such a fan of American capitalism as the engine of strong economies. My family—Grandpa, Grandma, Mom, Dad, and cousins came through the Great Depression. Their lives were the actual story of the Oklahoma family—the Joads—depicted in the 1940 classic film, *The Grapes of Wrath*, who, after abandoning their farm during the Dust Bowl and Great Depression of the 1930s, became migrant workers and ended up in California. They were the rugged individuals and "new pioneers" short on cash but high in faith who later provided the perfect role models for me and my generation to learn from concerning those things in life that should really matter and be cherished. They've been gone now for many years, and with them most of the Great Generation. But when by contrast I consider the things people like Bernie Sanders value today, I tremble. We live during a time when it is tempting for college kids—who, because of historical revisionism, often have no idea where our greatness as a nation came from—to feel "entitled" to things they have not earned and, according to polls, increasingly believe others who *have* worked hard to succeed owe them, including things like free higher education, free universal health care, housing assistance, and so on. This represents a crossroads that, whether you like Trump or not (and believe me, there are a lot of things that frustrate me with the Donald), is reflected in the current election cycle. Old-timers know and others can sense that our country has entered dangerous political waters in which a growing number of citizens either never knew about or have forgotten the lessons of the communist countries whose disastrous, failed policies caused their economies to crumble like dominoes following the Cold War. Among the growing cast of Americans who are ignorant of these facts are those who actually prefer a turn from free-market capitalism (which built the most powerful, progressive, and giving society in history) to socialism. Recent Barna polling confirms this scary trend, with current surveys showing that a mind-numbing 40 percent of US citizens now affirm that they prefer socialism to capitalism.[24] Such people are cozy with ideas like a "Universal Basic Income" that, for all intents and purposes, would enslave them as subordinates to a machine of "goods and services" production for redistribution to others. This stands at diametric opposition to the capitalist system our forefathers died to protect, in which individual efforts are rewarded and outweigh the collective (i.e., the New Testament model that puts for that if you won't work, you don't eat), wherein the free market determines the distribution of goods.

Derek Gilbert has much to say about this later in this book, but suffice it to recognize the irony here. While socialism promises a shared level ground, it actually lowers the living standard for all while providing little method or motivation for advancement or prosperity by hard-working and ambitious individuals, while conversely, American capitalism historically resulted in the abundance of capital that fed the hungry of the world and built the hospitals and care facilities that to this day assist the needy. This is one reason I believe America needs an awakening. First, we need a spiritual revival, and second, we need a cultural awakening defined by the reestablishment of Great Generation principles and behavior that could positively strengthen, recharacterize, and rejuvenate our society. Donald Trump, as inarticulate as he is, has captured the essence of this longing with his political jargon, "We can be great again" and "We can win again." I'd like to believe that on those points Mr. Trump is right. I'd like to think that America can once more be a nation of winners, of rugged individualism and pioneering determination. Yet I also understand that very powerful forces, both spiritual and political, are devoted to the opposite—the enslavement of all mankind beneath a socialist umbrella under which national boundaries dissolve and ethnic groups, ideologies, religions, and economics from around the world orchestrate a single and dominant sovereignty. Prophecy says that this is coming, and that, at the head of this "utopian" administration, a single personality is going to surface. He will at first appear to be a man of distinguished character, but will ultimately become "a king of fierce countenance" (Daniel 8:23). With imperious decree, he will facilitate a One-World Government, universal religion, and global socialism. Those who refuse his New World Order will inevitably be imprisoned or destroyed until at last he exalts himself "above all that is called God, or that is worshiped, so that he, as God, sitteth in the temple of God, showing himself that he is God" (2 Thessalonians 2:4).

Between current and former national American leaders, there are candidates among them who not only see themselves in the role of this leader, but they covet the position. Even the tenets of their own ancient occultism tell them the day is nearing when "The Secret Destiny of America" will produce a moment when one of them could rise to become the destroyer of worlds.

But before I get to that, I have invited two of my good friends to submit chapters to Saboteurs that build on what I have said thus far. They are best-selling author Carl Gallups, who in the next chapter discusses "Nationalism vs. Globalism" and whether the elite have surrendered their NWO vision in light of the 2016 presidential election, and Lt. Colonel Robert Maginnis, whose day job is as senior analyst at the Pentagon—the headquarters of the United States Department of Defense. His chapter on whether Donald Trump can actually drain the Washington swamp (one of Trump's campaign pledges) should concern you.

chapter two

Nationalism vs. Globalism

Have the Elite Surrendered the NWO Vision?

By Carl Gallups

One day there will be no borders, no boundaries, no flags and no countries and the only passport will be the heart.

—CARLOS SANTANA[25]

W alter Cronkite was known as "The Most Trusted Man in America" during his almost twenty-year stint as anchor of the *CBS Evening News*. In 1999, Cronkite spoke before the United Nations as he accepted the Norman Cousins Global Governance Award from the World Federalists Association. He told those gathered for the occasion that the first step toward achieving the goal of a one-world government was to strengthen the United Nations. Cronkite then announced that global government was his "personal dream."

During his speech, Cronkite asserted:

It seems to many of us that if we are to avoid the eventual catastrophic world conflict we must strengthen the United Nations as a first step toward a world government patterned after our own government with a legislature, executive and judiciary, and police to enforce its international laws and keep the peace. To do that, of course, we Americans will have to yield up some of our sovereignty. That would be a bitter pill. It would take a lot of courage, a lot of faith in the new order.

Cronkite sardonically added:

Pat Robertson has written in a book a few years ago that we should have a world government, but only when the Messiah arrives. He wrote, literally, any attempt to achieve world order before that time must be the work of the devil. Well, join me. I'm glad to sit here at the right hand of Satan.[26]

It's Coming

The shifting tides of intertribal entanglements have existed since the earliest days of recorded history. But once those populations developed into the more classic definition of nation-states, the relationships among them became increasingly complex as well. Many of the resulting international wranglings resulted in the positive provisions of military alliances, negotiations of borders, and/or innovative trade associations. On the other hand, a number of geopolitical tidal shifts have also been responsible for catastrophic world wars, millions of deaths, global transfer of power, the enslavement of entire people-groups, rampant disease and plagues, and even the horrors of wanton genocide.

But only once in world history did the sweeping current of intricate multinational associations bring about the startling, foretold resurrection of an ancient biblical nation—the nation of Israel. In the decades following the appearance of that revenant nation, the planet has never been the same. This factor figures into the equation of "what's really going on" in today's world, and it also helps to understand the deeply spiritual element of the globalist agenda. More on that later.

Globalism

The definition of "globalism" for our current examination is the notion of a human-crafted *Utopia*—a global community with no borders, no distinctive national heritages, a unified legal system, and enforcing a common goal: to live and to be ruled by humanity's own "heart." Sounds pretty good—at the surface.

However, the idea is at least as old as the Tower of Babel. In fact, many would argue that the continual playing-out of history's empire-building scenarios is really nothing more than this same spiritual war attempting to capture more territory. After all, they would claim, what was the purpose behind the Egyptian, Assyrian, Babylonian, Persian, Greek, Roman, and Ottoman Empires, or even the British Empire? Wasn't the underlying driving force simply the yearning to rule the world as a global community under the headship of one king? Suffice it to say, this idea of a humanistic paradise is not something invented by the 1960s *Age of Aquarius* hippy generation…it has been with us for a long, long time. And, its roots are diabolical.

Nationalism

Nationalism is the understanding that people generally function better when they are grouped by common goals and heritages and are set apart in individual nations/states. Of course, a healthy nation will also allow the legally controlled and gradual influx of other ideas and people-groups, while still retaining its foundational underpinnings of national sovereignty and rule of law.

Nationalism is a biblical ideal. It is God's decree. Globalism (the way we have defined it) is an aberrant idea, born from the heart of Heaven's adversary—Satan. It is his scheme of possessing the world as his own and setting up his own glorious kingdom—and unwary human subjects, rulers, and governments are his eternally expendable pawns.

For the last hundred years or so, the world has again witnessed the massive ebb and flow of that cosmic struggle—often without even realizing the divine clash of unseen principalities that are involved. But the Word of God is not silent on the matter. Those who are familiar with the contextual study of biblical prophecy understand that much of what is happening in our own little part of history is leaping right off the pages of those ancient prophecies.

The Bible is clear: There will indeed be an age in which an indisputably wicked sort of globalism finally wins the day—at least for a short while. Like it or not, *it will happen*.

Biblical and Historical Context

As a matter of fact, the topic of a demonically inspired globalism is one of the central themes of the eschatology of the book of Daniel, the writings of the apostle Paul, and John's Revelation.

We know from the Scriptures that Daniel, John, and Paul each had experiences of being "caught up before the throne of God." They all had heavenly revelations of the very last days of man's rule on the earth, and each described, to one degree or another, an end-times globalist leader who will operate a one-world system of defiance towards the Lord of Heaven. Intrigue, deceit, terror, spiritual/religious deception, signs and wonders, and out-and-out blasphemy will be the predominant tools of his demonic rule.

The coming globalist regime will be headed by the Antichrist, the one who "throws truth to the ground" and "leads the whole world astray." Paul calls him the "man of lawlessness" and the "man doomed to destruction." John is the only biblical writer to tag him with the moniker of Antichrist. He does this in the biblical books we know as 1 and 2 John. The term means something akin to: "opposed to Christ," "other than Christ," or "a fake Christ." He will be "Satan's man" embodied by Satan himself, but he will be presented to the world as the ultimate Messiah.

Daniel says this last-days globalist leader is the one who will ultimately set up the "abomination that causes desolation" and will attack the saints of God. In Matthew 24, Jesus Himself referred to Daniel's description of that horrible time:

> So when you see standing in the holy place the abomination that causes desolation, spoken of through the prophet Daniel—let the reader understand—then let those who are in Judea flee to the mountains. Let no one on the housetop go down to take anything out of the house. Let no one in the field go back to get their cloak. How dreadful it will be in those days for pregnant women and nursing mothers! Pray that your flight will not take place in winter or on the Sabbath. For then there will be great distress, unequaled from the beginning of the world until now—and never to be equaled again. (Matthew 24:15–21, NIV)

That coming universal potentate of biblical fame will eventually bring about the complete obedience of the nations of the world. Ultimately, he will require everyone to take a "mark" of allegiance (Revelation 13). He is also the one who will stand opposed to Yahweh and the returned Israel of Yahweh's last-days' promise (Ezekiel 38, Zechariah 12:3, and Psalm 83). Ultimately, the Antichrist will battle against the returning King of Kings and Lord of Lords—Yeshua/Jesus Christ (Revelation 16:12–16).

Global Participation v. Globalism—There Is a Difference

Now that we have the biblical facts laid out, let's take a moment to make certain we do not mix concepts to the point that we tag everything spoken of as *globalist* as being declared *antichrist* in nature. Because, in the bigger scheme of things, there is a sense in which international cooperative goals are crucial to national survival, and also reflect certain biblical principles of order.

Even the ancient nation of Israel quickly learned that international trade relations as well as freedom of travel agreements and military alliances were crucial to maintaining prudent interactions with the surrounding nations. In so doing, these cooperation paradigms actually helped protect and enrich Israel's national sovereignty as well as its overall standard of living. We see prominent examples of these truths in the reigns of King David and King Solomon, as well as in the succession of many of the kings in the Divided Kingdom.

Accordingly, there is a sense in which contributing to the global community in a mutually agreeable manner is not an "evil" thing at all. For example, national leaders might agree to sign peace treaties, make certain relational compromises, join military alliances, and construct trade agreements. Nations might have deeply connected contracts with a multiplicity of nations without necessarily being guilty of contributing to the antichrist spirit of the satanic *Globalist Empire* that is to come.

God and Government—Our Responsibility

In the meantime, exactly what role does God intend to fulfill through the ordained institution of human government? What is the Christian's place in God's intentions? After all, institutions of earthly administration are the mechanisms through which societal rules, national sovereignty, and domestic boundaries are expressed and protected.

The Word of God is plain in the answering of that question. The Lord entrusts civil authorities with: preserving a stable societal order, establishing rule of law, penalizing malefactors, and—ultimately—protecting citizens within that society. Of course, an inevitable "judgment of the nations" will call into account how faithfully, or unfaithfully, God's trust was administered by the nations and their leaders (Matthew 25:31–46). In the meantime, the instructions to God's people are clear. Romans 13 states the principle like this:

Let everyone be subject to the governing authorities, for there is no authority except that which God has established. The authorities that exist have been established by God. Consequently, whoever rebels against the authority is rebelling against what God has instituted, and those who do so will bring judgment on themselves.

For rulers hold no terror for those who do right, but for those who do wrong. Do you want to be free from fear of the one in authority? Then do what is right and you will be commended. For the one in authority is God's servant for your good. But if you do wrong, be afraid, for rulers do not bear the sword for no reason. They are God's servants, agents of wrath to bring punishment on the wrongdoer. Therefore, it is necessary to submit to the authorities, not only because of possible punishment but also as a matter of conscience.

This is also why you pay taxes, for the authorities are God's servants, who give their full time to governing. Give to everyone what you owe them: If you owe taxes, pay taxes; if revenue, then revenue; if respect, then respect; if honor, then honor. (Romans 13:1–7, NIV)

First Peter 2:13–17 and Titus 3:1 contain messages comparable to Romans 13. Contextual understanding of the matter presents a clear command to God's people: good citizenship, whenever possible, without compromising one's faith in Jesus Christ, is one method through which we express our reverence for God's order of things. After all, the opposite of national order is *anarchy.* The opposite of law-abiding citizenship is rebellion and disorder. And the opposite of national sovereignty is global oligarchy. Each of these descriptions more aptly applies to Satan's realm of operation rather than to routine Christian living.

The message of the Bible is strong regarding the topic: *National sovereignty, with benevolent and lawful rule-of-law structure, is ordained and blessed by the Lord.* And without doubt, God's people are to respect God's order. Our daily endeavor must be as follows: "If it is possible, as far as it depends on you, live at peace with everyone" (Romans 12:18, NIV).

It is also vital that we take Jesus' command to be the salt and light in a literal sense (Matthew 5:13–16). That is, we should endeavor to engage the political processes of our culture, and to *stay* engaged—"not growing weary in doing good" (Galatians 6:9). After all, it is the engagement of the culture around us—preaching, ministry endeavors, feeding and clothing the poor, voting and running for office, and courageous truth-telling, as well as praying and supporting those Christians who do run for office—that keeps the "lights" turned on in the work of Kingdom advancement. By engaging in these endeavors, we honor the Lord with our lives in a biblically genuine fashion. That is why we are here. We represent Jesus Christ Himself; We are his ambassadors (2 Corinthians 5:20ff).

God and Borders—Blessings and Curses

That leads us to another related biblical theme: God honors the concept of *borders and boundaries* in numerous areas of our lives. He holds us personally accountable for the maintenance of those "borders."

Consider the following examples of biblical *border* responsibilities and the punishments that come with violating them. We are instructed to guard the boundaries of: our minds and spirits (Romans 12:1ff), our bodies (1 Corinthians 6:18), the womb (Psalm 139:13ff), childhood (Matthew 28:6ff), marriage (Matthew 19:4ff), sexuality (1 Corinthians 6:18), and our allegiance of worship (John 4:24). Failure to revere these borders brings consequences. And sometimes, when a nation collectively and consistently violates the aforementioned borders, the Lord brings upon that nation a curse, which manifests itself in the degradation of another particularly important boundary—*national border security.*

To the surprise of many, the Lord is also a God of national and geographic borders. He originated the concept. And, He declares blessings and curses concerning the matter. Not quite convinced of this assertion? Consider the declaration of Deuteronomy 32:8:

> When the Most High gave nations as their inheritance, when he separated the human race, he set boundaries for the people according to the number of the children of God. (ISV)

It is particularly interesting that the "dividing of all mankind," spoken of in the Deuteronomy 32 passage, occurred at the Tower of Babel (Genesis 11). Here was humankind's first recorded attempt to have a purely globalistic community—a one-world rulership seeking to "reach the gods"—but, Yahweh expressly forbade it. Consequently, He divided the peoples into nations, each with distinct national borders.

The passages of Numbers 34:1–15 and Ezekiel 47:13–23 spell out the border markers that God gave the children of Israel even as they entered the Promised Land. Not only were national borders declared, but tribal borders were also delineated. God even used the "collapse" of national borders as an instrument of His judgment upon the nations—including Israel, the nation that had been set apart as His own.

Second Chronicles 36 describes the decline of Judah and the recurrent disobedience on the part of God's people. This woeful account tells of the Babylonian conquest of Israel and the judgment that came with the subsequent national captivity. All of this occurred through the vehicle of continual border encroachment by the surrounding nations—the enemies of God's people. As Israel wantonly continued to violate its spiritual borders, the Lord weakened their geographical borders. The spiritual law of border collapse is clear. Israel serves as the example of it.

Deuteronomy 28:43–48 further lays out the divine judgment of weak national borders:

The foreigners who reside among you will rise above you higher and higher, but you will sink lower and lower. They will lend to you, but you will not lend to them. They will be the head, but you will be the tail. All these curses will come on you. They will pursue you and overtake you until you are destroyed, because you did not obey the Lord your God and observe the commands and decrees he gave you. They will be a sign and a wonder to you and your descendants forever. Because you did not serve the Lord your God joyfully and gladly in the time of prosperity, therefore in hunger and thirst, in nakedness and dire poverty, you will serve the enemies the Lord sends against you. He will put an iron yoke on your neck until he has destroyed you. (NIV)

In light of these clear scriptural examples, how then can a serious Bible student deny God's intention concerning national borders? How can we doubt that He uses them to either bless or discipline the nations?

And never doubt: Hand-in-hand with that divine discipline is the continual scheming of the "prince of this world." He knows the "rules" of Heaven. Satan is aware of the divine discipline that is invoked upon a nation that begins with reverence for the Lord and then turns its heart to debauchery. This is why the Great Deceiver is so invested in destroying the national soul of America by attacking and destroying its foundational roots of reverence toward the Word of God.

A New World Order

It is Satan's goal to bring about his ultimate *New World Order*—a one-rule, one-religion, and one-currency globalist community; a universal society dedicated to worshipping the satanically *embodied one* who throws truth to the ground and exalts himself above Yahweh of Heaven. In order to accomplish his goal, national sovereignty and rule of law must first be eradicated—or at least it must become so watered down as to logistically b nonexistent.

So, Satan's target is America's borders—*all of them*. As those boundaries collapse within the life of our culture, one by one, the *evil one* is ever closer to fulfilling his lust for global power. Like a celestial game of Risk, he maneuvers the players throughout the nations until all the world succumbs to the victor. Do today's world, America's consistent slide toward debauchery, and the increasingly dangerous geopolitical climate make a bit more sense to you now?

And so it is that, for many decades, millions of people living within the borders of our great nation have been distraught over the consistent breaking down of our societal boundaries, rules of law, marriage and sexual boundaries, boundaries of the womb and sanctity of life, national heritage, and the basic principles of our constitutional republic.

We are now at a historically unmatched precipice, one in which all the powers of perdition are battling against one of the greatest stumbling blocks to the final establishment of the Antichrist kingdom. What is that stumbling block? One of the grandest prizes to the globalist schemers is nothing less than destroying the national sovereignty of the largest Christian nation and the greatest superpower the planet has ever known—the United States of America.

Movements That Illustrate the Battle—Brexit

In the minds of many biblical experts, 2016 proved to be a year that pulled back the veil exposing the spiritual powers and principalities desperately vying for globalist control (Ephesians 6:8ff). In that year, it appeared that Satan's kingdom plans suffered a few serious setbacks. Nevertheless, a number of those experts saw the perceived defeats only as a "throwing down of the gauntlet" in the ever-unfolding saga of end-time eschatology. The battle is not nearly over, they surmised; rather, the cosmic clash had only heated up, and like never before.

A few months prior to the November 2016 United States presidential election, the Brexit vote in Great Britain rocked the planet. Prophecy researchers looked on with awe as the jockeying of power and national sovereignty issues struck a mighty blow in what many of those scholars considered to be the heart of the potential "beast" of Revelation, a revived Roman Empire—the European Union.

Academics are divided on the ultimate nationalistic makeup of the end-time beast of Daniel and Revelation. However, it cannot be denied that a very large portion of biblical scholarship has pointed to the rise of some type of globalist union involving the bulk of the European nations as the potential fulfillment of that prophecy.

The European Union was birthed on November 1, 1993, at Maastricht, Netherlands. That multinational coalition is now comprised of twenty-eight member states, nineteen of which use only one currency, the euro. The Union is an economic and political partnership designed to create a "single market" among the member nations as well as the virtual elimination of borders and the eradication of strict national sovereignty. Is there any wonder that numerous Bible scholars see in the European Union the potential beginnings of the ultimate system of the Antichrist that is to come?[27]

However, on June 23, 2016, the panicking populace of Great Britain held a referendum to determine whether the United Kingdom should leave or remain in the European Union. Leave-the-Union votes won by 52 percent to 48 percent. The referendum turnout was 71.8 percent, with more than thirty million people voting.[28]

As anti-globalists around the world celebrated with Britain, the globalist visionaries went into a state of utter outrage. Their angst was expressed in headline news reports around the world. The globalists feared the nationalistic fervor of Brexit might spread to other member nations of their perceived EU utopia—maybe even branching out to nonmember nations as well.

What many people did not realize was that the Brexit referendum stipulated that in order for the UK to actually exit the EU, Britain would be required to appeal to an agreement called "Article 50 of the Lisbon Treaty." That treaty gives the two sides a total of two years to approve the terms of the split. Many within the leadership of Great Britain projected that the UK would leave the EU by the summer of 2019. However, much has happened between the Brexit vote of early 2016 and the middle of 2019. And, most likely, much will continue to happen. [29]

Movements That Illustrate the Battle—Donald Trump

And there was the rub. At least one enormous event did explode upon the geopolitical scene. The United States of America held a presidential election only seven months after the Brexit vote. By January 2017, not only had a new U.S. president who was touting "national sovereignty" as his main platform been installed, but the political maneuvering over just how the Brexit deal would actually unfold simultaneously heated up within the legal system of Great Britain. [30]

On November 4, 2016, a pugnacious, brash, multibillionaire businessman—builder, entertainment industry tycoon, and fiery national sovereignty presidential candidate—seized the larger part of America's heart. Donald Trump not only won the Electoral College vote with a sweeping victory, but he also pulled along in his wake the capture of both the House and the Senate majorities. This stunning turn of events almost guaranteed that the newly elected president would have the power and clout to pull off at least the majority of his planned agenda, one that was decidedly *not* "globalist." As a matter of fact, Trump's program actually represented a step-by-step undoing of the global elitists' often-expressed desire to eventually disassemble America.

Not only did the Trump victory trigger a Washington DC Republican majority, but his win also was, according to many analysts, the catalyst for the taking of thirty-three governors' offices and sixty-eight chambers of state legislatures. Not since the Civil War had the Democrats suffered such a humiliating defeat. [31]

Donald Trump's victory came with promises of opting out of several controversial global trade agreements; reinforcing America's national borders utilizing a literal wall; limiting immigration from among Islamic nations; strengthening the US military; ending socialization of the U.S. medical industry; solidifying America's infrastructure; and speedily restoring millions of American jobs. All of these things were to be done in conjunction with the promise of huge tax incentives and imploring many of the multinational corporations, who had previously fled the United States, to "come home." Additionally, within days of President Trump's victory, media sources were already reporting congressional plans to consider a United States' withdrawal from the United Nations. It seemed that the globalist paradigm might be in for a seismic shift. [32]

The epic "Trump factor," together with the "Brexit shock," appeared to mark the setting-back of the globalists' schedule—perhaps by several generations. However, as exciting as all that might have sounded to the anti-globalists, many prophecy experts believed the globalists elite would not give up without a hellish fight. Even now those elitists seem to be regrouping, with a revamped effort to move their plans forward with renewed vigor. It was *game on!*

Many prophecy watchers even believed they saw, within the context of those current events, shades of Revelation chapter 12's dire warnings. That passage speaks to the times during the prophetic, last-days, final outpouring of evil: "But woe to the earth and the sea, because the devil has gone down to you! He is filled with fury, because he knows that his time is short" (Revelation 12:12, NIV).

The Globalists Begin to Panic

But what really turned out to be the dead giveaway of the demonic realm's outrage toward Brexit and the election of Donald Trump came very shortly after the Trump victory. In less than a week after that landslide Electoral College win, the United Nations stepped up its implementation plans for its controversial Agenda 2030.

On November 9, 2016, UN General Assembly President Peter Thomson set up a special team to vigorously promote the speeded application of the agenda's Sustainable Development Goals (SDGs), "'leaving no-one behind,' ensuring human rights for all, and engaging young people."[33, 34]

In that UN global conclave, the agenda's elite enactment team was commissioned with the task of rousing everyone at global, regional, national, and even local community levels in an attempt to vigorously promote the execution of the United Nation's decidedly globalist goals—and *before* 2030 if possible. The gauntlet of nationalistic fervor (Brexit's and Trump's anti-globalism agendas) had been thrown down, and the globalist leaders were now responding with alarm.

So, what was the rush concerning the moving up of the 2030 objectives? Couched within the agenda's flowery language of "world peace" and "security for all" is a little-known aim the United Nations plans to put into place the "biometric identification" of every human on the planet by 2030. They plan to pull off this feat in the name of "peace and security."[35]

Not only is a global identification system one of the clearly defined goals of the agenda, but the tech companies necessary to accomplish the undertaking have already been tapped by the United Nations. Furthermore, these enterprises boast on their websites of their partnership in the stated goals of UN Agenda 2030.

As if to dramatically underscore the globalists' 2017 panic, in late January of 2017, *The Bulletin of the Atomic Scientists*, through their Science and Security Board, updated their *Doomsday Clock*. Observe their statement of dire alarm, as well as the dramatic appeal to the global community:

2017: For the last two years, the minute hand of the Doomsday Clock stayed set at three minutes before the hour, the closest it had been to midnight since the early 1980s. In its two most recent annual announcements on the Clock, the Science and Security Board warned: "The probability of global catastrophe is very high, and the actions needed to reduce the risks of disaster must be taken very soon." In 2017, we find the danger to be even greater, the need for action more urgent. It is two and a half minutes to midnight, the Clock is ticking, global danger looms. Wise public officials should act immediately, guiding humanity away from the brink. If they do not, wise citizens must step forward and lead the way.[36]

In that same update, the Board explained why they only moved the clock a half minute closer to their predicted doomsday: " [because]…as this statement is issued, Donald Trump has been the U.S. president only a matter of days."

The Board further railed against President Trump, mentioning the heated differences that they believe continue to divide Russia and the United States, the two nations that currently possess 90 percent of the world's viable nuclear weapons.

Observe the globalist agenda-speak of the Science and Security Board:

This already-threatening world situation was the backdrop for a rise in strident nationalism worldwide in 2016, including in a U.S. presidential campaign during which the eventual victor, Donald Trump, made disturbing comments about the use and proliferation of nuclear weapons and expressed disbelief in the overwhelming scientific consensus on climate change.[37]

An End to the Globalist Agenda?

In the months following the Brexit vote and the Trump presidential election, conservative analysts were announcing what they deemed to be an "unstoppable" nationalistic fervor. In the wake of Donald Trump's presidential victory, an article appeared at *American Thinker. com* excitedly proclaiming the utter defeat of globalism. Even the title suggested a *coup d'état* of historical proportions: "Donald Trump and the Death of Utopianism." Consider a few paragraphs from that article. Take note of the emphasis that I have added to a number of important words:

> Their agenda is global and *humanity-wide* in scope; their countrymen are not the highest in the order of value, but merely take their place among the *family of mankind. A rebellion against this view* was at the core of the election result.
>
> The election of *Donald Trump, Brexit, and the growing anti-EU* and *anti-globalist mood sweeping Europe and the world* show that rejection of the progressive utopian neo-Jacobin liberal program is not an American phenomenon alone.
>
> The election of 2016, perhaps the most significant in American history, was about more than another peaceful transfer of American political power. *An ideology has been defeated, not just a candidate.*
>
> *The bubble of utopian fantasies has burst.* A lesson learned from the horrors of history has re-emerged at the most advantageous time: *there is no utopia.*[38]

While admiring the expressed enthusiasm of the article, numerous students of biblical prophecy approached the matter a bit more cautiously, because there is truly one thing the Bible makes perfectly clear: There will be a period of time when the globalists, under the Antichrist, will rule the day.

"Not So Fast," Says Great Britain

However, during the very first week of President Trump's tenure, we witnessed another striking example of the globalists' attempt to "soften" the ultranationalist position of the new American president. The message was clear: *We aren't giving up.*

Avowed globalist British Prime Minister Theresa May became the first foreign leader to visit the shores of the United States during a Donald Trump presidency. Her visit was touted in the headlines of most mainstream media as a great success of cooperation and mutual agenda agreements. However, May's own words, in her January 26, 2017, Philadelphia speech, told a much different story.

Breitbart news organization published an article about Prime Minister May's speech, serving as a stark illustration of her full-on support of the major philosophies and institutions of the leftist agenda. The headline of the story reads: "Britain's Theresa May in U.S.: Islam is Peaceful, Globalism Good, Climate Change a Priority."

The Breitbart report revealed:

> Her speech was also littered with politically correct terms, as well as left and center-left talking points regarding international institutions, Islam, and radical Islamic terrorism, the latter of which she called "Islamist extremism."…. She hailed the United Nations, praised the World Bank, and called NATO "the cornerstone" of Western defense…. May also spoke of the necessity for multilateralism in stark contrast with the line pushed by the

White House.... She cited the need to tackle "climate change" as one of the reasons to back globalist institutions.... [May] is perhaps best known in the United Kingdom for an unprecedented expansion of the surveillance state and indeed mass migration at historic levels.[39]

As perhaps the most telling sign that indicated May was still in full alignment with the globalist agenda, particularly as it involved the European Union, Breitbart reported:

Curiously, despite Britain's Brexit vote, Mrs. May said of the European Union: "We will build a new partnership with our friends in Europe. We are not turning our back on them, or on the interests and the values that we share. It remains overwhelmingly in our interests—and in those of the wider world—that the EU should succeed."

While most prophecy experts would agree that a victory of historic proportions was achieved in these latest world-changing elections, a last-days resurrection of globalist power is still, most certainly, on the way. Ms. May is only the tip of the spear; there is much more to come. Exactly when that day of full global resurgence will finally arrive, and the specific catalyst that will set it off is anybody's guess. However, given the prophetic and volatile geopolitical climate of our day, many believe it will most likely be sooner rather than later.

The First Historical Generation

Think with me for just a moment: We are the first historical generation to experience a prophetically revived Israel and perhaps the beginning stages of the Ezekiel 38 alignment of nations against that returned Israel. Presently, we have Russia (Magog?) planted in the Middle East (Syria) conducting military strikes—at the same time making strong alliances with Persia (Iran). Even respected orthodox Jewish scholars believe that Ezekiel's prophesied alignment is taking place before our eyes. [40]

On top of those developments, China is also in the Middle East with a military presence and in cooperation with Russia—another first in history. Additionally, 2011 marked the outbreak of Arab Spring, the resulting fall of Syria into an unresolvable civil war, and also the meteoric rise of ISIS. With the birth of ISIS' horrific terror campaign has come a refugee crisis of monumental proportions, affecting the European Union nations in what some are calling an irrecoverable travesty. Political, religious, and military global leaders are warning of a looming World War III. Some have declared we are "already in the beginning stages of World War III." [41]

By late January 2017, Mikhail Gorbachev, former president of the Soviet Union, weighed in on the matter: "It all looks as if the world is preparing for war." And, of course, to whom did Mr. Gorbachev make his appeal to "do something" about the looming world war he feared? His entreaty was made to the globalist organization from which the Trump administration was giving serious consideration of withdrawing—the United Nations. [42]

Moreover, the stealth invasion of the Islamization of Europe is proceeding, and at lightning speed. Entire nations are in the throes of being upended in favor of Islamic sharia law and culture. [43]

Additionally, the world is witnessing a resurrection of the dreaded Ottoman Empire. Turkey is currently on the brink of melting completely away as a Middle Eastern democracy and a dependable NATO ally. The nation now appears to be desirous of becoming the headquarters for a global Islamic caliphate. [44]

And let us not forget Turkey is the exact location of the people to whom the book of Revelation was first addressed: the seven churches of Asia Minor. To further punctuate the importance of this implication is the fact that the church at Pergamum was warned twice: "I know where you are, you live where Satan has his throne on earth" (Revelation 2:13). Think of it: The last book of the Bible, which describes the very last days before the return of Jesus Christ, lists Turkey as the seat of Satan, his earthly place of rule.

The foregoing does not even take into account the prophetically foretold eventuality of the international hatred that would culminate towards the revenant nation of Israel in the last days (Zechariah 12:3). We are watching that prophecy unfolding like a tidal wave.

From a steady stream of anti-Israel United Nations edicts to the heretical teaching of Replacement Theology (Supersessionism) sweeping Western churches to the escalating Boycott, Divestment, and Sanctions (BDS) movement, right up to eight grueling years of the Israel-jabbing Obama administration—with its continual call for Israel to return to its 1967 borders—we are living in the midst of the unfolding of biblical prophecy.

There are still other indicators of our prophetic age. In just the last few years, the largest Christian nation in history, the only superpower on the planet to begin its existence by calling upon the God of Heaven in its founding documents, decided that it doesn't know what constitutes a real marriage. We have even codified that biblical travesty by declaration of a Supreme Court ruling.

Moreover, through shifting cultural norms and Obama-regime executive orders, we have avowed to the face of God that sexuality and gender identity are also an "undefined" element of our culture. Sadly, most of America's pulpits seldom address any of the matters we have just examined. [45]

Nor have we scratched the surface concerning the demonically inspired technological advancements that are so boldly proclaimed in mainstream headlines: sex robots, killer robots, military robots, and robots that will soon "learn and think." We are also making startling strides in genetic splicing between animals and humans, as well as continual progress in transhumanism technologies.

Add to that mix the latest developments in DNA and stem-cell manipulation that might result in the creation of human infants—without the need for opposite sexual union in order to accomplish the feat. This new technological marvel is being proclaimed by humanistic scientists as the "perfect solution" for homosexual partners who wish to have "their own family." Oh yes, the "perfect" solution, indeed. What could go wrong with this last-days horror?[46]

Each of these advancements has only emanated in the last handful of years. Do Jesus' words of prophetic warning, "The coming of the Son of Man will be like it was in the days of Noah…and in the days of Lot" (Luke 17:26–28), strike a chord with you yet?

This is not to throw cold water on the hot flames of our glorious, Heaven-sent victories that come to us along the way. Even when the world seems to be completely off its rocker, the Lord knows how to provide a little breathing room for His own. Consider the particularly apropos warnings and declarations of Psalm 2:1–12:

Why do the nations conspire and the peoples plot in vain?
The kings of the earth rise up and the rulers band together
    against the Lord and against his anointed, saying,
Let us break their chains and throw off their shackles.
The One enthroned in heaven laughs; the Lord scoffs at them.
He rebukes them in his anger and terrifies them in his wrath,
    saying,
I have installed my king on Zion, my holy mountain.
I will proclaim the Lord's decree: He said to me, You are my
    son; today I have become your father.
"Ask me, and I will make the nations your inheritance, the
    ends of the earth your possession.
"You will break them with a rod of iron; you will dash them to
    pieces like pottery.
Therefore, you kings, be wise; be warned, you rulers of the earth.

Serve the Lord with fear and celebrate his rule with trembling. Kiss his son, or he will be angry and your way will lead to your destruction, for his wrath can flare up in a moment. *Blessed are all who take refuge in him.* (emphasis added, NIV)

Note the last words of that Psalm, "Blessed are all who take refuge in him." In the midst of the plotting, raging, and evil schemes of "the nations"—as they take their collective (*Tower of Babel*) stand against the Lord, He provides refuge and respite—*for His people*. Hallelujah! What a gracious God we serve. Let us humbly claim that blessing, especially in our prophetically significant days.

Perhaps now those amazing biblical words so many of us have studied, preached, taught, and listened to over our lifetime will take on a richer meaning as we compare them to the current upheaval among "the nations" of our age:

For our struggle is not against flesh and blood, but against the rulers, against the authorities, against the powers of this dark world and against the spiritual forces of evil in the heavenly realms. Therefore put on the full armor of God, so that when the day of evil comes, you may be able to stand your ground, and after you have done everything, to stand. (Ephesians 6:12–13, NIV)

As the World Turns...

Observe the haunting lament coming from the memoirs of a woman who lived through the days of the Great War, *World War I*:

When I was a girl...I imagined that life was individual, one's own affair; that the events happening in the world outside were important enough in their own way, but were personally quite irrelevant. Now, like the rest of my generation, I have had to learn again and again the terrible truth…that no life is really private, or isolated, or self-sufficient. People's lives were entirely their own, perhaps—and more justifiably—when the world seemed enormous, and all its comings and goings were slow and deliberate.

But this is so no longer, and never will be again, since man's inventions have eliminated so much of distance and time; for better, for worse, we are now each of us part of the surge and swell of great economic and political movements, and whatever we do, as individuals or as nations, deeply affects everyone else.[47]

Those words were penned by Vera Brittain. She recorded her thoughts in her book titled, *Testament of Youth: An Autobiographical Study of the Years 1900–1925*.

We may, at first, be tempted to think of the days immediately following the close of World War I as "ancient days of yore." The reality, however, is that those days are only one hundred years removed from us at the time of this writing. In the scope of the entirety of humanity's history, a hundred years is just a miniscule speck along the timeline. Look what has happened in our world and nation since those swift hundred years have passed. It is almost unfathomable.

There has been an exponential burst in technology's explosive arrival into the global present, as well as its projection into the near future. And, so much of today's knowledge smacks of the technologies of the last days prophesied about in the Word of God more than two thousand years ago.

Ms. Brittain spoke prophetically in that referenced selection without quoting Scripture or even speaking of spiritual things. She knew that somehow the earth's first global war, the most catastrophic in history up to that point, had changed *everything*. She knew that technology would be the driving force behind a global shift of power and borders. She also sensed that the world was rapidly becoming a global community. She could not have been more correct.

Then, only a few decades later, World War II would grow out of the event upon which Ms. Brittain had lamented. As if World War I wasn't enough, the Second Great War would absolutely ensure that the planet would never be the same—and, in unspeakable ways.

Out of World War II came nuclear technology, and along with it came global nuclear-weapons proliferation and the international Doomsday Clock. A major realignment of the nations and a global power structure swelled to the forefront. Visions of a New World Order began to dance through the heads of the world's elite, drunk with the possibilities of realizing a new Tower of Babel dream. They finally had the power with which to terrorize and manipulate the nations. The global human will was beginning to bend. The inhabitants of earth were, at long last, literally crying out for "something or someone" to save them. *Perfect.*

Also, out of World War II came the biblically prophesied rebirth of Israel. That event indubitably started the prophetic clock in motion. All of these events were kicked off by World War I, the experience about which Ms. Brittain writes. We are the first historical generation to see this happen, and the first that can accurately be called "the generation of World Wars." As already noted, many global leaders believe we may now be on the brink of a horrific World War III.

We are in the midst of an ultimate cosmic clash, the war of the powers and principalities in heavenly realms that Paul spoke of in Ephesians 6. It is the battle for the hearts and souls of human beings, and it is the war being waged by the ultimate narcissist of the universe—who thinks he can ultimately "ascend to the throne of the Most High" (Isaiah 14, Ezekiel 28). It was so from the Garden, and will be so until Jesus returns and brings the end to Satan's wicked plot. Until then, the mêlée thunders on.

Won't They Give Up?

In March of 2017, a news headliner on the Internet's top-ranked Drudge Report exclaimed, "Without World Government, Technological Advances Will Destroy Humans."

The announcement corresponded to the following words spoken by, arguably, the world's most famous scientist, Dr. Stephen Hawking:

Technology has advanced at such a pace that [its potential future] aggression may destroy us all by nuclear or biological war. We need to control this inherited instinct by our logic and reason. We need to be quicker to identify such threats and act before they get out of control. This might mean some form of world government.[48]

Then, just two days later, former president Bill Clinton delivered a passionate speech in Washington, DC, Brookings Institute—less than two months after the inauguration of President Donald Trump. Following is a portion of Clinton's remarks:

People who claim to want the nation-state are actually trying to have a pan-national movement to institutionalize separatism and division within borders all over the world. And it always comes down to two things—are we going to live in an us-and-them world, or a world that we live in together? If you got that, in every age and time, the challenges we face can be resolved in a way to keep us going forward instead of taking us to the edge of destruction. The whole history of humankind is basically the definition of who is us and who is them, and the question of whether we should all live under the same set of rules.[49]

Everyone from popes, former presidents, renowned scientists, media elites, United Nations statesmen, world financial magnates, and celebrated educators and authors to technology industry leaders continually sounds the clarion call to install a globalist ruling authority. They desperately long to inaugurate a manmade dreamland of a New World Order—a paradise on earth. In other words, they yearn for a world without the lordship of Yahweh. And, according to the Word of God, they will finally have it, if only for a short while.

The question of what actually will bring about the one-world, Antichrist government system is a subject continually speculated upon within the world of prophecy examination. The globalists elite are discussing everything from a monumental environmental crisis and World War III to a looming financial meltdown, a technology nightmare scenario, and even an "alien invasion" as possibilities that could be used to actuate their dream. The search is never-ending for the one "key" factor that will finally flip the switch and cause the world to "insist" upon a one-world leader and government.

The globalist New World Order elites will not disappear. They have been possessed with a demonic spirit. It is the diabolical, biblically prophesied spirit of our age. That spirit comes straight from the throne of Satan.

Most Christians are thankful that Donald Trump, an avowed nationalist, won the 2016 election. With that win, the Church just might achieve some much-needed breathing room. Certainly, had there been a Hillary Clinton victory, many are convinced that the globalist agenda would have dissolutely barreled ahead—perhaps bowling over America's evangelical Church along the way.

How long will the current respite last? Will the United States finally begin to correct its cultural decay? Will the Church rise to the occasion while there is still a little light shining the way? Will born-again Christians in America determine to "make the Church great again?"

Will Christians use this window of opportunity to advance the Kingdom of Jesus Christ like never before? Or will we sit back in comfort, crying "peace, peace, Donald Trump will save us! We have won!" when that peace may be soon snatched from underneath us? These are good questions. They are serious matters of concern. Let me answer them with three prophetic words, "We shall see."

In the meantime, never forget: If these truly are the prophetic times we believe them to be, and since God has placed us squarely in the midst of these specific days, how can we not be aware that perhaps…just perhaps…we have been raised up *for such a time as this*?

Now, let's get to work! Time is short. Satan is furious. He will not relent. And neither shall the people of God. We have been promised that ultimately the gates of Hell will not prevail. So, let us live that promise in power, and with sound minds.

Even so, Lord Jesus—*come.*

chapter three

Trump's Promise to Drain the Washington Swamp

By Robert Lee Maginnis

onald Trump came to the presidency on a populist wave expecting his nonpolitical business savvy to grant him special insight
into how to fix what's wrong with Washington. Certainly during
the 2016 presidential campaign, Mr. Trump famously promised to do
just that by invoking a common anti-Washington metaphor, "drain the
swamp," which drew widespread applause and seeded expectations that
just maybe a New York billionaire, nonpolitician was the type of person
to finally clean-up Washington.

The newly minted President Trump didn't waste any time recon-
firming his campaign commitment to clean up the mess in Washington.
Moments after taking the oath of office, he stood behind the inaugural
podium looking out across hundreds of thousands of Americans on the
National Mall, then unabashedly let loose on the Washington political
elite hovering nearby in their VIP seats. "For too long, a small group
in our nation's Capital has reaped the rewards of government while the
people have borne the cost. Washington flourished—but the people
did not share in its wealth," Trump declared. The political elite poised
on their cushioned seats hung on Trump's every word, and many likely
squirmed uncomfortably as the new commander-in-chief declared,

"January 20th 2017, will be remembered as the day the people became the rulers of this nation again."[50]

Recent American history demonstrates that fulfilling Trump's campaign promise to drain Washington's political swamp will be a daunting, albeit elusive, challenge that will require great tenacity, a tolerance for massive criticism, and the sobering realization that the new president will only have a brief opportunity to make a dent in the government quagmire before he inevitably must turn his attention to seeking a second term. Can President Trump succeed where all others have failed?

President Trump must quickly tackle an assortment of complex problems that makes Washington a political swamp or, like those who came before him, he, too, will end up in the same slimy vortex that trapped other well-intended leaders such as former President Ronald Reagan, who grudgingly admitted only a year after taking office: "I know it's hard when you're up to your armpits in alligators to remember you came here to drain the swamp."[51]

Although Reagan came to the presidency promising to drain the swamp of big government, his two-term record is mixed at best on that subject and largely due to the unpredictable alligators such as nuclear-arms-reduction talks, the Iran-Contra Affair, air strikes in Libya, and the invasion of Grenada that haunted his presidency. To his credit, Reagan did reduce government spending and stood up against air traffic controllers who illegally went on strike, but in the end, he made only a marginal impact on the well-entrenched Washington quagmire in spite of his campaign promise.[52]

Promising to do something about the political bog in Washington has become part of America's political folklore, which was chronicled three-quarters of a century ago by Hollywood on the widescreen. In 1939, famed producer/director Frank Capra released the classic comedy-drama, *Mr. Smith Goes to Washington*, starring actor James Stewart as a newly minted U.S. senator who fought against a corrupt political system and won, albeit a momentary and small victory.

Much like Mr. Trump, who surprised most political observers by winning the 2016 election, the *Mr. Smith Goes to Washington* movie surprisingly won wide acclaim by earning eleven academy award nominations, winning for best original story—and, in 1989, the Library of Congress added the movie to the U.S. National Film Registry for being "culturally, historically, or aesthetically significant."[53]

The movie's message of exposing Washington corruption was at the time very popular, and that same message evidently enjoys widespread support today, as evidenced by Mr. Trump's electoral victory, which is attributable in part to his promise to "#drain the swamp."

Like the movie character Senator Smith, Mr. Trump faced a lot of criticism throughout the 2016 campaign, especially among the so-called Washington politically elite who expressed little confidence in his lack of a political background. Remember the "Never Trump" crowd and the Republican establishment who ran from Trump? On the other hand, some of the smug Washington elite who did give him an outside chance of defeating Hillary Clinton perceived the businessman as politically naïve and possibly easy to manipulate. They were very wrong on all fronts.

The movie's conniving and corrupt politicians set up Smith for a fall due to his unwillingness to cooperate with their scheme. They turned to the equally corrupt Washington press corps to make a public spectacle of Smith by tarnishing his reputation and branding him a bumpkin. Mr. Trump faced similar opposition.

Just as the attacks against Smith reached a crestfall, the senator launched a filibuster on the Senate floor over the questionable appropriations project intended to line the pockets of his corrupt adversaries. Smith's filibuster stretched almost twenty-four hours, gaining significant media attention, affirming the American ideals of freedom, and disclosing the true motives of the corrupt political system.

Smith collapsed to the Senate floor in exhaustion, and his fellow state senator who conspired against him was overcome with guilt, raced out of the Senate chamber, and attempted to commit suicide—but failed. He returned to the Senate chamber, shouted a confession to the whole corrupt scheme, insisted that he should be expelled, and affirmed Smith's innocence.

One of the most memorable lines from the movie was spoken by Smith, who said, "Well, I'm gettin' out of this town so fast, away from all the words and all the monuments and the whole rotten show." That's a statement of disgust with Washington's corrupt political swamp and a sentiment echoed in a tweet by Mr. Trump during the 2016 presidential campaign: "I will make our government honest again—believe me. But first, I'm going to have to #drain the swamp."[54] Trump knows our government has lost the confidence of the American people. His election is a mandate to quickly expose Washington's corruption and to drain the swamp if he dare.

Draining the Washington Political Swamp

Americans of all stripes are distrustful of their government. In fact, according to polls over the past few decades, the average American senses that our country is going in a very bad direction, and as a result, they have lost confidence in most of the nation's leading institutions such as Congress.[55] That, in part, explains why Mr. Trump's anti-Washington message resonated with many voters. He promised radical change, and those who voted for him now expectantly pray he is the man to turn Washington and the country around.

Mr. Trump employed the "drain the swamp" metaphor during the presidential campaign to communicate his intent to address what the average American believes about the wayward government. That metaphor has been part of campaign fodder for more than a century and used by the political class of every stripe to mean ridding Washington of all that's so distasteful: elitism, corruption, too-big government, over-regulation, high taxes, and so much more.

The metaphor was first used by Mary Harris "Mother" Jones, a prominent nineteenth-century labor and community organizer who promised to drain the Washington swamp of capitalists. More recently, as indicated earlier in this chapter, then-presidential candidate Ronald Reagan invoked the term, and even former Secretary of Defense Donald Rumsfeld used a version of the expression after the September 11, 2001, attacks on America, promising the US would go after terrorists by moving "to drain the swamp they live in."[56]

Democrats have invoked the same term as well. The then newly minted Speaker of the House Nancy Pelosi promised in 2007 to "drain the swamp," which for her meant to clean up the Congress after a decade under Republican leadership, as well as to break the link between lobbyists and congressional legislation.[57]

President Barak Obama invoked the metaphor when he promised to bar presidential appointees from seeking lobbying jobs in Washington and prohibited former lobbyists from working in his administration.[58] He, too, understood the common sentiment that Washington's ecology was broken and distasteful to the average voter.[59]

It's fair to ask: Why has this expression become associated with American political folklore to mean everything that's wrong with Washington, and in particular, our federal government?

Let's begin by disabusing you of the rumor that Washington was built on a literal swamp.

Washington Was Not Built on a Swamp

No, Washington was not built on a swamp, but the land under it once included some marshy areas and river banks prone to periodic flooding.

It is useful to review some American history as it relates to Washington, District of Columbia. The country's Constitution, which took effect in early 1789, gave Congress the authority to establish a federal district up to ten miles square in size.

Mr. Pierre "Peter" Charles L'Enfant, a French-born American architect and civil engineer, had previously asked President George Washington to be commissioned to plan the proposed city, a commission not granted until 1790, after the first Congress passed the "Residence Act," setting the site of the new capital to be on the shores of the Potomac River, the future District of Columbia.[60]

Peter L'Enfant began surveying the site in March 1791 and presented his first plan for the federal city to President Washington on August 19, 1791. L'Enfant found the future site of the nation's capital included fields of tobacco and corn, small forests, and some waterside bluffs and wetlands. The few marshy areas were mostly along the Potomac because of tidal fluctuations and occasional flooding. Even today, the District has many water sources that include Rock Creek, the Potomac River, and the Anacostia River, plus other, smaller feeder creeks.[61]

Part of L'Enfant's survey included the selection of appropriate sites for important government buildings. He selected the top of Jenkins Hill as the future site of the capitol building, and another site was selected for the future White House.

By the way, Jenkins Hill (the present-day site of Capitol Hill) rests at least eighty-eight feet above the level of the nearby Potomac River.[62] It was never a marshland (swamp).

The nineteenth-century Potomac River, as surveyed by L'Enfant, was much wider than it is today, which was changed to accommodate the tidal basin area that now includes the Washington Monument (thirty feet above sea level),[63] the Lincoln Memorial (thirty-three feet above sea level),[64] and the Jefferson Memorial (ten feet above sea level).[65] The present National Mall was once a large, flat and low area used for grazing animals.

America's Experience Draining Swamps & Folklore

The process of preparing the land for the nation's capital included considerable effort to fix the banks of the Potomac River and bring in fill dirt, a common effort seen across America as settlers created useable land from our vast wetlands. Yes, Americans have a lot of experience "draining swamps," which in part may explain why the term migrated into our political vernacular and folklore.

The purpose of draining an actual swamp, other than to create useable land like that for our nation's capital, is to get rid of disease-carrying mosquitoes and other undesirable swamp creatures. That effort begins by building trenches and canals to allow the water to flow out with the help of gravity. Sometimes pumps are needed, especially if the wetland/ swamp is lower than the surrounding areas, a common challenge. Frequently, the drained swamp is then backfilled with dry dirt to preclude future accumulation of water. This is a familiar process, according to a 1989 Department of the Interior study, which found that since the 1780s to present, the US has drained 221 million of 392 million acres of American wetlands, which included many actual, creature-infested swamps.[66]

One of the common reasons to drain a swamp, as outlined above, is to exterminate creatures (like mosquitoes, alligators, and snakes) that are harmful and contribute to the spread of diseases. Perhaps this explains why the metaphor became so politically popular among Americans who understand the draining process and intent. After all, many Americans are deeply suspicious of the Washington political elite, so it made sense to apply their understanding of draining swamps to the political scene in order to get rid of harmful critters like corrupt elitist politicians, bloodsucking lobbyists, and their Washington, self-sustaining, disease-ridden eco-system.

That widely held view explains in part why the movie *Mr. Smith Goes to Washington* became incredibly successful, a perspective not lost on the average American today. Many of our citizens rightly hold to the "outside-the-Beltway" view that Washington's political elites, with their incestuous cronyism, look down their collective noses at the rest of the nation, which they call America's "Fly-Over Country."

Mr. Trump tapped into that widespread resentment, the feeling of being disenfranchised from our bloated and corrupt, self-serving, elite government. For example, as only Trump could illustrate, he explained that corruption by indicating that, over his business career, he has given loads of money to politicians with the unspoken expectation that he can ask them for special treatment—the essence of crony capitalism.

Trump explained how crony capitalism works to reinforce the widespread distaste for Washington's political elite. Specifically, he contributed $100,000 to the Clinton Foundation, and in August 2015, he explained:

> When they [politicians] call, I give. And you know what? When I need something from them two years later, three years later, I call them, they are there for me…. With Hillary Clinton, I said be at my wedding, and she came to my wedding. You know why? She didn't have a choice, because I gave. I gave to a foundation that, frankly, that foundation is supposed to do well. I didn't know her money would be used on private jets going all over the world.[67]

Crony capitalism is just the tip of the diseased Washington elite swamp, however. We also saw during the Obama administration some of the worst abuse of government institutions for elitist political purposes. Remember how the Internal Revenue Service (IRS) targeted anti-Obama conservative groups?

Obama's IRS eventually grudgingly admitted to targeting anti-Obama Tea Party groups for intrusive scrutiny. Federal courts forced Obama's tax agency to provide a list of 426 organizations it targeted for extra (read "illegal") scrutiny.[68]

Tea Party and conservative groups said they were the target of unusually heavy IRS investigations and long delays for their nonprofit applications. So far, no investigation has found any direct order from the

Obama White House to conduct the targeting. However, congressional Republicans said Obama's IRS commissioner John Koskinsen failed and even misled Congress during their investigation, which explains why some Republicans pursued impeachment against Mr. Koskinsen, accusing him of defying a subpoena for former senior IRS executive Lois G. Lerner's e-mails by allowing computer backup tapes to be destroyed, allegedly vanishing evidence of IRS criminal wrongdoing.[69]

Even our justice system was corrupted by the Obama administration for political purposes. The nonprofit Judicial Watch found that Obama's Operation Fast and Furious, a Department of Justice program that officially intended to capture drug dealers in violent Mexican drug cartels, was a politically corrupted effort. It eventually became clear that Mr. Obama's real intent for Fast and Furious was to create an excuse for more gun control, a key liberal political agenda item. The program ended up as part of a scandal involving Obama's presidency that found itself tied to at least sixty-nine killings, to include U.S. Border Patrol Agent Brian Terry.[70]

The Democrats, in the wake of the 2016 presidential campaign, complained that the Federal Bureau of Investigation (FBI) Director James Comey likely helped Mr. Trump's election chances by twice targeting Hillary Clinton for investigations of her illegal e-mail server and thousands of WikiLeaks-published e-mails that illegally released classified information and demonstrated political manipulation and rank corruption. The FBI's alleged role in the election is now a matter under investigation by the Justice Department inspector general, an issue that may never be satisfactorily answered—but that is yet another example of perceived government corruption.

The whole tangled, corrupt relationship between the Obama Justice Department and the Clinton campaign was exposed to the public when former President Clinton was caught secretly meeting with Attorney General Loretta Lynch in Phoenix in June 2016. The meeting took place ahead of the public release of the House Benghazi Committee's report on the 2012 attack on a US consulate in Libya. Remember, that incident brought into question Hillary Clinton's competence as secretary of state. The Phoenix meeting, which Lynch characterized as no more than a social exchange of family greetings, rightly raised questions about the independence of the Justice Department, which at the time was investigating Hillary Clinton's e-mail server scandal and might have been compromised.[71]

The Obama administration was also famously known for wasting taxpayer money on wrong-headed projects, another sign of government corruption. Obama used our Export-Import Bank to grant funds to favored American companies to advance their competitive edge, in itself not necessarily an indicator of corruption. But, in a sign of political hypocrisy, the Obama administration spent at least $34 billion supporting seventy fossil-fuel projects around the world, an unexpected footnote to Obama's own radical climate change legacy. After all, Obama called global warming "terrifying" and helped broker the world's first agreement to tackle it, yet he approved billions in grants to push the planet even closer to climate disaster, albeit it with overseas firms in developing nations.[72]

Obama took a different tactic at home when he heaped praise for renewable energy projects—not fossil-fuel projects like overseas—and poured taxpayer funds into the pockets of that industry. One report indicated that by 2011, Obama visited twenty-two clean-tech projects to emphasize his economic recovery program, which included a $90 billion stimulus program to promote energy independence.[73] Who can forget how Obama siphoned half a billion dollars to one of his favorite green energy companies, Solyndra, a Silicon Valley startup, which eventually went bankrupt, leaving the taxpayer to pay the bill?[74]

Similar corruption was associated with Obama's foreign-policy deals. Remember how the Obama administration secretly laundered $400 million in cash in Swiss francs and euros, palletized the loot, and then shipped it in the dead of night in an unmarked charter jet to Iran? Then Obama's administration illegally wired billions to Iran. Both payoffs

happened in the shadows to seal Mr. Obama's foreign-policy legacy—
the so-called Iran nuclear deal known as the 2015 Joint Comprehensive
Plan of Action.

The corruption goes much deeper. The Obama administration created a mechanism to funnel perhaps billions of taxpayer dollars to leftist
organizations and politicians willing to promote liberal policies, according to the *Wall Street Journal*. The Residential Mortgage-Backed Securities Working Group (RMBS), a collaborative effort by the Department
of Justice and other government entities, was created in 2012 to find
"evidence of false or misleading statements, deception, or other mis-
conduct by market participants (such as loan originators, sponsors,
underwriters, trustees, and others) in the creation, packaging, and sale
of mortgage-backed securities."[75]

What the RMBS actually did is fleece the American taxpayer to line
the pockets of Obama's liberal cronies. It reached: "multibillion-dollar
settlements with essentially every major bank in America, such as the
$5.06 billion grant given to Goldman Sachs for what the Justice Depart-
ment said was conspicuous packaging, marketing, and sales of mortgage-backed securities the company sold consumers from 2005–2007."
The Bank of America received the largest settlement of $16.65 billion
dollars to "resolve federal and state claims against Bank of America and
its former and current subsidiaries."[76]

The rest of the story is that those same banks then were required
to pay $11 billion in consumer relief to those who lost assets due to
bank mismanagement. But in the middle of this so-called relief was a
sweet deal for the big banks. For example, Bank of America was able to
reduce its penalty by simply "giving millions of dollars to liberal groups
approved by the Obama administration." Or, as one writer put it, "The
Obama administration shook down private sector banks in order to funnel cash into the coffers of left wing groups it approved."[77]

The Washington swamp is bad enough at the macro level, but arguably some of the swamp critters are worse. Washington has elite political

figures known for their arrogance, boastfulness, self-pride, greed, and avarice. Remember the brouhaha about Hillary Clinton's leaked e-mails that revealed a seedy, self-serving, haughty crowd of malcontents surrounding the Democrat nominee who felt entitled to special treatment?

There are plenty of tell-all books written by former Washington insiders who either served or were among Washington's elite political class that expose a raft of despicable personal foibles. Just ask the Secret Service, military personnel, and other public servants who had close contact with some political elites—those at the White House, on Capitol Hill, and even among appointees in government. You'll hear about constant, demeaning comments hurled at those who serve elites and demand special favors.

Then consider that the power that comes with Washington elected-office and political appointments can be especially intoxicating for some, further exposing the wretchedness of the swamp ecosystem. It is so addictive that some Washington elite cling to that power for as long as possible, and that sense of entitlement keeps them detached from the electorate and unresponsive to the common citizen. That phenomenon explains why many remain in Washington think tanks and lobbying organizations long after they leave office.

There are many ugly examples of this avarice. How many former members of Congress and government appointees are still in Washington working as high-salaried lobbyists? Lots. Consider the poster child for this "revolving door" to the Washington swamp.

Rep. Billy Tauzin of Louisiana served twelve terms in Congress, and in his final years (2001–2004), he was the chairman of the House Commerce Committee that pushed Medicare legislation to make drugs cheaper for the taxpayer. Ultimately, Tauzin's "cheaper" Medicare drug legislation cost the taxpayer $549 billion over nine years, and meanwhile, he left Congress to collect a cool $2 million annual salary as a lobbyist for the pharmaceutical companies that profited from his drug legislation.

Imagine the corruption that likely occurs when one considers there are battalions of Washington lobbyists doling out billions annually to advance their pet causes.

Opensecrets.org, a nonprofit Washington watchdog organization, reports that as of October 2016 there were 10,886 registered lobbyists in Washington who spent $2.36 billion in 2016 alone. The three top lobbying firms for 2016 were Akin, Gump, et al ($27,700,000); Brownstein, Hyatt, et al ($19,590,000); and the Podesta Group ($17,970,000).[78] It is noteworthy that John Podesta of the Podesta Group was Hillary Clinton's campaign manager in 2016.

Podesta's leaked e-mails were especially telling, providing insight into the corrupt swamp. They told us that Clinton hates "everyday Americans;" Clinton lied about the Saudis funding ISIS; and, according to Podesta's leaked e-mail, most Clinton Foundation donors are not Americans.[79] Perhaps one of the most bizarre e-mails revealed Podesta's invitation to a "spirit cooking dinner" hosted by performance artist Marina Abramovic, to take part in an occult ritual founded by satanist Aleister Crowley.[80]

Obviously, Washington's federal government and its related ecosystem is a swamp full of harmful creatures. How should Mr. Trump go about draining the swamp and getting rid of the dangerous critters?

Draining the Swamp Is Really Hard

Mr. Trump must learn to appreciate the complexity of draining the swamp and the major obstacles. Once those challenges are tackled, then he should consider two parallel major approaches that might truly satisfy the voters who sent him to the White House.

The first approach is to transform government agencies through a deliberate process that improves their efficiency. The second approach is far more radical. Specifically, Mr. Trump should use a figurative machete to chop off many of the heads of the federal bureaucratic swamp hydra, and hopefully that effort won't end up being like the Lernaean Hydra, the many-headed serpent in Greek mythology that, every time someone cut off one of its heads, two more grew out of the stump.[81]

First, consider the more tepid approach of reforming the federal bureaucracy. An outstanding reforming approach is proposed by Frank Ostroff, a management consultant, who wrote in the *Harvard Business Review*, "Change Management in Government," where he first identified four obstacles to reform and then six steps to reform the federal departments.

Ostroff's four obstacles to reform federal departments are tough and pragmatic.

The first is getting the right people with the right skills. Unfortunately, with few exceptions, new administrations tend to fill top federal department jobs with political appointees on the basis of their contributions, campaign work, and, in the best of circumstances, their command of policy, technical expertise, or political connections.

The second obstacle is insufficient time for reform. The presidential nomination process can last months, and the last year of the term, the agency head is looking for a new job. Therefore, the average tenure of political appointees is effectively eighteen to twenty-four months—hardly enough time to make lasting reforms.

The third obstacle is government rules that create organizations that are significantly less flexible than those in the private sector. The top government leader can't fire people willy-nilly or reorganize departments without union objections, personnel complaints, and disrupting established processes that hurt workflow. Further, as Ostroff explains, "Public-sector managers know, too, that the penalties for failure are almost always greater than the rewards for exceptional performance."

The fourth obstacle is too much oversight. Government agencies have many constituencies that exercise oversight, and inevitably someone will disapprove of reform. Congress and its numerous committees can stall reformation by providing too much unhelpful oversight.

So, how does one truly reform the federal bureaucracy given these obstacles? Ostroff argues that every administration in the past forty years has launched initiatives to improve government performance. He identified five principles that characterize successful public-sector reform efforts that show promise to achieve the desired results, which Mr. Trump should consider to make the federal bureaucracy more efficient.

First, improve service to the public, something the taxpayer should expect by keeping the mission crystal clear. Ostroff states, "Once the mission has been articulated, agency leaders must put a stake in the ground by establishing improved performance against mission as the fundamental objective of the transformation effort." Then select clear performance-improvement goals and formulate specific initiatives.

Second, win over as many stakeholders as possible—both external and internal. Ostroff cites the example of the Government Accountability Office (GAO) to illustrate winning over stakeholders. "Theoretically, I have 535 bosses in the Senate and the House," David Walker, the US Comptroller General and GAO leader said in 1998. "I respect them all but have to concentrate on the ones with the most interest in an issue. We identify stakeholders and work hard to understand their issues and concerns." For example, he focused on the chairman and ranking member of the congressional committee with jurisdiction over the issue, as well as others with local interest.

There are also important internal stakeholders who must not be neglected. Many long-time public-sector employees can actually be helpful to a leader seeking change, because they know how their agencies run and where they fail. They can be important allies in the transformation effort.

Third, the reform leader needs a road map. GAO's Walker began reforming his department by talking with Congress members and the agency's two key internal groups. Another way of identifying areas that need change is to review internal reports and conduct interviews of senior managers as well as outside experts. Ultimately, the leader and his/her team must identify performance objectives, set priorities, and roll out the reformation program.

Fourth, the leader must take a comprehensive approach to reform that includes leadership, structure, processes, infrastructure (including technology), people, and performance management. Avoid putting too much emphasis on any single element, however.

Finally, reformation takes a leader, not a bean counter (bureaucrat). The leader must formulate a vision, be aware of present realities, generate broad-based support, and set a clear path. Then hold people accountable for both results and commitment to the change effort.

Federal agencies are complex and sometimes mysterious places. But, as Ostroff argues, the solutions to reform them are not that mysterious. "What's required is recognition that successful change is possible and that a proven set of techniques is available to get you there. Agencies with the vision and courage to undertake meaningful change can use these five principles to achieve their highest purpose."[82]

The above is an approach not so much about draining the swamp, per se, but about making the swamp more efficient. The process begins by understanding each government's department purpose, and then the agency leaders go about reforming their departments to make them as efficient as possible. But too often, reformation is too little and too late; more radical change is warranted. We move to the second approach—take out the machete.

Trump Needs to Take Three Draconian Actions—If He's Serious about "Draining the Swamp"

Making the swamp more efficient isn't enough, at least according to many public opinion surveys, and that's why President Trump needs to consider taking three drastic actions. First, he needs to take a machete to the size of the federal government workforce, and second, he needs to chop away at our significant and over-burdensome regulations. Third, he must scatter what's left of the federal workforce across the fruited plains of America. Collectively, those three actions will do more to change what's wrong with Washington than any reforming of the current federal bureaucratic swamp.

The good news is that just prior to Mr. Trump's inauguration, his transition team announced their intentions regarding federal government spending and staff cuts. Specifically, Trump "landing teams" were sent into each of the cabinet agencies immediately after the inauguration to find up to 10 percent in spending and 20 percent in staffing cuts. The teams were told to only target discretionary spending, not mandated programs such as Medicare and Social Security. Further, the staff cuts are expected to be made over four years through attrition, but there will also be hiring freezes and reorganization.[83]

That announcement won cheers from conservatives, anti-tax and anti-spending groups that have long sought massive cuts in the federal bureaucracy. Time will tell whether Mr. Trump's "landing teams" were successful. However, until the results of those efforts are fully realized, the reader should understand the scope of the problem Trump inherited.

The taxpayer will be interested to know that under President Obama, the federal workforce jumped 10 percent to 1.4 million people other than military personnel. President George W. Bush's record was worse than Obama in terms of percent expansion of the workforce over his two terms. Bush hiked the workforce 17 percent.[84] Meanwhile, to his credit, President Obama reversed a workforce trend that started with President Clinton by cutting government employees and replacing them with contractors to do their jobs. "Obama has worked hard to insource them again, as his union allies have pushed for," said Chris Edwards, director of tax policy at the Washington-based Cato Institute.

Unfortunately, when considering the size of government over many decades, there is every indication it will continue to expand in terms of workforce and expenditures, and it doesn't matter which major political party controls Washington. Specifically, given the assumption that the size of government is a reflection of federal spending, since 1946, the average annual increase in government spending was 2.4 percent under a Democratic and 2.2 percent under a Republican president. The same is true when considering federal spending as a percentage of gross domestic product (GDP). Since 1946, Democratic-led governments spent on average 19 percent of GDP compared to Republican administrations, which spent slightly more, 19.6 percent.[85]

Federal spending levels are not sustainable, another obvious problem for Mr. Trump. The federal government spent $4 trillion in 2016, and annual federal outlays are expected to rise to $5.1 trillion by 2021. Meanwhile, the federal deficit is expected to rise to $23.2 trillion by 2021.[86] The Congressional Budget Office projects that if current laws remain unchanged, then by 2026, the president's budget will be considerably larger as a share of the nation's GDP than its average over the past fifty years, and the debt held by the public will reach 86 percent of GDP.[87]

The increase in federal spending is not necessarily the fault of the bloated workforce. When we set aside Social Security and Medicare, federal spending has fallen below its forty-year historical average and is projected to decline even further. But the fact is further radical change is needed to prevent the inevitable federal default.[88]

Yet, the federal government has plenty of fat ready for cutting, and much of that is duplicative. For example, there are sixteen intelligence agencies serving the US government. Why do we need that many separate intelligence agencies? We don't! Combine them into one agency and then assign intelligence experts to support other government agencies. Consolidating our intelligence agencies will save considerable overhead and the costs associated with redundant infrastructure, and likely it will allow for a significant reduction among the federal intelligence workforce.

The Department of Defense is a bloated organization with four military services, a Joint Staff, an expansive Office of the Secretary of Defense, twenty Defense Agencies, eight Defense Field Activities, six geographical combatant commands, and much more. Although the 1984 Goldwater-Nichols Act was intended to streamline defense operations and find economies to scale, it left in place the terribly redundant dual staffs for each military department. Specifically, the Secretary of the Army has a full staff, and so does the Chief of Staff of the Army. Why does the Army need two duplicative staffs located inside the Pentagon? The same is true with the Departments of the Navy and the Air Force.

Hopefully, Mr. Trump's so-called landing teams identified similar duplicative staffs for cuts across the entire federal government.

Any serious effort to cut government waste must also dust off the Constitution for inspiration to return to the States what rightly belongs to them. The Tenth Amendment to our Constitution provides that any powers not expressly delegated to the federal government are "reserved to the states respectively, or to the people." One doesn't have to scrub the list of federal departments and agencies to make a long list of functions like education that rightly ought to return to the states.

The tug of war between the federal and state governments over the interpretation of the Tenth Amendment is long and bloody, however. In the late 1960s and early 1970s, then President Richard Nixon tried to reverse the flow of power to the federal government back to the states. President Ronald Reagan claimed in the 1980s that the federal government, in its attempts to improve society, was eroding individual freedoms by federalizing so many issues that our founders intended for the states. Even the 1994 Republican-controlled Congress mounted what they called the "Devolution Revolution" to return many functions to the states. Unfortunately, the expansion and consolidation of power by big government in Washington continues.[89]

Once Mr. Trump downsizes the federal workforce, he must next take a machete to out-of-control federal regulations that are a major drain on America's economy.

The Obama administration was responsible for a massive expansion of the regulatory state, which according to the Heritage Foundation, costs taxpayers at least $108 billion annually. The actual costs are likely much greater because the worst effects of overregulation tend to be intangible, such as the loss of freedom and opportunity.[90]

Obama's overzealous rule-making was evident across the entire federal government. Consider a few recent examples of overregulation.

The Environmental Protection Agency's "Clean Power Plan," a 1,560-page regulation, imposed higher energy costs for so-called meaningful climate benefits. Even though the "climate benefits" are elusive, what's clear is that the regulations shifted energy consumption away from plentiful coal—a big job killer—and raised costs for consumers.[91]

The Food and Drug Administration ought to be renamed the food police. In 2011, Congress passed and Obama signed the Food Safety Modernization Act, which dictates how the "federal government expects farmers to produce fruits and vegetables, including rules governing soil, water, hygiene, packing, temperatures, and even what animals may roam which fields and when." The new rules meant higher food costs across the board without any evidence that consumers benefited.[92]

The Democrat-controlled Congress and President Obama gave us hundreds of regulations mandated by the 2010 Dodd-Frank Wall Street Reform and Consumer Protection Act, a response to the 2008 financial crisis, which generated billions of dollars in new annual costs. That new set of regulations is 850 pages of text. Then Dodd-Frank created the Consumer Financial Protection Bureau, which produced 797 pages of additional rules that is far more intrusive than the original law. We are still looking for the benefits to the consumers.[93]

Obama and his Democrat congressional majority created a true regulatory albatross in the name of the Affordable Car Act, better known as Obamacare. The healthcare law created a regulatory juggernaut with 2,700 pages of complex rules that resulted in at least $45 billion in new costs and demanded hundreds of millions of hours of paperwork to comply, according to the American Action Forum. The Obamacare regulations also included hundreds of guidance documents published across the many federal government agencies to "assist" with citizen compliance.[94]

We should remember that Obamacare was famously supported by Speaker of the House Pelosi, who coined the phrase, "We need to pass the bill in order to find out what's in it." This should be an alarm to all that rational governance is not a strong suit of the liberals.

Finally, Obama's Federal Communications Commission created rules governing the Internet. The "Open Internet order" did two things. It reclassified "Internet access" as a common carrier service that subjects service providers to comprehensive FCC regulation of their businesses. The new rules also imposed "network neutrality" requirements, which chill investment and growth.[95] Once again, there is no obvious benefit to the average American consumer.

This avalanche of new rules acts as a stealth tax on the American people by some estimates that amount to more than $2 trillion annually. That's why Mr. Trump needs to move quickly to turn back the snowballing of government regulations. Further, the Republican-controlled Congress must make reforms that require all legislation to undergo an impact analysis before any vote in Congress, and any new rules must have a sunset deadline.

Once the size of government is reduced and federal regulations are downsized to the bone, the final and perhaps most radical change is to move much of the federal bureaucracy out of Washington.

Any serious consideration of "draining the swamp" must include moving all or major parts of the federal government out of Washington. After all, Mr. Trump pledged to rebuild America's troubled inner cities and restore confidence in their government. Why not make good on that promise by moving federal government agencies out of Washington and closer to the citizens they serve in cities like Detroit and Milwaukee?

There are many good reasons for scattering the federal workforce. One of those reasons includes sharing the wealth, because rightly many Americans view the federal government as a money machine for bureaucrats and Washington elites. According to the 2010 U.S. Census, eleven of the twenty richest counties in America are in the Washington, DC, metro area. That wealth is attributed to generous federal payrolls, but also to the lobbyists and contractors who swarm like flies around federal agencies.[96]

There is also a compelling security reason for relocating the federal workforce. Concentrating them in mostly one metro area makes the government especially vulnerable to a major terrorist attack. A 2016 paper by scholars from the London School of Economics and MIT anticipates the chances of either a biological or nuclear attack at 76 percent by the year 2050. The center of mass of the US government is a prime target for such an attack.[97]

So scatter federal agencies across the nation to preserve the integrity of the government's workforce in today's terrorist-rich environment, and at the same time bolster many local economies by creating new jobs and adding new infrastructure across the country. Just as important as relocating parts of the federal workforce to the fly over parts of America is the renewal of faith that our government really exists not to serve the Washington elite, but the American people.[98]

An added benefit of the proposed Washington exodus would be to ensure that more Americans are given the opportunity to serve in the federal workforce. Right now, Washington bureaucracies tend to attract a large percentage of East Coast liberals. A major agency relocated to Omaha or Waco would soon be filled with Middle American conservatives and add balance to the groupthink currently in Washington's swamp.

There is no compelling reason not, for example, to relocate most of the Department of Defense to Fort Bragg, North Carolina, or Fort Riley, Kansas, where the cost of living is far less and there is plenty of land. Put the State Department in New York City, where many of the world governments already have a significant presence.

Imagine what relocating the Federal Bureau of Investigation (FBI) to Detroit would do for that area. Moving eleven thousand FBI employees to Detroit would create $2.5 billion in construction spending and provide a major boost to the local economy. Besides, government acquisition and building and maintenance costs are likely to shrink in Detroit, and so will the costs for contractors who service the government.

There's a reasonable chance that relocating federal bureaucracies will have other benefits, such as providing a massive infrastructure and stimulus. Relocating would also save on federal salaries that are pumped up because of the metro DC cost-of-living premium. Congress should welcome the benefit of a much cheaper federal labor cost.

Finally, modern technology exists today to scatter government agencies across the land without creating major problems while enjoying very significant benefits. This is an issue ripe for Mr. Trump.

Can the swamp really be drained?

Let's be realistic. "Drain the swamp" is an attractive metaphor to win votes. But no politician has ever accomplished that promise. I suspect that Trump's success will end up looking like something less than a new, level, productive farm field devoid of evil swamp creatures.

It wasn't surprising when Trump's first campaign manager, Corey Lewandowsky, lowered expectations about the president's "drain the swamp" campaign promise. What Trump meant by using the metaphor, according to Lewandowsky, is he intends to cut the federal bureaucracy and create more jobs. Don't get me wrong; that will be a great accomplishment, but realistically, it's a far cry from the common perception of what "drain the swamp" really means for many Americans—especially among those who voted for Mr. Trump.[99]

Lewandowski's statement was an effort to give Trump's supporters a dose of reality. But Mr. Trump promised to do more than just cut the bureaucracy and create jobs, and we wish him success.

On October 17, 2016, Trump promised very specific steps that target Washington's institutional corruption: Impose a ban on executive officials from lobbying for five years; ask Congress to do the same for its own members and staff; expand the legal definition of lobbying "so we close all the loopholes that former government officials use by labeling themselves consultants and advisers when we all know they are lobbyists"; ban senior administration officials from lobbying for foreign governments; and stop foreign lobbyists from raising money for US elections.[100]

Unfortunately, those actions could end up being the best we can reasonably expect. After all, campaign promises aren't enforceable, and besides, Congress has shown no interest in strengthening its own lobbying ban. Besides, the Trump administration seems to have already violated one of the tenets of its anti-swamp rhetoric by hiring outside consultants, such as the firm led by Brad Parscale, whose digital consulting firm earned $70 million from the Trump campaign.[101]

Frankly, and I must say with some disappointment, it appears Mr. Trump is vulnerable to falling into the same slimy Washington political swamp that sucked in his predecessors. After all, swamps are replete with quicksand.

Remember when Trump criticized Hillary Clinton during the 2016 campaign for being "crooked" and making a fortune on the backs of hard-working Americans? In fact, at the time, he tweeted an advertisement accusing Clinton of profiting from her government service.[102] But Mr. Trump better watch his step as well. His rich cronies, some who are fellow billionaire cabinet officials like Rex Tillerson, should keep short accounts lest they commit Clinton-esqe offenses either during their service or later. The temptations associated with federal executive service are great, and we humans are vulnerable.

Hopefully, President Trump will succeed at minimizing the influence of special interests by culling lobbyists from his administration and reducing the likelihood of future corruption by running accountable government agencies. However, chances are, unless Mr. Trump takes a long view and personally engages with subordinate officials to reform, downsize the government workforce, cut regulations and federal spending, and then ship much of the bureaucracy to new homes across America, the Washington swamp will continue its old corrupt and elitist ways.

Finally, the real hope of success for America and for Mr. Trump's promise to "drain the swamp" and "Make America Great Again" rests on whether God blesses the new administration. Will Mr. Trump tap into God's offer of help?

Just prior to attending the inauguration ceremony, President-elect Trump attended a private service at St. John's Episcopal Church led by Rev. Robert Jeffress, a Southern Baptist supporter. Jeffress' sermon was drawn from the story of Nehemiah, a great leader God chose thousands of years ago to rebuild Israel.[103]

Nehemiah was neither politician nor priest, just a man called to build a wall around Jerusalem to protect its citizens from enemy attack. Nehemiah succeeded for three reasons, and so might Mr. Trump, if he remains faithful to his calling.

First, Mr. Trump must refuse to allow his critics to distract him. Like Nehemiah, he must expect to face criticism. Two of Nehemiah's antagonists, Sanballat and Tobiah, hounded and spread false rumors about him. "Stop and come down to meet with us," his critics insisted. To which Nehemiah said, "I'm doing a great work…why should I stop the work and come down to you?" (Nehemiah 6:3).

Second, Nehemiah refused to allow setbacks such as lack of money, terrorist attacks, and discouragement among the Israelites. Nehemiah never gave into those setbacks, and neither should Mr. Trump.

Third, Nehemiah was a gifted natural leader, but his secret was God's divine help. "O Lord, let your ear be attentive to the prayer of this your servant who delights in revering your name. Give your servant success today" (Nehemiah 1:11).

Mr. Trump possesses significant leadership skills, but his challenges are greater than his natural abilities. He must tap into God's power.

The good news is that God is willing to help Mr. Trump. Psalm

50:15 promises: "Call upon me in the day of trouble I shall rescue you and you will honor me."[104]

Time will tell whether Mr. Trump taps into God's power, and if he does, then he will succeed in draining the Washington political swamp and leading America into a bright future. We must all pray for his success!

chapter four

Was Zenith 2016 Just Fulfilled?

Now that we know who the important Saboteurs, deep-state, and shadow government players are, what globalists are scheming, and what it will actually take for Trump to drain the DC swamp, the time has come for me to spend a few chapters examining a more profound spiritual question: Is the arrival of Donald Trump something that God was behind for reasons beyond what can be discerned through the lens of political and election analysis?

If you ask retired firefighter Mark Taylor that question, his answer would be a resounding "yes!" A "word" came to Taylor in April 2011 in the middle of a most debilitating sickness, and it was very specific (written down in 2011, shared with his doctor, and recorded on radio shows between then and 2015). God was going to allow Trump to become president against all odds; the stock market would respond positively even though deep-state antagonists would attack the Republican candidate like none other before; the US and Israel would strengthen their relationship; and a specific number of Supreme Court justices would be appointed. Those, as well as a whole list of other foresights listed by Taylor, at the time I am writing this book, continue to materialize in the way that he—or God—said they would (with Trump's victory only the beginning and numerous other very specific events scheduled to transpire between now and 2024, according to Taylor's new best-selling book, *The Trump Prophecies* [Defender Publishing, 2017]).

But the difference between Mark Taylor's personal prophetic word and reasons other religious folks may have voted for (or against) Trump lies in a deeper question having to do with *providence.*

In theology, divine providence refers to God's oversight, management, and involvement in the world with a distinction usually made between "general providence," which represents God's sustaining of the natural order of the universe, and "special providence," which refers to His intervention in history for people (such as a healing miracle), governments (such as placing a king in power), and nations (such as helping win a world war).

Unless you are atheist, agnostic, deist, or something like them, at some level you believe in the providence of God and that He was and is involved in this type of creation and management of the cosmos, with earth holding a special place in His plans.

Does this imply that God is involved in everything that happens to every person on the planet every day? Did He ordain that you mowed your lawn yesterday, or that your neighbor stubbed her toe on the sidewalk? If He's not involved in those types of menial things, how about major events that influence the affairs of nations? Most scholars reject the former idea in favor of the latter—that God does not necessary direct your steps over what color curtains you decide to buy, but is often involved in matters of state, at least to the degree that citizens and nations can be blessed or cursed as a result of national leadership (1 Timothy 2:1–3).

With that in mind, did God, "who works all things together for good" (Romans 8:28) ordain the election of Donald Trump?

Those members of the clergy who laid hands on him and prayed at the New Spirit Revival Center in Cleveland Heights, September 21,

2016, must have thought so, as did other prominent Christian leaders during the campaign and most of the clergy who offered invocations at his unforgettable inauguration. Some of these Christians trust in Trump's statement of faith, while others simply see him as imperfect but chosen by God.

For instance, Dr. Lance Wallnau refers to Trump as God's "chaos" president, a line he borrowed from Jeb Bush, who had coined the phrase in describing Trump during the final Republican debate. Wallnau draws analogies between Trump and Cyrus "the Great," the pagan Persian king whom Isaiah prophesied by name two hundred years in advance (Isaiah 44:28), saying that he would conquer Babylon (that happened in 539 BC); the waters of the Euphrates would "dry up" to make way for the army; and the city's gates would "not be shut," and thereby, the Jews would be liberated and return to Jerusalem, where they would rebuild the temple—all of which happened just as the prophet foresaw many years in advance. According to Wallnau, Trump was chosen by God to similarly rescue America from its catastrophic alternative (Hillary).

Others, like Messianic Rabbi Curt Landry, have drawn the same Cyrus analogies and note how it seems beyond random chance that 2017 is the Hebrew year 5777, and on January 20, 2017, the first day Trump took office as forty-fifth president, he turned 70 years, 7 months and 7 days of age. [105] Also of interest is how, as forty-fifth president, this matches Isaiah 45, where the prophecies of Cyrus were given.

Curiously, Cyrus isn't the only example of a pagan leader used by God to providentially influence the ancient Jewish nation. Nebuchadnezzar was also called "the Servant of the Most High God," and I understand why many modern believers prefer not to think about that example. Unlike Cyrus the deliverer, Nebuchadnezzar was the instrument of God's chastisement against Judah, resulting in most of the people (approximately seventy thousand) being brought into captivity with desolation upon their land. This was the providence of God, too, because they would not listen to His words (Jeremiah 25:8ff). The prophet Habakkuk bemoaned God using such a heathen to spank His own children, but God told him it was necessary, and that Nebuchadnezzar would be dealt with later (Habakkuk 1:5–11; cf. Jeremiah 25:12ff).

Assyria and Babylon are two more examples of pagan entities used by God to correct His people after they had fallen into apostasy. The Assyrians went to war against Israel under Tiglath-pileser (2 Kings 15:29; 16:7–9), and again under Shalmaneser and Sargon—all because they would not obey "the voice of Jehovah their God" (2 Kings 18:9–12).

These contrasting illustrations raise a serious question. If God did through providence choose Trump to become America's president, is he our Cyrus (deliverer) or Nebuchadnezzar (agent of judgment)? I want to believe Trump was God's way of putting his foot down on the socialist-globalist runaway agenda to allow a respite and opportunity for spiritual awakening in this country. But what if I'm wrong?

Speaking of Nebuchadnezzar, his example also illustrates how in times past God sometimes used pagans to utter divine insights. An amazing case in point is when God chose to reveal a prophecy spanning from 605 BC through the Scond Coming of Christ to the arrogant, narcissistic, idol-worshipping Nebuchadnezzar. Of course, it required God's holy servant, Daniel, to interpret the dream. Similarly, God used Balaam, a sorcerer hired by Balak, a Moabite king, who was exceedingly fearful of the encroaching multitude of Israelites. Accordingly, the king sent for Balaam, a darkened wizard who now lives in prophetic infamy (2 Peter 2:15; Jude 11; Revelation 2:14). Despite Balaam's incorrigible status, God used him to prophesy, "I shall see him, but not now: I shall behold him, but not nigh: there shall come a Star out of Jacob, and a Sceptre shall rise out of Israel" (Numbers 24:17). Ronald Allen, professor of Hebrew Scripture at Western Baptist Seminary, writes, "In agreement with many in the early church and in early Judaism, we believe this text speaks unmistakably of the coming of the Messiah. That this prophecy should come from one who was unworthy makes it all the more dramatic and startling." Thus, we see that God uses the most unlikely characters and situations to get His message across and work done. This Pethorian prophecy was well over one thousand years before the birth of Christ and from a hostile source, yet it is probably what led the Magi to Bethlehem.

Another interesting thing about Trump and unlikely agents who lead wise men to Bethlehem is the mysterious and metaphysical logic some currently share involving God's possible providence in the arrival of Trump as a "savior" figure. Nowhere is this language more pronounced than in the Holy Land itself, where several respected Rabbis and kabbalists have insinuated that America's new president is a forerunner of Messiah and the final redemption.

"Donald Trump (424) is the Gematria of 'Messiah for the House of David' (דוד בן משיח)," wrote Adam Eliyahu Berkowitz for *Breaking Israel News* on May 16, 2016. "That is not to say that Donald Trump is the Messiah, but that his presidency will usher in the Messianic era."[106]

Others, including Rabbi Matityahu Glazerson, who accurately predicted the Trump victory before the election using Bible Codes,[107] have chimed in. He found various connections between Trump and "moshiach" (messiah) in the codes, which in Hebrew means "anointed," and led Glazerson to conclude his election is connected to the coming of Messiah.

Rabbi Hillel Weiss is a Trump-Messiah-connection believer too, and he also sees in the president the agent of God's favor for building the Third Temple, another Cyrus linking.[108]

And then there is the Sanhedrin in Israel, the nascent tribunal who have styled themselves after the Second Temple-era Jewish court. They have sent letters to Donald Trump and Russian President Vladimir Putin, asking them to join forces to build the Third Temple for Messiah.

Professor Weiss is a spokesman for the Sanhedrin and notes how Donald Trump made support for Israel and recognition of Jerusalem as their capital part of public discourse during 2016. Combining that with Putin's expressed opinion that the Third Temple ought to be built now caused him to say that both men should do what King Cyrus did 2,500 years ago and build the religious complex for the benefit of all Jews and the world. "We are poised to rebuild the Temple," Weiss said, and "the leaders of Russia and America can lead the nations of the world to global peace through building the Temple, the source of peace."[109]

Rabbi Yosef Berger, who oversees King David's tomb in Jerusalem, takes it a step farther. He believes Trump actually won the election through "the power of Moshiach [Messiah], which gave him the boost he needed" and is "connected to the Messianic process which is happening right now."[110]

When I brought all this up not long ago on *The Jim Bakker Show,* I noted how many Jewish leaders view Trump as connected to end-times prophecy in general and/or to the Messiah specifically, extreme leftists at Right Wing Watch couldn't help but jump on the "fake news" bandwagon and use the opportunity to once again misconstrue everything I said to make it sound like I was pitching the Donald as a modern John the Baptist or as the Messiah Himself. Of course, they've made a career out of hating Jim Bakker and trolling his shows, but their ridiculous headline this time was really over the top: "End Times Pastor: Donald Trump Could Be the Messiah or His Forerunner" followed by:

> One of Bakker's guests, Tom Horn, a prolific author of Last Days-themed books, spent an entire segment of the program explaining that "rabbis" have revealed that Trump may be the messiah, or a harbinger to the arrival of the messiah akin to John the Baptist.
>
> "They're looking at Donald Trump" as the messiah, Horn said of "the rabbis," saying that Trump's name "actually means 'messiah.'"

Right Wing Watch was mostly fair to this point, but then, as usual, their straw man couldn't resist the opportunity to misrepresent what I said, which anybody can verify for themselves by watching the archive of the program on the *Jim Bakker Show* website.

Right Wing Watch continued:

> Among the clues that Trump may be the messiah, he [me] said, is that the president-elect is a kingly and warrior-like leader committed to protecting Israel and, according to Horn, rebuilding the Temple of Jerusalem.

Eh, no, I didn't say that either. This is again a classic misdirection from context that no legitimate journalist would make, as I never insinuated any "clues that Trump may be the Messiah," never said he was a kingly or a warrior-like leader, or that he was going to rebuild the temple, but rather stated that the rabbis were saying this.

But the beat went on…

> Horn said that if Trump is not the messiah, then he is likely "the forerunner" to the messiah who "will start the message in the wilderness and the messiah is going to come in on his heels"

This was their biggest lie and, again, I said no such thing. This was just more blatant misdirection, as I specifically cited that some rabbis believe that Trump is a forerunner, which they do, and have said so. But, *sigh*, what more could I have expected from a washed-up fake-news publishing hack like Right Wing Watch?[111]

Now I can hardly wait to see what Right Wing Watch says in 2022, if they are still around. This will be midway through Trump's second term, according to Mark Taylor, when for the first time in recorded history, people will witness with the naked eye a brand-new star. According to astronomers at Apache Point and the University of Wyoming,[112] it will suddenly appear and be the brightest in the sky for six months, precisely the celestial phenomenon the Jews in the Zohar and Torah and

Christians from the New Testament book of Matthew believe will mark the arrival of Messiah.

> And then the sign of the Son of Man will appear in the sky, and then all the tribes of the earth will mourn, and they will see the Son of Man coming on the clouds of the sky with power and great glory. (Matthew 24:30)

All of this brings me to another important point involving messianic prophecies: political players, providence, the year of Trump's election specifically (2016), and the prophetic ramifications of where we may be headed.

Was Zenith 2016 Just Fulfilled?

In 2009, I released the book *Apollyon Rising* that was later updated and rereleased as *Zenith 2016* due to important information I came across after publishing of the first version, which many consider my seminal work and *magnum opus*. I hope, with the release of *Saboteurs*, to find similar accolades, as I truly believe this to be the most important and timely research I've released since.

Besides having a full year in 2009 to travel, interview, and research related topics as well as taking the sabbatical I needed for the actual writing, what made *Zenith* unusual was the big question about why so many ancients—some from hundreds of years ago and some from much farther back—foresaw the year 2016 specifically as the date when the Messiah, or, alternatively, the Antichrist, would arrive on earth, with most believing "his" presence would become known to a select few in 2016 but remain unrecognized by wider populations until slowly "he" is revealed for who and what he actually is at the appropriate time in the immediate years following. Even a major Sunni website set these dates years before Trump's election after studying the ancient Quran and

Hadith, saying:

> Based on our numerical analysis…the official beginning of the
> End of Time and the coming of the Imam Mahdi [their Mes-
> siah, but for others like Joel Richardson, the Antichrist] will
> most likely be in…2016 and Jesus Christ will come down from
> Heaven to Earth in 2022 [that's the date when the new star
> appears in the heavens, which was not published or known at
> the time these Muslims set their dates].[113]

The most ancient prognosticators that intrigued me in *Zenith* for
whom the year 2016 appeared prophetically significant are as follows:

Prophecy from the *Zohar* on Messiah's Arrival

Widely considered the most important work of Jewish Kabbalah,
the *Zohar* is a collection of books written in medieval Aramaic
over seven hundred years ago containing mystical commentary
on the Pentateuch (five books of Moses, the Torah). In addition
to interpreting Scripture, the Vaera section (volume 3, section
34) includes, "The signs heralding Mashiach," or, "The coming
of the Messiah." The fascinating date for "his" secret presenta-
tion to the rabbis in Israel was set in the *Zohar* for 2012–2013
(given the rejection of Jesus by orthodox Jews as Messiah, evangelicals would say this seven-hundred-year-old prediction indi-
cates the Antichrist could have arrived circa 2012–2013).

And, sure enough, on the heels of that date, some of Israel's
foremost rabbis began behaving as if they knew something the
rest of the world does not involving the arrival of "Messiah." In
addition to the ones I quoted earlier in this chapter who believe
the Messianic era has started, Chaim Kanievsky—one of Israel's
most prominent rabbis, a leader of the Haredi branch of Judaism, and a recognized authority on Jewish law—has recently

been warning his students not to leave the Holy Land, because, "The Messiah is already here. He will reveal himself very soon…. Don't travel."[114]

The Eight-Hundred-Year-Old Prophecy of Rabbi Judah Ben Samuel

Will the years immediately following 2016 be prophetically important for Israel and the world? According to an eight-hundred-year-old prophecy, it certainly could. Before he died of cancer, J. R. Church analyzed the ancient predictions of Rabbi Judah Ben Samuel and noted:

> Ludwig Schneider, writing for *Israel Today* (March 2008) said, "Some 800 years ago in Germany, Rabbi Judah Ben Samuel was a top Talmudic scholar with an inclination for the mystical. Before he died in the year 1217, he prophesied that the Ottoman Turks would conquer Jerusalem and rule the Holy City for 'eight Jubilee Years.'" A biblical Jubilee year consists of 50 years. Fifty multiplied by eight equals 400 years.
>
> Afterwards, according to Ben Samuel, the Ottomans would be driven out of Jerusalem, which would remain a no-man's land for one Jubilee year. In the tenth Jubilee year [2017]…the Messianic end times would begin.…
>
> Looking back at Ben Samuel's prediction, we should note that the Ottoman Empire did conquer Jerusalem in 1517, exactly 300 years after the rabbi's death, and was defeated 400 years later in 1917.
>
> In *Israel Today*, Ludwig Schneider continues, "This came to pass 300 years after Ben Samuel's death. He could not have based this prophecy on events that could be foreseen, but only on the results of his study of the Bible.
>
> "According to Leviticus 25, the nation is reunited with its land in the year of Jubilee. Therefore, the Jubilee year plays an

important role in Israel's history. In this case, the Jubilee began with the defeat and conquest of the Mamelukes in Jerusalem by the Ottoman Kingdom in 1517. The Turks reigned over Jerusalem until the British General Edmund Allenby defeated them exactly eight Jubilees later in 1917.

"Ben Samuel's prophecy was fulfilled precisely because 1517 to 1917 is exactly 400 years. Afterward, Jerusalem was a no-man's land for 50 years during the time of the British Mandate (1917–1967) and the time of Jordanian rule (1947–1967), another Jubilee year. During the Six Day War in 1967, Israel captured Jerusalem from Jordan and the city returned to the Jewish people after nearly two millennia of exile. After that, the countdown for the Messianic age began."

Schneider assumes that since Rabbi Judah Ben Samuel's prediction appears to be fulfilled to date, then 2017 should launch the beginning of the Messianic era. [115]

Protestant Reformers and What They Believed Would Start In 2016

Among the turn-of-the-century Protestant reformers, an astonishing number of theologians believed the False Prophet and Antichrist would assume places of authority in 2016 and shortly thereafter ascend the world stage. The famous preacher Jonathan Edwards was convinced of this possibility and held a postmillennial view based on the 1,260 days the woman is in the wilderness in Revelation 12:6. He interpreted those days as the years when the true Church was to be oppressed by the papists. Clarence Goen writes of this, "Edwards considered that the most likely time for the...reign of Antichrist was 1260 years after AD 756 (the acceding of temporal power to the Pope)," [116] which would place the (beginning) of Antichrist's power squarely in 2016. When we were doing research for the book, *Petrus Romanus: The Final Pope Is Here*, we learned of this belief by Edwards and sought to verify it by examining a collection of his voluminous personal writings. We found confirmation within a series of his sermons preached at Northampton, Massachusetts, in 1739, on how history and prophecy coincide:

> I am far from pretending to determine the time when the reign of Antichrist began, which is a point that has been so much controverted among divines and expositors. It is certain that the twelve hundred and sixty days, or years, which are so often in Scripture mentioned as the time of the continuance of Antichrist's reign, did not commence before the year of Christ four hundred and seventy-nine; because if they did, they would have ended, and Antichrist would have fallen before now. The rise of Antichrist was gradual. The Christian church corrupted itself in many things presently after Constantine's time; growing more and more superstitious in its worship and by degrees bringing in many ceremonies into the worship of God, till at length they brought in the worship of saints, and set up images in their churches. The clergy in general, and especially the bishop of Rome, assumed more and more authority to himself. In the primitive times, he was only a minister of a congregation; then a standing moderator of a presbytery; then a diocesan bishop; then a metropolitan, which is equivalent to an archbishop; then a patriarch. Afterwards he claimed the power of universal bishop over the whole Christian church; wherein he was opposed for a while, but afterwards was confirmed in it by the civil power of the emperor in the year six hundred and six. After that he claimed the power of a temporal prince, and so was wont to carry two swords, to signify that both the temporal and spiritual sword was his. He claimed more and more authority, till at length, as Christ's vice-regent on earth, he claimed the very same power that Christ would have done, if he was present on earth reigning on his throne; or the same power that belongs to God,

and was used to be called *God on earth*; to be submitted to by all the princes of Christendom.[117]

We also found this letter by Edwards that addresses the 1,260 days specifically:

To the Rev. Mr. M'Culloch.
Northampton, Oct. 7, 1748.
Rev. and Dear Sir,

[edited out first section]

With respect to your very ingenious conjectures, concerning the period of *forty-two months*, or *one thousand two hundred and sixty days*, of the outer court and holy city's being trodden under-foot of the Gentiles; you know, Sir, that that forty-two months, or one thousand two hundred and sixty days, spoken of Rev. xi. 2. has been universally understood, as being the very same period with the 1260 days of the witnesses prophesying in sackcloth, spoken of in the next verse; and the one thousand two hundred and sixty days of the woman's being led in the wilderness, chap. xii. 6. and the time, times, and half a time, of her being nourished in the wilderness from the face of the serpent, ver. 14. and the forty-two months of the continuance of the beast, chap. xiii. 5. But it does not appear to me probable that these forty-two months of the continuance of the beast, means the sum of the diverse periods in which the *plat of ground*, whereon the ancient literal Jerusalem stood, was under the dominion of the Romans, Saracens, Persians, and Turks; but the space of time during which the reign of antichrist or the popish hierarchy continues; and as to the particular time of the downfall of antichrist, you see my reasons in the forementioned pamphlet, why I think it certain that it will not be known till it be accomplished: I cannot but think that the Scripture is plain in that matter, and that it does, in effect, require us to rest satisfied in ignorance till *the time of the end* comes.

However, I should be very foolish, if I were dogmatical in my thoughts concerning the interpretation of the prophecies: especially in opposition to those who have had so much more opportunity to be well acquainted with things of this nature. But since you have insisted on my thoughts, I conclude you will not be displeased that I have mentioned them, though not altogether agreeable to yours. I am nevertheless greatly obliged to you for your condescension in communicating your thoughts to me. If we do not exactly agree in our thoughts about these things, yet in our prayers for the accomplishment of these glorious events in God's time, and for God's gracious presence with us, and his assistance in endeavours to promote his kingdom and interests, in the meantime, we may be entirely agreed and united. That we may be so, is the earnest desire of, dear Sir,

Your Affectionate Brother and Servant,

In Our Common Lord,

Jonathan Edwards[118]

As we endeavored to demonstrate in *Petrus Romanus*, the pope's rise to temporal power began when Pope Stephen began courting Pepin around 751 and then became a reality in 756 with the expulsion of the Lombards. We wrote how 756 placed the target sometime in 2016. Around that same time during our investigation, we became aware of a sermon collection from the 1800s titled, "Lectures on the Revelation," by the Reverend William J. Reid, pastor of First United Presbyterian Church in Pittsburgh, Pennsylvania, which were given over a period of time ending in March of 1876. Like Jonathan Edwards had over a hundred years earlier, Reid deduced that the False Prophet and Antichrist would arrive sometime around 2016. Soon we uncovered numerous other ancient examples in which the year 2016 was specifically foreseen as when the False Prophet and the Antichrist would be on earth, followed by the destruction of Rome. These included:

- *The Theological Dictionary of Princeton University* (1830)
- *Critical Commentary and Paraphrase on the Old and New Testament by Lowth and Lowman* (1822)
- *The American Biblical Repo*sitory (1840)
- *Notes on the Revelation of St. John by Lowman* (1773)
- *The Christian Spectator,* "The Monthly" (1885)
- *Abridgement of Ecclesiastical History* (1776)
- *The Works of the Rev. P. Doddridge, DD* (1804)
- The International Sunday School Lessons Pub (1878)
- *Character and Prospects on the Church of Rome in Two Discourses* by the Rev. William Mackray (1829)
- *The Panoplist and Missionary* magazine (1809)
- *Lectures on Romanism* by Joseph F. Berg (1840)
- The *Congregational Magazine for the Year* (1834)
- *The Presbyterian Magazine* (1858)

Petrus Romanus and the Final Conclave

As stated in our bestselling book, *Petrus Romanus,* the idea by some Catholics that the final pope from St. Malachy's list heralds the beginning of "great apostasy" followed by "great tribulation" sets the stage for the imminent unfolding of apocalyptic events, something many non-Catholics would agree with. This could give rise to the False Prophet, who, according to the book of Revelation, leads the world's *religious* communities into embracing a *political* leader known as the Antichrist. This marriage of Church and secular government would give unprecedented global influence to the Man of Sin during the period known as the Great Tribulation.

In recent history, several Catholic priests—some deceased now—have been surprisingly outspoken on what they have seen as the inevitable danger of the False Prophet rising from within the ranks of Catholicism as a result of secret satanic "Illuminati-Masonic" influences. These priests used the term "Illuminati" not strictly as a reference to the Bavarian movement founded May 1, 1776, by Jesuit-taught Adam Weishaupt, but as indicative of a modern multinational power elite, the occult hierarchy operating behind current supranatural and global political machinations, such as Donald Trump is now learning about. According to Catholic priests such as Father John F. O'Connor, Father Alfred Kunz, Father Malachi Martin, and others, among this secret society are sinister false Catholic infiltrators who understand that, as the Roman Catholic Church represents one-sixth of the world's population and over half of all professing Christians, it is indispensable for controlling future global elements in matters of church and state.

In *Petrus,* we especially featured retired professor of the Pontifical Biblical Institute, eminent Catholic theologian, and former Jesuit priest, Malachi Martin, who was a close personal friend of Pope Paul VI and worked within the Holy See doing research on the Dead Sea Scrolls, publishing articles in journals on Semitic paleography, and teaching Aramaic, Hebrew, and Sacred Scripture. In 1965, Paul VI granted Martin a dispensation from his Jesuit and priestly duties, and Martin moved to New York, where he dedicated himself to writing about—and sometimes speaking out on—a variety of issues stemming from the Second Vatican Council, to detailed insider accounts of papal history, Catholic dogma, and geopolitics. As a member of the Vatican Advisory Council and personal secretary to renowned Jesuit Cardinal Augustin Bea, Martin had privileged information pertaining to secretive Church and world issues, including the Third Secret of Fátima, which many believe has never been released and that Martin hinted spelled out parts of a plan to formally install the dreaded False Prophet during a "Final Conclave." In light of Pope Benedict's resignation, which Cris Putnam and I accurately predicted to the month and year in our influential work, and the election of the first Jesuit to the pontificate, Martin's book, *Windswept House*—in which he depicted how a pope would be secretly forced from office (Benedict?) and replaced by a Jesuit-backed leader who would help them establish a New World Order (Francis?)—comes vividly into view. Martin's claim that this Illuminati-empowered group had infiltrated the highest levels of Vatican administration and was working to bring about this New World Order may also have led to involvement by operatives of the same group concerning his untimely—some say "suspicious"—death in 1999. Was he murdered by the Masonic "Superforce" he had warned about as working behind the scenes, secretly acting to use the Vatican to bring about a global Antichrist system?

We investigated this conspiracy extensively in *Petrus Romanus*, and if you have not read that book, you should do so as soon as you can.

Why?

Because a growing number of Catholic theologians, priests, and laity are increasingly concerned that Pope Francis may not only be the man from Malachy's ancient "Prophecy of the Popes," but the one Malachi Martin feared. [119]

And it isn't just conspiracy fruit-loops thinking this way. In fact, the pope's personal secretary, emeritus Pope Benedict, and even Pope Francis himself may agree.

In a shocking 2014 interview titled *Is Francis the Last Pope?* published by the two largest Catholic News agencies in the world (CAN and EWTN News), the personal secretary to Pope Benedict and Prefect of the Papal Household for Pope Francis, Archbishop George Gänswein was specifically asked about the "Prophesy of Malachy," the retirement of Benedict, and whether Francis believes he is the last pontiff.

The interview began by making direct reference to questions I (Tom Horn) had raised regarding the dual lightning strikes atop St. Peter's Basilica on the evening of February 11, 2013, on the same day of Benedict's resignation. I followed that with commentary about the inauguration of

Francis and how, "for a few adepts of history and secret orders," this sign from Heaven was deliciously staged. The term "inaugurate" is from the Latin *inauguratio*, and refers to the archaic ceremony by which the Roman *augurs* ("soothsayers") approved a king or ruler (or other action) through omens as being "sanctioned by the gods." As for Petrus Romanus, his "inauguration" was sealed by the same omen the ancient augurs used in determining the will of the gods for a king in that part of Rome—thunder and lightning as the most important auspice and sign that Jupiter—the father of Apollo—was watching.

It turns out that I was not alone in my ponderings, as "many observers chose to interpret this as a divine reaction to the historical announcement of Pope Benedict's resignation, made that very morning" the Catholic news agencies confirmed. "As his personal secretary, Archbishop Gänswein, reminisced about how both he and Benedict only found out about the lightning strike after the event. 'The impression was one of a sign from above, a reaction,' he told Badde [who conducted the interview]. When he showed Benedict images of the spectacular incident a few days later, the pope asked whether this was some kind of digital montage, Gänswein said, adding: "however, nature had spoken,'"[120] he said, echoing what I had published online in 2013.

The astonishing report continued:

> During the interview, Paul Badde referenced... The "Prophecy of the Popes"—according to which, Pope Francis may be considered to be the last pope. "Indeed, when looking at the prophecy, and considering how there was always a sound reference to popes mentioned in its history—that gives me the shivers," Archbishop Gänswein admitted... "speaking from historical experience, one has to say: Yes, it is a wake-up call."[121]

Given that both current popes and their closest advisors at the Vatican have considered whether Pope Francis is Petrus Romanus, that the reality "gives them the shivers," and that it is perceived as "a wake-up call," is it any wonder that conservative scholars within the Church have taken an increasingly careful view of the new pope? And is the subsequent question of whether Pope Francis is the "False Prophet" the reason Canon Lawyers and Theologians for the Vatican hosted a Conference in Paris in March of 2017 to discuss "how to depose a heretical pope"?[122]

Accusations of apostasy are stacking up against Francis elsewhere, too, with numerous top Catholic websites, blogs, and discussion forums deliberating how he is leading the Church toward schism, ironically a fulfillment of the pope's namesake, Francis of Assisi, who famously predicted about the final pope:

> At the time of this tribulation a man, not canonically elected, will be raised to the Pontificate, who, by his cunning, will endeavor to draw many into error and death.... Some preachers will keep silence about the truth, and others will trample it under foot and deny it...for in those days Jesus Christ will send them not a true Pastor, but a destroyer.[123]

A respected Italian monsignor and former consultor to the Vatican's Congregation for the Doctrine of Faith has even gone on record saying that Pope Francis needs to stop the "confusion and apostasy" he is sowing among priests and bishops by "correcting" his "ambiguous and erroneous words and acts."[124]

But Francis has been quick to expunge those from leadership who oppose him and to replace them with allies including Jesuits like himself, another Malichi Martin warning.

As I am writing this chapter, Reuters News Agency just reported a "major shake-up of the Vatican's administration" in which Pope Francis replaced Catholicism's top theologian, Cardinal Gerhard Ludwig Mueller, who was the head of the department charged with defending Catholic doctrine—the Congregation for the Doctrine of the Faith.

The position is the most important one that a pope fills in the Vatican hierarchy after the Secretary of State. Most incumbents keep it until they retire, which in Mueller's case would have been in six years.[125]

Mueller, 69, was appointed by emeritus Pope Benedict in 2012 and is replaced by Pope Francis' confederate, Jesuit Archbishop Luis Francisco Ladaria Ferrer.

Another influential Catholic television network director named Jose Galat is even publicly claiming that Pope Francis is the "false prophet" who, he says, is "paving the way for the Antichrist." He claims the "real pope" is Benedict XVI, who was somehow forced to resign in 2013. Francis "was elected by a mafia of cardinals," he argues, agreeing with those other Catholics who see a conspiracy behind this first ever Jesuit pope.[126]

And then there is Benedict himself who recently said the Catholic Church is "on the verge of capsizing."[127]

Perhaps strangest of all is a current inquiry (also underway as I write this chapter) in which the Vatican has launched an investigation into a Catholic group of exorcists (the Heralds) who, *after having discussions with Satan, have determined that Petrus Romanus "is the Devil's man."*[128]

But what if Francis is not Petrus Romanus, the final pope of Malachy's prophecy? What if that dark Superforce (Catholic Freemasons) that Malachi Martin warned about is using Francis and his left-leaning theology to play a complex end-times game aimed at manipulating and reconfiguring Rome into a Socialist-Marxist instrument for the real Final Pope's arrival? What if the same George Soros-globalist one-worlders who have teamed up against Trump are working with Francis to lay the groundwork for Antichrist's global order ala the book of Revelation?

Too crazy to believe?

Here is what popular Catholic website LIFE SITE recently said:

Most astonishingly, the Vatican itself seems involved as Pope Francis, the German bishops and others around him have openly developed close relationships with many leading One-Worlders, inviting them to the Vatican to give talks and advice. This has been a radical change from all past popes. Reports suggest George Soros favored Bergoglio [Pope Francis] during the Conclave that elected him pope. For the first time ever, the New World Order movement has gained powerful public backing for many of their agendas from the head of the Roman Catholic Church, who has aggressively insisted that climate change, open borders, anti-capitalism and more are now issues of moral and religious obligation for a new, worldly Catholic Church. It also appears that some in the Vatican may be laying the groundwork for a moral and religious case in favor of population control…. Many signs point to this.[129]

And what if I told you the rabbit hole of evidence to support this global conspiracy does not stop there, and actually ties the resignation of Pope Benedict, the election of Pope Francis, George Soros, Obama, Hillary, John Podesta, the possible arrival of the False Prophet, Antichrist, Final Pope, discussions of a Messiah, and the years 2012 and 2016 to the Saboteurs now at work to overthrow the Trump administration's agenda?

Are you aware that a group of respected Catholic leaders recently sent a letter to President Trump asking him to launch an official investigation into activities connected to the people mentioned above? It appears that Team Obama was involved in a different coup similar to the one currently focused on Trump, but this time against the Vatican and which the authors of the letter believe forced the aging Pope Benedict to step down for sinister reasons.

In a top-notch piece of investigative journalism, William F. Jasper at the *New American* asks:

> Did billionaire speculator George Soros, President Barack Obama, Secretary of State Hillary Clinton, Vice President Joe Biden, and Obama/Clinton adviser John Podesta conspire to overthrow the conservative Pope Benedict XVI and replace him with a radical, Pope Francis? Did they use America's intelligence agencies, and our nation's diplomatic machinery, political muscle, and financial power to coerce and blackmail "regime change" in the Roman Catholic Church?
>
> Far from being some wild conspiracy theory, there is sound prima facie evidence to indicate that this is a serious effort to expose a political scandal of the highest order, involving flagrant, criminal abuse of power at the top levels of the U.S. government.[130]

Here is the letter that Jasper refers to in its entirety that was written and sent by Catholic leaders from *The Remnant* newspaper:

Dear President Trump:

The campaign slogan "Make America Great Again," resonated with millions of common Americans and your tenacity in pushing back against many of the most harmful recent trends has been most inspiring. We all look forward to seeing a continued reversal of the collectivist trends of recent decades.

Reversing recent collectivist trends will, by necessity, require a reversal of many of the actions taken by the previous administration. Among those actions we believe that there is one that remains cloaked in secrecy. Specifically, we have reason to believe that a Vatican "regime change" was engineered by the Obama administration.

We were alarmed to discover that, during the third year of the first term of the Obama administration your previous opponent, Secretary of State Hillary Clinton, and other government officials with whom she associated proposed a Catholic "revolution" in which the final demise of what was left of the Catholic Church in America would be realized. Approximately a year after this e-mail discussion, which was never intended to be made public, we find that Pope Benedict XVI abdicated under highly unusual circumstances and was replaced by a pope whose apparent mission is to provide a spiritual component to the radical ideological agenda of the international left. The Pontificate of Pope Francis has subsequently called into question its own legitimacy on a multitude of occasions.

During the 2016 presidential campaign we were astonished to witness Pope Francis actively campaigning against your proposed policies concerning the securing of our borders, and even going so far as to suggest that you are not a Christian. We appreciated your prompt and pointed response to this disgraceful accusation.

We remain puzzled by the behavior of this ideologically charged Pope, whose mission seems to be one of advancing secular agendas of the left rather than guiding the Catholic Church in Her sacred mission. It is simply not the proper role of a Pope to be involved in politics to the point that he is considered to be the leader of the international left.

While we share your stated goal for America, we believe that the path to "greatness" is for America to be "good" again, to paraphrase de Tocqueville. We understand that good character cannot be forced on people, but the opportunity to live our lives as good Catholics has been made increasingly difficult by what appears to be a collusion between a hostile United States government and a pope who seems to hold as much ill will towards followers of perennial Catholic teachings as he seems to hold toward yourself.

With all of this in mind, and wishing the best for our country as well as for Catholics worldwide, we believe it to be the responsibility of loyal and informed United States Catholics to petition you to authorize an investigation into the following questions:

- To what end was the National Security Agency monitoring the conclave that elected Pope Francis?

- What other covert operations were carried out by US government operatives concerning the resignation of Pope Benedict or the conclave that elected Pope Francis?

- Did US government operatives have contact with the "Cardinal Danneels Mafia"?

- International monetary transactions with the Vatican were suspended during the last few days prior to the resignation of Pope Benedict. Were any U.S. Government agencies involved in this?

- Why were international monetary transactions resumed on February 12, 2013, the day after Benedict XVI announced his resignation? Was this pure coincidence?

- What actions, if any, were actually taken by John Podesta, Hillary Clinton, and others tied to the Obama administration who were involved in the discussion proposing the fomenting of a "Catholic Spring"?

- What was the purpose and nature of the secret meeting between Vice President Joseph Biden and Pope Benedict XVI at the Vatican on or about June 3, 2011?

- What roles were played by George Soros and other international financiers who may be currently residing in United States territory?

We believe that the very existence of these unanswered questions provides sufficient evidence to warrant this request for an investigation.

Should such an investigation reveal that the U.S. government interfered inappropriately into the affairs of the Catholic Church, we further request the release of the results so that Catholics may request appropriate action from those elements of our hierarchy who remain loyal to the teachings of the Catholic Church.

Please understand that we are not requesting an investigation into the Catholic Church; we are simply asking for an investigation into recent activities of the U.S. Government, of which you are now the chief executive.

Thank you again, and be assured of our most sincere prayers.
Respectfully,
David L. Sonnier, LTC US ARMY (Retired)
Michael J. Matt, Editor of The Remnant
Christopher A. Ferrara (President of The American Catholic Lawyers Association, Inc.)
Chris Jackson, Catholics4Trump.com
Elizabeth Yore, Esq., Founder of YoreChildren

At the end of the letter above on the Remnant's official website,[131] they provide links to documents and articles that support their charges, including some released by WikiLeaks, which caught Soros, Clinton, and Podesta conferring on how to bring the "middle ages dictatorship" at the Vatican to an end.

In another *New American* report from last October, the e-mails in question were investigated involving the Clinton campaign's secret anti-Catholic agenda. They noted:

Podesta, a longtime Clinton adviser/confidante and hand-picked top activist for left-wing funder George Soros, revealed in a 2011 e-mail that he and other activists were working to effect a "Catholic Spring" revolution within the Catholic Church, an obvious reference to the disastrous "Arab Spring" coups organized that same year by the Obama-Clinton-Soros team that destabilized the Middle East and brought radical Islamist regimes and terrorist groups to power in the region. The Podesta e-mail is a response to another Soros-funded radical—Sandy Newman, founder of the "progressive" Voices for Progress. Newman had written to Podesta seeking advice on the best way to "plant the seeds of the revolution" in the Catholic Church, which he described as a "middle ages [sic] dictatorship."[132]

Of special interest to me in the letter to Trump from the concerned Catholics is where they specifically note: "Approximately a year after this e-mail discussion, which was never intended to be made public, we find that Pope Benedict XVI abdicated under highly unusual circumstances and was replaced by a pope whose apparent mission is to provide a spiritual component to the radical ideological agenda of the international left" and that they "remain puzzled by the behavior of this ideologically charged Pope, whose mission seems to be one of advancing secular agendas of the left rather than guiding the Catholic Church in Her sacred mission.... It is simply not the proper role of a Pope to be involved in politics to the point that he is considered to be the leader of the international left."

With all this in mind, and given my personal exhaustive investigation into the Vatican, my extensive research into the Prophecy of the Popes, the correct predictions we made regarding the resignation of Benedict before the fact, and our follow-up probe into the conclave that elected Francis, I have a bombshell announcement to make. I have come to believe that Pope Francis will either retire soon or be taken out of the way, and that this really is tied to something strange that unfolded in bringing him temporarily to the pontificate. In other words, I believe Francis was not "canonically elected," as his namesake originally predicted. And the Catholics already cited above are only the tip of the iceberg of those who will eventually voice how "illegitimate" activity went on behind closed doors during the last papal election,[133] and that, for reasons we do not yet understand, Francis was put in as a temporary "placeholder" until the real Pope #112 (Petrus Romanus) could be installed. The mysterious reasons surrounding this "placeholder" false pope may never fully be known, but was foreseen by such mystics as Father Herman Bernard Kramer in his work, *The Book of Destiny*. During an unusual interpretation he made of the twelfth chapter of the book of Revelation concerning "the great wonder" mentioned in verse 1, Father Kramer wrote:

> The "sign" in heaven is that of a woman with child crying out in her travail and anguish of delivery. In that travail, she gives birth to some definite "person" who is to RULE the Church with a rod of iron (verse 5). It then points to a conflict waged within the Church to elect one who was to "rule all nations" in the manner clearly stated. In accord with the text this is unmistakably a PAPAL ELECTION, for only Christ and his Vicar have the divine right to rule ALL NATIONS.... But at this time the great powers may take a menacing attitude to hinder the election of the logical and expected candidate by threats of a general apostasy, assassination or imprisonment of this candidate if elected. (capitalized emphasis in original)[134]

Although I disagree with Kramer's interpretation of the book of Revelation, his fear that "great powers may take a menacing attitude to hinder the election of the logical and expected candidate" echoes the sentiment of priests mentioned elsewhere in *Petrus Romanus*, who saw a crisis for the Church coming, and the False Prophet and Antichrist rising as a result.

This, too, was in the news recently when a report was published by Sébastien Maillard, Vatican correspondent for La Croix, in Rome. He noted how a large array of conservative bishops fear that Francis is bypassing critical Church doctrine and fear he has already gone too far. Even those cardinals who voted for Francis now want him to step down so that the Holy See's secretary of state, Cardinal Pietro Parolin, can be elected the real pope.[135] And these electors understand something else, too. Parolin's name means "Peter the Roman" from the final line of the *Prophecy of the Popes.*

chapter five

Have We Entered the "Fourth Turning"?

n 2008 and again in 2012, with input from Steve Quayle and me, my good friend Sue Bradley, an investigative journalist and blogger who has since gone home to be with Jesus (April 26, 2013) had started work on what would be one of her last articles. It was titled "The Fourth Turning: The Protocols and the Grey Champion." A couple of months before she departed this life, she had e-mailed me from her hospital room and said she was about to expand her "Fourth Turning" work based on some *Zenith 2016* material I had just shared with her. Unfortunately, like with the passing of David Flynn, the world will never know what Sue was about to reveal. What we do understand now is that it was connected to a primary player in the new Trump administration—a man some believe is the actual power behind the throne in Washington, DC, today—Steve Bannon. This is because Sue's unfinished research was partially based on a book published in 1997, *The Fourth Turning*, which seems to have deeply influenced Bannon's worldview and possibly his eschatology. *Turning* describes itself as a work "that turns history into prophecy." It explains cycles of life and generational archetypes through the examination of Western historical paradigms over the past five centuries. By surveying the past and identifying contemporary markers, William Strauss and Neil Howe, the authors of the study, determined an astoundingly prescient forecast in which they saw a cascade of incidents that would ultimately lead to chaos and the "Fourth Turning." Keep in mind they made these predictions twenty years ago, long before the September 11, 2001, attacks on America or the financial issues of today. Among the scenarios they foresaw were:

The first could be economic distress with a government beset by fiscal crisis, the state laying claim to federal tax monies, federal marshals enforcing orders, tax rebellions, special forces, and an ensuing constitutional crisis;

The second is a terrorist attack involving an airliner, a military response, authorization for house-to-house searches, and false flag accusations against the administration;

The third scenario is an economic disaster involving Wall Street and a federal budget impasse that results in a stalemate;

The fourth consideration is eco-environmental malaise with the Centers for Disease Control announcing the spread of a new communicable virus with quarantines and relocations;

The fifth projection is geopolitical in nature, with growing anarchy throughout the former Soviet republics prompting Russia to conduct training exercises around its borders, a Russian alliance with Iran, soaring gold and silver prices, and global military responses.

In describing these insightful scenarios, Strauss and Howe felt a catalyst would unfold as a result of a specific dynamic, and, "An initial spark will trigger a chain reaction of unyielding responses and further emergencies."[136]

According to Strauss and Howe in 1997, this chain reaction was already prepped to unfold as the result of natural cycles or "Turnings" in which generations are doomed to forget—and thus to repeat—the mistakes of the past. The authors describe a Turning as "an era with a characteristic social mood, a new twist on how people feel about themselves and their nation. It results from the aging of the generation [before it]."[137] A society enters a Turning once every twenty years or so, when all living generations begin to enter their next phases of life. The living generations, or *saeculae*, comprise four cyclical Turnings, characterized as:

The First Turning (THE HIGH): An era of enthusiastic collective strengthening and civic development, having burned the brush and swept the ashes of preceding structure.

The Second Turning (THE AWAKENING): Built on the energies and accomplishments of the High but finds increasing yearning for introspection with a high tolerance for spiritual expression outside the parameters of predetermined standards.

The Third Turning (THE UNRAVELING): Begins as the "society-wide embrace of the liberating cultural forces" loosed by the Awakening shows signs of civic disorder and decay, a heightened sense of self-reliance and an increasing withdrawal of public trust. This builds to a near crisis of downcast pessimism and a palpable pall that can only be remedied by yielding to the next.

The Fourth Turning (THE CRISES and the era we have now entered): By far, the most perilous as societies pass through the greatest and most dangerous gates of history. As desperate solutions are sought for "sudden threats" on multiple cultural fronts, confrontation is passionate and decisions are often reactive, aggressive. "Government governs, community obstacles are removed, and laws and customs that resisted change for decades are swiftly shunted aside. A grim preoccupation with civic peril causes spiritual curiosity to decline.... Public order tightens, private risk-taking abates, and...child-rearing reaches a smothering degree of protection and structure. The young focus their energy on worldly achievements, leaving values in the hands of the old. Wars are fought with fury and for maximum result."[138]

Through the examination of an enormous amount of political and cultural history, Strauss and Howe processed over five hundred years of Anglo-American cultural nuance into remarkable, well-organized, and predictable cycles, and it is from this reservoir they finally stake an uncanny claim:

Just after the millennium, America will enter a new era that will culminate with a crisis comparable to the American Revolution, the Civil War, the Great Depression, and World War II. The very survival of the nation will almost certainly be at stake.[139]

Strauss and Howe saw the United States of that time (1997) in the Third Turning, "midway through an Unraveling," roughly a decade away from the next Crisis or Fourth Turning:

America feels like it's unraveling. Although we live in an era of relative peace and comfort, we have settled into a mood of pessimism about the long-term future, fearful that our superpower nation is somehow rotting from within.

The next Fourth Turning is due to begin shortly after the new millennium.... Real hardship will beset the land, with severe distress that could involve questions of class, race, nation, and empire...

The very survival of the nation will feel at stake.

Sometime before the year 2025, America will pass through a great gate in history, commensurate with the American Revolution, Civil War, and twin emergencies of the Great Depression and World War II.

The risk of catastrophe will be very high. The nation could erupt into insurrection or civil violence, crack up geographically, or succumb to authoritarian rule. If there is a war, it is likely to be one of maximum risk and efforts—in other words, a TOTAL WAR.[140]

The striking details contained within the Fourth Turning illustrate the precision that was distilled with a close examination of historical patterns and contemporary application.

Although the authors note that the events described are not absolute, they also insist that the cycles, these Turnings, cannot be interrupted. As summer follows spring, an Unraveling precedes a Crisis of Faustian proportions:

> It will require us to lend a new seasonal interpretation to our revered American Dream. And it will require us to admit that our faith in linear progress has often amounted to a Faustian bargain with our children.
>
> Faust always ups the ante, and every bet is double-or-nothing. Through much of the Third Turning, we have managed to postpone the reckoning. But history warns that we can't defer it beyond the next bend in time.[141]

While a "Faustian bargain" sounds ominous, there is little evidence that the Anglo-American "Dream" has undergone the introspection and discipline necessary to buffer the arrogant recklessness of this generation and its administration.

NBC's Chuck Todd noted, on the evening of November 4, 2008, that Barack Obama was a changing of the guard in the United States from the Baby Boomer presidencies of William Clinton and George W. Bush. The *Toronto Globe and Mail* referred to President-elect Obama as being a member of Generation X, being born in 1961. And Strauss and Howe assigned Generation X—the Thirteenth Generation—to those who brought America to chaos and the start of the current Fourth Turning.

Fast forward to today and ask yourself: What does this have to do with Steve Bannon and the Trump administration?

In 2009, Bannon called historian David Kaiser on the phone. At the time, professor Kaiser worked at the Naval War College in Newport, Rhode Island. Bannon wanted to know if Kaiser, an expert on "the Fourth Turning," would appear in a documentary he was producing based on Strauss and Howe's generational theory (the film was released in 2010, titled "Generation Zero").

Kaiser agreed to be part of the film and traveled to the Washington headquarters of Citizens United, where Bannon was at the time, to be interviewed. At one point during the recordings, Kaiser says Bannon pressured him to agree with something he doesn't believe. "He was talking about the wars of the fourth turnings," Kaiser said, recalling how Bannon seemed sharply focused on making the point that another world war was on the horizon and that it would be a catalyst for the arrival of an international leader—the *Grey Champion* that Sue Bradley had named her unfinished investigation after.

"You have the American Revolution, you have the Civil War, you have the Second World War; they're getting bigger and bigger," Bannon allegedly emphasized to Kaiser.

"Clearly, he was anticipating that in this 'fourth turning' there would be one at least as big. And he really made an effort, I remember, to get me to say that on the air."[142]

In a feature article for *Huffington Post*, Paul Blumenthal and J. M. Rieger echo Kaiser's suspicions, but see a darker underlying worldview in Bannon's thinking. They wrote:

Bannon, who's now ensconced in the West Wing as President Donald Trump's closest adviser, has been portrayed as Trump's main ideas guy. But in interviews, speeches and writing—and especially in his embrace of Strauss and Howe—he has made clear that he is, first and foremost, an apocalypticist.

In Bannon's view, we are in the midst of an existential war, and everything is a part of that conflict. Treaties must be torn up, enemies named, culture changed. Global conflagration, should it occur, would only prove the theory correct. For Bannon, the Fourth Turning has arrived. The Grey Champion, a messianic strongman figure, may have already emerged. The apocalypse is now.[143]

According to Strauss and Howe, an unexpected national leader would emerge during the current Fourth Turning against all odds from an older generation to become a "hero" who leads the globe into a New World Order. This commander—whom they call the Grey Champion (and who some of us could worry is Antichrist)—will continue in power as a result of war or conflict that keeps his regime in command (a second term for a US president or continuance as executive during presidential war powers or martial law that suspends elections?).

"The winners will now have the power to pursue the more potent, less incrementalist agenda about which they had long dreamed and against which their adversaries had darkly warned," says the Fourth Turning. "This new regime will enthrone itself for the duration of the Crisis. Regardless of its ideology, that new leadership will assert public authority and demand private sacrifice. Where leaders had once been inclined to alleviate societal pressures, they will now aggravate them to command the nation's attention."[144]

Strauss and Howe were convinced when they wrote this thesis twenty years ago that the United States was in the Third Turning then, and that the next crises period or Fourth Turning would begin sometime following 2005 and end around 2025. In between these dates, the Grey Champion would appear.

Remarkably enough, most economists today point to the Lehman crisis in 2008 to explain the ramifications of the next global financial crisis, which the world's leading authorities such as the Bank for International Settlements are now saying is going to hit global markets soon with a vengeance.[145]

Does this mean we are in the middle now of the Fourth Turning?

It's hard to argue against facts.

The foundations that once supported America's stability and clout have weakened to the point that our institutions and infrastructure are crumbling. From illegal immigration to social programs to mounting debt, we have reached an unsustainable reality so reminiscent of Strauss and Howe's generational prediction it's getting harder each day to deny.

And then there is that "risk of catastrophe" in which the "nation could erupt into insurrection or civil violence" the professors foresaw. Will the Soros and Obama-backed agitators currently wreaking havoc across America ignite the circumstances that lead to the Grey Champion's authoritarian rule?

"Emboldened by a mainstream media apparatus which functions as a mouthpiece of Deep State interests, these activists are determined to overturn democratically elected officials and overturn law and order on the grounds that they personally disagree with the results" warned Michael Hart at StockBoardAsset earlier this year.[146]

He continued:

As we have seen in recent months, Trump supporters, conservatives, and other patriots are not afraid to confront leftist activists in the streets, and this is likely to intensify as these DNC-backed groups become more desperate and confrontational in their tactics.

James Comey's congressional testimony...showed that the Trump administration is indeed attempting to break the old political order and its far-too-powerful Deep State. The cracks are surfacing now, and this will likely shatter and spill into many facets of social life outside of the realm of politics.

This crises-creation machine emanating from the manufacturers of descent who despise the new Republican president and who want the old order eclipsed by a revolutionary new world system are the very appliance that threatens to give rise to the Fourth Turning described by Strauss and Howe, and perhaps to the Grey Champion of the apocalypse of Daniel and Revelation.

According to the Fourth Turning, America has experienced three such major crises before: the Revolutionary War, the Civil War, and the Great Depression and World War II, each followed by their respective periods of reconstruction.

These times were marked by social decay and civil dread that required Americans to carry a tremendous burden after massive conflict and substantial loss in order to rebuild and reinvent a better future.

Are we nearing the trigger event(s) or chaos stage of another Fourth Turning?

If so, are Bannon and company the cause of it, or are they simply astute enough to prepare for the inevitable as a result of their knowledge of an endgame under construction by occult Saboteurs working behind the scenes in Washington, DC?

Ordo ab Chao: How Elements for the Fourth Turning and the Arrival of the Grey Champion Were Envisioned Long Before Strauss, Howe, or Steve Bannon

Nancy Pelosi, at the first session of the 110th Congress where she assumed her role as speaker of the house, infused a loaded statement concerning the founding fathers, saying they were so confident in "the America they were advancing, they put on the seal, the great seal of the United States, '*novus ordo seclorum*'—a new order for the centuries."

Pelosi didn't explain the significance behind *Novus ordo seclorum* (Latin, "new order of the ages") to her listening audience during this momentous changeover in governmental control, she didn't give any clarification of this "new order," and she made no attempt to enlighten anyone with why our Great Seal pictures the all-seeing eye of Osiris/ Horus—but she didn't have to. To the illuminated ones in the nation's capital, the address was an important edition in a larger series of carefully crafted speeches in which line-by-line analysis of her and other DC insider public references were, according to biblical scholar Bruce Lincoln and *American Dynasty* author Kevin Phillips "a medium for the voice of God" in which the inside elite enlist specialized hermeneutical skills they have cultivated to encourage those in the know "to probe beneath the surface," where in *sotto voce* ("under voice"), they will understand and sympathize with what is actually being communicated, even if requirements of the public side of their office constrain them from speaking plainly.[147] Thus, Pelosi wasn't saying those words for the benefit of the country's citizens. She knew very well that there were certain individuals whose ears would perk to those expressions: people who would know precisely what they meant; those who knew that the "In *God* We Trust" and "one nation, under *God*" mottoes of the country were intentionally ambiguous—that they point to and revere another spirit that will someday soon possess the one that some may call the Grey Champion. Without a specified "god" to which we could point to since our foundation, we essentially can—*and have*—dedicated our land to the supervision (translation: "perversion") of whichever lowercase-g god the founding fathers and architects revered.

Besides the giant pentagram that forms the layout of Washington, DC (discussed later), many other symbols appear in the fabrics of our nation's identity that cause one to stop and consider their ultimate occultic intentions. Such example of this is the Great Seal—the symbolism of which is richly pagan. Highly venerated 33rd-Degree Freemason and mystic Manly P. Hall once referred to the Great Seal as "the signature" of that exalted body of Masons who designed America for a "peculiar and particular purpose." Interestingly, when Christians in the 1800s argued that a hypothetical annihilation of the US would lead to "antiquaries of succeeding centuries" concluding that America had been a heathen nation based on symbolism of the Great Seal, Congress was pushed to create something reflecting the Christian faith of so many of its citizens to quiet the voices of those who saw through the esoteric imagery. Though US President and Freemason Theodore Roosevelt strongly opposed this idea, certain powerful and Masonic leaders stood to approve it, and thus, "In God We Trust" was implemented as the national and official motto.

To illustrate the intentional ambiguity of the motto by our early leaders, follow this fictional trail:

- It is the year 4300, and the earth has been all but annihilated. Humans are extinct, but their planet remains.

- Space travelers from another planet land on major cities and kingdoms across the earth—starting with the earliest Mesopotamian populations and onward, eventually arriving in Egypt. They dig through the debris and become rapidly fluent in ancient languages and writings of the Egyptians and the surrounding territories.

- Notes are made by the team regarding the phallic/pregnant belly designs gracing Egypt's archaic structures and the beliefs associated with them. The all-seeing eye of Horus/Osiris, the belly of Isis, the pentagrams, the sun circles, and the astrological alignments of old-world architecture and monuments are all compared.

- The team comes to the obvious conclusion that the Egyptian pharaohs believed in using these symbols and structures to reincarnate Horus/Osiris himself into the host bodies of each leader, who would then, through the enlightenment of the gods, carry the perfect torch of leadership. The space travelers have no reason to believe that the reincarnation was impossible; they were never raised (as we Americans have been) to disregard such a sensational belief system through any kind of cultural bias. To the travelers, the Egyptian symbolism represents actual world history as it pertains to the souls that inhabited the planet long ago.

- The team moves on from Egypt and continues to study each land in the order it ws formed, coming to the US in due course. Many other world religions are studied along the way, including Christianity, which spoke of a man called the Antichrist who would greatly deceive many and lead mankind into the ultimate destruction as foretold in a book called "Revelation" written by one "John of Patmos." The team learns that when the canonical Holy Bible was formed, this book of Revelation was included. Without any cultural imprinting of one interpretation or another regarding Revelation's implications (premillennial, postmillennial, amillennial, etc.), they assume that the prophecies contained therein pointed to a literal fulfilment.

- The travelers discover over the progression of this earth assignment that Horus/Osiris was also known by influential Masons/Freemasons/Rosicrucians throughout history and across many nations as the venerated "Apollo" and/or "Nimrod."

- When "In God We Trust," stamped on US currency, is found, the dollar bill is taken to their team captain. The question of which "God" the people placed their trust in is raised, and the captain immediately concludes that this "America" was either founded by a subsequent generation of Egyptians who journeyed to this secondary land, or by a different tribe/clan of people altogether who held the same beliefs as the ancient Egyptians. The symbolism throughout the capital city is a match—especially the Horus/Osiris all-seeing eye hovering over the unfinished Egyptian pyramid on the nation's very seal—so the "God" the Americans "trusted" was Osiris/Horus/Apollo/Nimrod.

- The captain then follows the thread to its reasonable close: A hidden divination in the Great Seal prophesied a time when this "God" Osiris/Horus/Apollo/Nimrod would return to earth in a physical host body upon US soil. His coming, according to the information gleaned from the draftsmen of the Great Seal, heralded a New World Order. This New World Order was based on ancient occultism that went hand in hand with satanic ritualism as practiced by followers of the secret fraternities from the Rosae Crucis Order in Egypt and forward. The prophecy of "John of Patmos" whose words in Revelation—given by Christ, Himself—warned of the day the Antichrist (identified in the New Testament as "Apollo") would greatly mislead all of humankind into end-times destruction. If John was correct when he relayed the words of this "Son of God" known as "Jesus Christ" to these earthlings, then "Perhaps," the team captain postulates, "we have discovered the cause behind the annihilation of earth."

By no means am I suggesting that an annihilation of our planet is on the horizon. Nor do I wish to begin arguing my beliefs on the various interpretation methods of Revelation. I do believe, however—as well as many Christians—that the Bible is the holy and inspired written Word of God, and that its words regarding the Antichrist are real and prophetic, pointing to a day when this Grey Champion *will* arrive to deceive the masses into following a World Order that has every potential of annihilating life—at least the life we know now. And if that is truly going to happen, it appears that there are some suspicious monuments, structures, architecture, symbols, and ambiguous mottos that appear to be welcoming that very Antichrist to our capital city. At times, it's not only the glaring symbolism, but the particular timing structures were laid.

David Ovason, whose work, *The Secret Architecture of Our Nation's Capital: The Masons and the Building of Washington DC,* has been endorsed by numerous experts and leaders among the Freemasons, notes how the dedication of the US Capitol building cornerstone had to be done at a certain astrological time related to the zodiacal constellation Virgo ("Isis" to the Egyptians), while Jupiter was rising in Scorpio, because "the cornerstone ceremonial was designed not only to gain the approval of the spiritual beings, but also to ensure that these were content that the building was being brought into the world at the right time."[148] He later adds more directly, "Whoever arranged for Virgo to be so consistently operative during foundation and cornerstone ceremonies, must have been alert to the fact that *they were inviting some archetype, or spiritual being, to direct the destiny of the city.*"[149]

Julia Duin, American journalist and author of *Quitting Church* and other books on religion, made note of the interesting correlation between our capital city and the stars above it when she wrote:

Washington's stellar design was no coincidence.... Masonic founders oriented the District of Columbia around Virgo.

Every Aug. 10, an astrological event takes place in the sky over Washington that some say ties the city to a pagan goddess. At dusk, as golden light turns brick facades a dusty rose, the shimmering sun floats a few degrees just to the left of Pennsylvania Avenue, gradually inching to the right until it sets directly over the famous street. If the horizon remains cloudless, three stars are visible in a straight line from the Capitol to the White House to the skies in the west. Known as Regulus, Arcturus and Spica, the stars form a right-angled triangle framing the constellation of Virgo.

Washington's founders deliberately aligned the city with the stars, consecrating it to Virgo—also known as the Egyptian goddess Isis.[150]

In light of these facts and like Pelosi did, George W. Bush also carefully crafted deeply meaningful if not disturbing words in his 2004 acceptance speech to the Republic National Convention when he said, "Like generations *before us*, we have *a calling from beyond the stars*."[151] This statement, as many researchers on this topic have already pointed out, is a reference to the communication between man and the "Elder Gods" of Babylon in H. P. Lovecraft's satanic work, *Necronomicon* (which was translated into English by none other than Bloody Mary's prized sorcerer and Freemasonic forerunner, John Dee). According to Lovecraft's narrative—which, though fiction, was based on texts by the ancient Syrians regarding the liaisons between mankind and the gods and later praised by dark fraternities for its insights—these same "Elder" entities sent a scribe as emissary to divulge great secrets to those deemed worthy of enlightenment. The narrative reads:

This is the book of the laws and practices of the sleeping dead, written by myself, Abd Al-Hazred—the great sorcerer and poet. With the secrets in this book I have spoken with dark spirits, who have furnished me with many riches, both in the form of money and knowledge, I have even learned the unlearnable knowledge of the divine ones, such is the power of what I learned. I have also learned of the Old Spirits, who lived before man, and still live dreaming, and they are very terrible. It was a face of one of these very spirits that initiated me into this powerful magic. [So far, we see that Al-Hazred was initiated into powerful magic by terrible Old Spirits...]

The wolves carry my name in their midnight speeches, and that quiet, subtle Voice is summoning me from afar. And a Voice much closer shall shout into my ear with unholy impatience. The weight of my soul shall decide its final resting place. Before that time, I must put down here all that I can concerning the horrors that stalk Without, and which lie in wait at the door of every man, for this is the ancient arcana that has been handed down of old, but which has been forgotten by all but a few men, the worshippers of the Old Ones....

Let all who read this book be warned thereby that the habitation of men are seen and surveyed [or "watched"] by that Ancient Race of gods and demons from a time before time [i.e., "generations before us," as Bush stated], and that they seek revenge for that forgotten battle that took place somewhere in the Cosmos and rent the Worlds in the days before the creation of Man, when the Elder Gods walked the Spaces....

Know, then, that I have trod all the Zones of the Gods, and also the places of the Old Ones, and have descended unto the foul places of Death and Eternal Thirst…which was built in the EMPTY SPACE, in the days before Babylon was.

Know, too, that I have spoken with all manner of spirit and daemon, whose names are no longer known in the societies of Man, or were never known [secrets given to men from demonic spirits so ancient that some were never identified but to the select chosen few]. And the seals of some of these are writ herein [the seals of these ancient demons are referred to here and later in his words regarding the amulet]; yet others I must take with me when I leave ye.…

I have traveled beneath the Seas, in search of the Palace of Our Master, and found the stone of monuments of vanquished civilisations, and deciphered the writings of some of these; while still others remain mysteries to any man who lives. And these civilisations were destroyed because of the knowledge contained in this book.

I have summoned the ghosts of my ancestors to real and visible appearance on the tops of temples built to reach the stars [sounds like Nimrod's tower of Babel].[152]

The narrative goes on to tell how Abd Al-Hazred discovered a stone with mysterious etchings upon it. He built a fire nearby and then cowered in fear as the stone began to hover above the ground. Suddenly, priests appeared in black robes, chanting in an unknown language. They had cut themselves all over their chests in exhortation of a mysterious power (like the priests of Ba'al). Al-Hazred, once spotted, fled the scene. A short chase ensued, and Al-Hazred, certain he was as good as dead, turned to see the priests were gone. On the ground around him were black robes, caught in the thorns and covered in a green odorous substance as if they had been vaporized by some kind of extraterrestrial weaponry. Al-Hazred returned to the site of the floating stone and found a small metal plate, also carved with etchings, but differing from those that had been on the stone. After he picked it up, his head began to pound, and the moonlight fell upon the face of the plate. This became the amulet of the Elder Gods:

My head began to ache as though a devil was pounding my skull, when a shaft of moonlight struck the metal amulet, for I know now what it was, and a voice entered into my head and told me the secrets of the scene I had witnessed in one word:

CTHULHU.

In that moment, as though whispered fiercely into my ear, I understood....

And this is the amulet that I held in my hand, and hold to this very day, around my neck as I write these words: Of the three carved symbols, the first is *the sign of our Race from beyond the Stars*, and is called ARRA in the tongue of the Scribe who taught it to me, an emissary of the Old Ones. In the tongue of the eldest city of Babylon, it was OUT OF SPACE. It is the Sigil of the Covenant of the Elder Gods, and when they see it, they who gave it to us, they shall not forget us. They have sworn!

Spirit of the Skies, Remember!

The second is the Elder Sign, and is the Key whereby the Powers of the Elder Gods may be summoned, when used with the proper words and shapes. It has a Name, and is called AGGA.

The third sign is the Sigil of the Watcher. It is called BANDAR. The Watcher is a Race sent by the Old Ones. It keeps vigil while one sleeps, provided the appropriate ritual and sacrifice has been performed,: else, if called, it shall turn upon ye.

These seals, to be effective, must be graven on stone and set in the ground [some kind of cornerstone, perhaps?]...for the Watcher must need to be reminded of the Covenant it has sworn with the Elder Gods and our Race, else it shall turn upon thee and slay thee and ravage thy town until succour is to be had from the Elder Gods by the tears of thy people and the wailing of thy women.[153]

Now the question must be asked: Why in the world would Bush (who is honored in the Pillars of Charity in the House of the Temple, the headquarters of the Supreme Council, 33°, Scottish Rite of Freemasonry for the millions of dollars he and his family have contributed to the cause of Freemasonry) be referencing such writings from the *Necronomicon* in his acceptance speech? Is it perhaps because he, too, respects a covenant-seal between man and the ancient elder gods who gave their blessing only upon those who know their secrets and place stones in the ground and images upon "seals" as a covenant?

Occultists around the world understand the power of these DC symbols and rituals and realize they are not only for conveying psychological concepts, but actually for coercing the mysterious and potent supernaturalism invited to take residence there. This belief is deeply preserved in all of the Babylonian, Egyptian, Greek, Roman, and Kabalistic symbolism that is a part of Masonic history, and according to famous Freemason Foster Bailey, these symbols and seals intentionally hide "a secret…which veils mysterious forces. These energies when released can have a potent effect."[154]

In the next few chapters, we will discuss where these mysterious forces are worshipped, by whom, and how the world's elite are presently scheming to release the "potent effect" that will give life to the personage—and image—of the Grey Champion.

chapter six

The Deep Occultism of the Deep State

One of Netflix's most popular political drama's is a series called *House of Cards* starring Kevin Spacey as Frank Underwood, a Democrat from South Carolina's 5th congressional district and House Majority Whip who later becomes president. Actress Robin Wright stars as his wife, Claire Underwood, who is nearly as ruthless and pragmatic as her cutthroat and manipulative husband.

Season 5 of the program raised a lot of eyebrows in 2017 when it depicted where Underwood derives some of his power and influence. Episode 8 opened in what is obviously the Bohemian Grove in Monte Rio, California, where in mid-July of each year, a three-weekend encampment hosts some of the world's most prominent men—from US presidents and politicians, to entertainment figures and notable businessmen, to power brokers and heads of state from other countries outside the US.

As the camera zooms in on the wooded area, a giant, owl-like figure with burning red eyes stands in the background as red-hooded figures circle before it chanting "Set us free," followed by the cloaked men sacrificing a human effigy on an altar.

As happens in *House of Cards* on somewhat of a regular basis, Mr. Underwood, who is also hooded and walking among the crowd, then looks at the camera and begins a monologue during which he describes the history of the Grove and how, if you really want to get things done— like winning another presidential election—this is where you come to arrange the deal.

As Peter Martin Phillips in a doctoral dissertation published in 1994 titled *A Relative Advantage: Sociology of the San Francisco Bohemian Club* pointed out regarding these movers, shakers, and dealmakers who meet at the Grove, this place is "unique in American clubdom because it puts 2,000 to 3,000 mostly elite men together in the forest for up to sixteen days every summer. Of the top 800 corporations in the U.S. in 1980 30% had at least one officer or director at the Grove."[155]

To give credit where credit is due, it is because of radio host Alex Jones that the public is aware this place actually exists and is indeed where the world's most powerful men gather to do more than practice druid worship, drink, and pee on a tree. Super-secret talks have included the planning for the Manhattan Project—which led to the creation of the atom bomb (as Underwood mentions in the TV show).

Having said that, the secret annual meeting also involves occult rituals.

When Alex Jones and a British filmmaker slipped into the Bohemian Grove thirty miles west of Santa Rosa, California, a few years ago, they recorded what is now known as the "Cremation of Care" ceremony. What Jones caught on camera is like something out of a Stanley Kubrick film. Hooded figures of some of the world's wealthiest, most powerful men (which has included acting and former U.S. presidents such as George W. Bush, George H. W. Bush, Vice President Dick Cheney, Bilderberg mastermind Henry Kissinger, and other participants) gathered beneath a forty-foot-tall stone owl surrounded by water. A child (or effigy) dubbed "Dull Care" was delivered by a ferryman on a small boat and placed on the altar before the owl, where it was burned as an offering for the purpose of magically alleviating the cares and concerns of those elitists making the sacrifice. Before Jones captured this astonishing ritual on film, American citizens were not even aware that such occultism is carried out under the cover of darkness by the world's most powerful and respected leaders. Does this not cause reasonable people to question what other sorcery is occurring behind the veil?

On his website, Jones says: "This is like something out of a Hollywood movie, where teenagers are out camping in the wilderness and come over a hill and witness some devil cult in black and red garb sacrificing some poor soul on a bloody altar." Jones has written about the similarity between the "Cremation of Care" rite and the ancient Canaanite worship of the owl god Molech, where children were sacrificed for nearly identical reasons. Scholars have debated whether the child sacrifices made to Molech were burned alive, or were slain elsewhere and then drained of blood and offered as food to the deity. If the former, a comparison is made between Molech and Kronos, from whose brazen arms children were rolled alive into an oven of fire. Like the Bohemian ritual, the ancient Baals Molech and Kronos were usually called upon to relieve the ones making the sacrifice of their earthly cares, and people who sought material prosperity believed their lives could be improved by offering the child as a sacrifice to the deity.

Three hundred years before Christ, the Greek author Kleitarchos recorded the dastardly process of sacrificing infants in "Cremations of Care" to Kronos:

> Out of reverence for Kronos, the Phoenicians, and especially the Carthaginians, whenever they seek to obtain some great favor, vow one of their children, burning it as a sacrifice to the deity, if they are especially eager to gain success. There stands in their midst a bronze statue of Kronos, its hands extended over a bronze brazier, the flames of which engulf the child. When the flames fall on the body, the limbs contract and the open mouth seems almost to be laughing [such areas of child sacrifice were often called "the place of laughing"], until the contracted body slips quietly into the brazier.[156]

127

The sacrifice of children in this way was widespread in antiquity and was practiced by the children of Israel under the reign of King Ahab and Queen Jezebel. A recent archeological find illustrated how far-reaching such offerings were when it unearthed the remains of more than twenty thousand infants who had been sacrificed to a single Baal.

For some, a better candidate than Molech for the deity represented at Bohemian Grove is the Mesopotamian storm demon Lilith, whose giant, horned statues once formed the highest competition to Yahweh. In Hebrew folklore, Lilith is "the dark wind of the storm" who takes the form of an owl (still worshipped in modern Beltane/Mayday rituals) and, among other things, overshadows the sacrifice of children. She is a powerful seductress who, before Eve's creation, was Adam's wife and lover, according to myth. The Cremation of Care ceremony conducted by US presidents and other elitists for her (or Molech) at Bohemian Grove is evidently especially seductive, given that metaphysicians among them believe the biblical version of Abraham's test on Moriah was sanitized by Moses in the Genesis account in an attempt to cover up the actual practice of human sacrifice among ancient Hebrews. Perhaps at places like Bohemian Grove they see magic in a "corrected" version of the story—a heretical retelling—where Isaac is extinguished beneath the dark-winged one who rides in the whirlwind and heals her power-hungry and seduced worshippers of their cares. Some claim the same occultists even hid the image of the owl in the Masonically designed US dollar bill for very important and related magical reasons.

Whether that is true or not, the intersection between Bohemian Grove-like mysticism and American politics has a far longer relationship than the average citizen may ever consider. It reaches back to ancient Babylon, where an unbroken thread from then until modern times has been vigilantly maintained by secret orders in Washington, DC, that, early in our nation's history, took residence as the designated keepers of the arcane wisdom. Russian occultist Madame H. P. Blavatsky once recognized this about America, and in her 1888 esoteric volumes *The Secret*

Doctrine, said, "It is in America that the transformation will take place, and has already silently commenced." [157]

Since then, hundreds of occult masters have echoed Blavatsky's recognition of America as the global power center for human apotheosis, designated by the founders and approved by the gods for what Manly P. Hall called "a secret destiny." As thoroughly documented in my book *Zenith 2016,* this marriage between American patriotic ideas and metaphysical spirituality is clearly seen in the motivation of Vice President Henry Wallace and President Franklin Roosevelt's decision to place the Great Seal on the US one-dollar bill. Both men were Freemasons who saw in the Seal a "Masonic prophecy" about a future leader—a Grey Champion—who would one day take the helm as leader of not only the US but the world at the birth of a new global order.

When President George W. Bush in his second inaugural address spoke of America's founders declaring "a new order of the ages," he was referring to this coming empire from the Masonically designed Great Seal (*novus ordo seclorum*), and Bush further acknowledged that the secret society members who oversaw the seal's prophetic design were acting on an "ancient hope that is meant to be fulfilled." [158]

Of course, it's not just Republicans who mix political stations with paranormal beliefs. Who can forget Bill Clinton's foray into Voodoo magic (as investigated by Judi McLeod in 2005 involving a March 31, 1995, "visit to Haiti under Aristide's restored rule" where "Clinton took part in a Voodoo initiative ceremony intended to keep him impervious to Republican attacks and to guarantee his reelection) [159] and Hillary who, during her husband's first term, came under heat for hosting "seances" in the White House with spirit-guide Jean Houston, during which she visited with the phantom of her political inspiration Eleanor Roosevelt. [160]

While speaking at a dedication ceremony for the Franklin D. Roosevelt Four Freedoms Park in New York City in 2012, Bill Clinton admitted Hillary talks with the dead and even channeled a message for him from a familiar spirit calling itself "Eleanor," which Hillary wanted him to let the family know about, which he seemed proud to repeat:

A special thanks to the members of the Roosevelt family who are here. And the one who is not, Eleanor, who made sure that the four freedoms were included in the preamble to the Universal Declaration of Human Rights in 1948. I know that because, as all of you famously learned when I served as president, my wife, now the secretary of State, was known to commune with Eleanor on a regular basis. And so she called me last night on her way home from Peru to remind me to say that. That Eleanor had talked to her and reminded her that I should say that.[161]

According to author and journalist Bob Woodward, who helped break the Watergate scandal, when Hillary's medium Jean Houston suggested she also talk with Jesus Christ, Hillary clammed up and refused to speak to the Son of God, which may be understandable, given recent Wikileaks discoveries that indicate something much creepier may have been transpiring between her and the dark side. Clinton insider Larry Nichols perhaps put his finger on part of the forbidden knowledge when he said Bill Clinton told him that Hillary was a member of a coven in California that regularly met to practice witchcraft.

Bill told me that she was going out there, she and a group of women, and she would be a part of a witch's church. Man, when Bill told me that, he could have hit me with a baseball bat. I tried to point out to him, "Do you realize what would happen if that got out?" Of course my job was to make sure it didn't get out.

Now I don't know…if Hillary still partakes in the witch ritual…. But for the better part of many years, Hillary would go quite often, whether it was regularly once a month, or maybe once every couple of months, she would go out on the weekend simply to be a part of it.[162]

Are such comments by Larry Nichols trustworthy?

Given that third-party information by anyone can be suspect, I find far more concerning the revelations from Wikileaks in which private e-mails between Hillary, John Podesta, and others from their own private computers were uncovered that disclose a radical level of occultism was indeed going on, and it is right out of the Libri of Aleister Crowley.

On this, Douglas Ernst of the *Washington Times* released a stunner of a headline November 4, 2016: "WikiLeaks: Podesta invited to 'Spirit' dinner; host's known 'recipes' demand breast milk, sperm." The feature story involved WikiLeaks' releases of stolen e-mails belonging to John Podesta, Hillary Clinton's campaign chairman at the time (besides WikiLeaks founder Julian Assange releasing Podesta and Hillary e-mails, federal agents had found documents linked to Mrs. Clinton's e-mail server while investigating former congressman, Anthony Weiner, who was later found guilty of sending illicit texts to a minor girl). The *Washington Times*' featured e-mail in the story was one from John's brother, Tony, inviting him to a "Spirit Cooking dinner" to be hosted at the home of Marina Abramovic, a so-called artist whose *Spirit Cooking with Essential Aphrodisiac Recipes* was released in 1996. Abramovic's recipes include ingredients similar to what infamous occultist Aliester Crowley taught his disciples to use when communicating with fallen angels— blood, urine, breast milk, sperm, and other elements that are consumed by satanists on particular nights to bring their actions and thoughts into contact with supernaturalism (New York's Museum of Modern Art even called Abramovic's "cookbook" a manual for "evocative instructions for actions or thoughts").

"Dear Tony, I am so looking forward to the Spirit Cooking dinner at my place," Ms. Abramovic says in a June 25 e-mail. "Do you think you will be able to let me know if your brother [John] is joining? All my love, Marina." Tony forwarded the e-mail to John, adding, "Are you in NYC Thursday July 9 Marina wants you to come to dinner?"

It is unknown if John Podesta attended the ceremony or what may have taken place if he did, but Ms. Abramovic is a self-proclaimed mystic whose "artistic" demonstrations include cutting and stabbing herself with sharp knives during masochistic rituals, depictions of cannibalism, getting naked and slithering about on the floor with snakes, and, under the right circumstances (she says), seeing through a dimensional veil into the future. Aliester Crowley claimed the same. We also know a bit about Ms. Abramovic's secret demonstrations from a thoroughly disgusting gala dinner she conducted and that was hosted at MOCA Grand Avenue on November 12, 2011, in Los Angeles, California. Seven hundred fifty guests were there that night, including celebrities like Will Ferrell, Gwen Stefani, Tilda Swinton, Pamela Anderson, Gov. Jerry Brown, Mayor Antonio Villaraigosa, and numerous others. They each paid $2,500 and more to be seated where human heads protruded as centerpieces through holes in dinner tables and food was served that included bloody-looking meats and spaghetti that appeared like human intestines and bowels. Elsewhere in the room that evening, nude "performers" lay on top of skeletons and "breathed life into them" while life-sized nude cake replicas of Abramovic and the evening's singer, Debbie Harry, were carried out and ritualistically "sacrificed" with large knives thrust into their hearts. The razor-sharp cutting devices exposed the "murdered" women's blood-red innards, followed by the evening's guests laughing and eating the two "ladies." When I watched the presentation for this and reviewed the published images (you can see them for yourself online, but be warned they are disturbing), I wondered where the outrage was among the women's rights advocates amidst these liberals! Really? Depicting the grotesque slaughter and consumption of female murder victims is fun and entertaining?

Beyond the absurdity of the symbolically satanic and revolting gala above, the fact that former highly placed Hillary staffers are on a first-name basis with people like Abramovic and participate in "spirit-cooking" rituals is not only concerning, but leaves reason to believe this is just the tip of the iceberg.

I say that because, as devotees of Crowley occultism are fully aware, a sinister secret can be perceived between the lines of the Podesta e-mails having to do with Hillary and a series of sex-magic rituals that were conducted between January through March in 1946. These ceremonies were called the Babalon Working.

I'll get to that and what it may have to do with Hillary (or at least what some of her esoteric friends may have thought it had to do with her) in a moment, but first, on this issue of "artistic" cannibalism, sex magic, Abramovic, and her intimate friends the Podestas, a private art collection belonging to Tony Podesta depicts numerous disturbing, Abramovic-like themes including cannibalism, decapitation, mutilation, and what some consider child porn.

For example, on April 28, 2016, *Time* magazine published a feature on John Podesta that showed him standing in front of one of his brother Tony's art pieces, which they described this way:

On the wall in his office at Hillary Clinton's Brooklyn headquarters, campaign chairman John Podesta has an oil painting on loan from his lobbyist brother, who is an avid art collector. The image shows two men hunched over a dining room table, bearing knives and forks. On the table lays a man in a suit, who looks vaguely like Podesta. "It's better to be the guy with the fork," Podesta quips to his colleagues, if they ask about the image, "than the guy on the table."[163]

The painting is eerily similar to another "art" scene where Abramovic and Lady Gaga eat "blood" off a simulated dead woman's naked body.[164]

Other examples of Tony Podesta's "art" includes Louise Bourgeois' "The Arch of Hysteria"—an eight-foot-long sculpture of a decapitated naked man's contorted body (which hangs from the ceiling of the Podestas' stairwell), a nude women immersed in what looks like blood, a naked dead Jesus, photographs of naked children from Katy Grannan that would get normal people arrested, and numerous works by Serbian painter Biljana Djurdjevic that depict near-naked, sad-looking children whose buttocks are red as if they have been punished.

On the decapitated sculpture, Harrison Koehli at SOTT.net (Signs of the Times) writes: "Whether intentional or not, the sculpture bears a resemblance to one of serial killer Jeffrey Dahmer's victims." Koehli then points to a link where one of Dahmer's fatalities was photographed, which for all intents and purposes looks identical to Podesta's headless art piece. A caption on the photograph of Dahmer's subject reads: "Dahmer photographed his victims' bodies in various positions that he found sexually significant." Koehli adds, "I could find no indication that Bourgeois (the artist that made Podesta's figurine) intentionally modelled the sculpture on the Dahmer photograph [but] the similarities are striking, including the arched position, the slender frame, the prominent ribs, and the lack of a head."[165]

Earlier in his editorial, Koehli made the following relevant point about the Podesta art collection, Podesta's friends of choice, and a so-called "Pizzagate" connection:

> The art is weird and disturbing and definitely speaks to the Podestas having deviant minds. The presence of Marina Abramovic says a lot about these people; "spirit cooking" is their idea of a good time…. The type of "events" hosted at Comet Ping Pong and the fact that convicted pedophile Jared Fogle frequented the venue, which is owned by James Alefantis, a Washington insider and close friend of Hillary Campaign manager John Podesta and his brother, is rather unnerving. Add in the Clintons' ties to convicted pedophile Jeffrey Epstein and their connection to Anthony Weiner, who allegedly sexted with an underage girl, and we're left with an impression of something very unsavory going on in the heart of American politics.[166]

Numerous alt-right bloggers and conspiracy sites that had paid attention to the Podesta brothers were quick in 2016 and 2017 to jump on the so-called Pizzagate bandwagon to infer that underage children were in fact being trafficked for use by powerful political and underworld figures connected to Bill and Hillary Clinton (and it doesn't help that the Wikileaks e-mails included one in which John Podesta mentions his close relationship with former Speaker of the House Dennis Hastert, who was sent to prison for fifteen months over sexually abusing boys and whom the judge called "a serial child molester"). Hastert himself, who was released after serving a little over a year of his sentence,[167] may have been linked to the Wikileaks e-mails where dozens of references to "pizza" (149 e-mails) combined with other foods were viewed as a coded system for pedophiles where words like "hotdog" with "pizza" equaled a little boy, "pasta" with "pizza" meant a girl, cheese was for a "little girl" and so on. The reason a conspiracy grew up around this is partly because of Tony Podesta's disturbing, some say occult pedophilic art collection, together with the pizza parties he often cohosted with his friend James Alefantis, a man considered to be one of the fifty most powerful people in Washington and the owner of the pizza and music restaurant named Comet Ping Pong. This restaurant is mentioned a dozen or so times in the leaked e-mails and is the dining establishment where Edgar Welch was arrested for taking an AR-15 rifle and handgun December 2016, where he later told police he was there investigating a story about Pizzagate and Hillary Clinton running a child-sex ring out of the eatery.

Some weeks after Welch was arrested, CBS46 evening anchor Ben Swann, whose popular "Truth in Media" website and "Reality Check" program had launched an investigation into the Pizzagate story, also framed the location as possibly connected with a child pornography ring being run out of DC. Swann questioned why authorities had been unwilling to conduct a full investigation into the allegations and pointed to music bands that play at Comet singing songs that joke about pedophilia and depicting artwork that matches known "boy-lover" symbols (numerous Podesta e-mails also mention "pizza" and "handkerchiefs," which are said to be coded language for pedophiles). Swann went on to note that two doors over from Comet Ping Pong is another parlor named Besta Pizza, where their logo matched what a 2007 FBI report depicted as a unique symbol commonly used by pedophiles to express their particular preferences in children—a winding triangle that stands for "boy love." Following Swann's report, Besta Pizza modified its logo.

A few days after his first broadcast on the subject, Swann's Truth in Media site disappeared, as did his Twitter, Instagram, and Facebook accounts.

Did somebody tell him to back off, or was it simply his bosses ordering him to quit the conspiracy-themed reporting?

On the heels of Swann abruptly abandoning the story, Alex Jones was likewise somehow pressured into publicly apologizing for promoting similar commentary involving Pizzagate. Whether he, too, had been threatened by a defamation suit or something else, he read from a prepared statement that to his knowledge, "neither Mr. Alefantis, nor his restaurant Comet Ping Pong, were involved in any human trafficking as was part of the theories about Pizzagate that were being written about in many media outlets and which we commented upon."[168]

And then there was Hillary Clinton tweeting about Pizzagate when Michael Flynn was forced to resign, rubbing it in his face and reminding him how his son had once accused her of running a child-sex ring out of Comet Ping Pong.

Regardless of whether everything surrounding this particular conspiracy was overblown and never had any real substance, a series of recent police raids on pedophile circles in the US with ties to international child trading illustrates that such crimes are not only alive and well, but often include the elite. President Trump responded to one of the recent arrests by holding a press conference in which he announced his plan to bring the "full force and weight" of the US government against this "epidemic of human trafficking."[169]

While former Congresswoman Cynthia McKinney—who once challenged the elite on the floor of the House about their participation in sex slavery—agreed with Trump's plan to take down child abusers, she offered a disquieting revelation of her own in the form of a warning to the new president: If you go after pedophiles, plan to make arrests of both Republicans and Democrats reaching all the way to the top in Washington DC.[170]

Reinforcing her allegation was a 2006 Immigration and Customs Enforcement investigation into the purchase of child pornography that "turned up more than 250 civilian and military employees of the Defense Department—including some with the highest available security clearance." Mysteriously, the Pentagon refused to further investigate these culprits.[171]

We could also discuss the Dutch whistleblower Ronald Bernard, who claimed in an interview with De Vrije Media earlier this year that he participated in secret sex-cult societies that included rituals and human sacrifice.[172]

Then there are the upper echelons of Hollywood, where veterans of the trade like Jon Robberson, Elijah Wood, Corey Feldman, and others claim that Hollywood hides its own dark secrets involving child sex abuse and cover up. Robberson in particular says the filmmaking capital's rampant pedophilia includes an occult element, too. He said in an interview:

> Much of what is used in Hollywood today [during sex abuse of children] that would be considered Luciferian in nature really comes from a lot of the Druidic incantations, the Druidic witchcraft, the worship of Gaia, of earth, in ninth and tenth century England. And prior to that, you can trace that through Kabbalistic witchcraft and Jewish mysticism all the way back, really, to what was going on in Babylon.

> There is a distinct through-line from the time of when the Babylonians were sacrificing kids to Moloch in the temple at the

top of the Tower of Babel. From the time that they attempted to slap God in the face with that stuff to Hollywood today, you could do an exhaustive study and find a distinct through-line in the practice of witchcraft.[173]

Even horror master and beloved actor Vincent Price was once a pitchman for satanism in Hollywood. In fact, you can still get one of Price's originally best-selling and now collector's items vinyl records providing step-by-ste,p how-to guidance for listeners to conjure spirits and demons—and even how to sell their soul to the devil.[174]

But what does all this have to do with Hillary Clinton, sex magic, and that thing I mentioned earlier called the Babalon Working?

After Vincent Price made his Hollywood debut in 1933, the occult became a hot commodity for the elite up through the early '70s. While the Jesus Freaks and Jesus Movement were spreading across North America, Europe, and Central America (as chronicled by Donna Howell in *Final Fire* [Defender Publishing, 2016]), this same time period was giving rise to a counterculture that preferred occult mysticism to knowing Jesus. This was especially true with many popular musicians, bohemian artists, and author-philosophers such as William Burroughs (largely considered a leader of the so-called Beat Generation of the 1950s that rejected conventional society and American Christianity and favored Zen Buddhism, free thinking, open sexuality, recreational drugs, and mysticism in which a renaissance of ceremonial magic and occult thought from spiritualists like Elophas Levi, Helena Blavatsky, and Aleister Crowley were experiencing a huge resurgence).

Rock music of the time also helped fuel interest in the occult through groups like the Beatles, with George Harrison's love for Eastern mysticism, and the influence of John Lennon, who was so captivated by Timothy Leary's teachings that he employed Leary's manual, based on the Tibetan Book of the Dead, in the song "Tomorrow Never Knows."

Many years ago, I even preached a sermon during which I brought up the cover of the Beatles' album *Sgt. Pepper's Lonely Hearts Club Band* and how among the group members on the vinyl record's cover were William Burroughs, Aleister Crowley, and Aldous Huxley—whose best-known work may have been *Brave New World* but whose other books like *The Doors of Perception* recalled his mind-portal-opening experiences when taking psychedelic drugs.

This was a time when free thinkers like Timothy Leary openly advocated the use of mind-expanding psychedelics for breaching hallucinogenic doorways, which theologians correctly worried might actually open mystical gateways of exposure to invisible entities that had been forbidden by Scripture. Leary himself understood this esoteric spirituality endemic of his philosophy and once said, "I rejoice to see our culture being taken over by joyful young messiahs who dispel our fears and charm us back into the pagan dance" (*The Lost Beatles Interviews* from Geoffrey Giuliano).[175] Later, he even penned an essay in which he said the Beatles were the reincarnation of a god: "He or she has come back as the four sided mandala–the Beatles. The means by which to spread the new gospel—music. The sacrament—drugs."[176]

Of course, the portal of choice for occultists, medicine men, and shamans has always been mind-altering substances. In the New Testament, the English word "sorcery" translates from the Greek *pharmakei n*, from which the later word "pharmacy" was derived (Galatians 5:20; Revelation 9:2, 18:23, 21:8, 22:15). The term was adopted into modern use because the original "pharmacists" were mixing potions to bring one into contact with the spirit world like a modern druggist would make cough syrup. Indigenous peoples worldwide have identified a multitude of drugs for accomplishing the task. Hume states, "The ingestion of perception-altering substances is commonly acknowledged cross-culturally as a way to journey into the non-material world of spirit." Although scant, there is a small body of scientific evidence concerning such biochemical portals.

Psychiatrist Rick Strassman's landmark study, using the psychoactive compound N, N-Dimethyltryptamine (DMT), was the first human psychedelic research in the United States after twenty years of censure. The study employed sixty volunteers—screened to prefer stable folks with positive past psychedelic drug experiences—who were injected with DMT under clinical supervision at the University of New Mexico's School of Medicine in Albuquerque, New Mexico, where Strassman was a tenured associate professor of psychiatry. Strassman, a Buddhist, holds degrees in biological sciences from Stanford University and an MD with honors from Albert Einstein College of Medicine of Yeshiva University and further studies at University of California, Davis. His groundbreaking research became a best-selling book and documentary.

Published in 2000, *DMT: The Spirit Molecule* makes a case that DMT, naturally released by the pineal gland, facilitates the soul's movement in and out of the body, enabling birth and death experiences, as well as deep, meditative states. More than half of the subjects reported similar experiences interacting with nonhuman beings, described by experiencers as "alien space insects" and "reptilian and humanoid." Furthermore, the resulting testimonies were remarkably consistent with near-death experiences, alien abductions, and various occult techniques.

The resulting evidence shocked Strassman, who conceded to himself, "This sounds like nothing I've ever heard about in my therapy patients' dream life. It is much more bizarre, well-remembered, and internally consistent." The uniform testimony of those who participated in the study was that the beings they interacted with were real. Author and consciousness researcher Graham Hancock asks:

> Are they simply quaint "brain fiction"? Most mainstream scientists would say so—although they cannot explain why evolution should have installed identical, highly imaginative Gothic novelists in all our brains. Or could it be that these strange, complex, universal experiences with evolving storylines are in some way as real as those we take for granted in normal states of consciousness?[177]

Most Western scientists simply assume that all such experiences are subjective hallucinations produced by a drugged brain. However, there is really no good reason to accept the reductionist interpretation. Strassman points out, "However, just as likely as the theory that these worlds exist 'only in our minds' is that they are, in reality, 'outside' of us and freestanding." I believe this is true, and, at first encounter, I was surprised that someone trained in Western schools would be open to the reality of the spirit realm, that is, until I discovered Strassman is an accomplished Buddhist.

In 1984, Strassman obtained "lay ordination in a Western Buddhist order," which probably explains why he seems eager to jettison the materialist consensus. In the introduction, he proposes: "DMT can allow our brains to perceive dark matter or parallel universes, realms of existence inhabited by conscious entities."[178] Frankly, it seems that way to theologians as well, and it is noteworthy when scientists discover evidence for spiritual realities the Bible disclosed thousands of years ago about the relationship between man's physical body made from the clay and God-breathed, immaterial soul.

Instead of thinking of the brain as a biological meat computer, Strassman offers the "receiver of reality" model for brain function. Like a television receives its content from the airwaves, consciousness or the mind resides outside of our bodies. If so, it explains why altered states of consciousness "change the channel" and allow one to view programming from other realms. Strassman corresponded with Oxford Professor of Physics David Deutsch, a proponent of the Many Worlds Interpretation (MWI) of quantum mechanics and the author of *The Fabric of Reality*, concerning DMT altering the brain to work as a receiver of information from parallel worlds.

Deutsch, a pioneer in quantum computing,[179] believes contact with such worlds is possible, but only through complex algorithms using the computers of the future. When Strassman proposed the idea that DMT facilitated biological quantum computation, it seemed impossible to

Deutsch, because such technology required a temperature near absolute zero. However, chemists have continually developed processes allowing superconductivity at higher and higher temperatures. Strassman suggests that DMT similarly changes the brain's physical properties so that quantum computing takes place at body temperature, accessing parallel universes.

I assert something like the above theory can be true without necessarily accepting the Many Worlds Interpretation. These could be very real intrusions into the spirit realm where angels and demons dwell. Consider Graham Hancock's assessment of the beings he encountered on psychedelics:

> My intuition was that I had been afforded glimpses, however brief and however distorted by my own cultural preconditioning, of beings that are absolutely real in some modality not yet understood by science, that exist around us and with us, *that even seem to be aware of us and to take an active interest in us,* but that vibrate at a frequency beyond the range of our senses and instruments and thus generally remain completely invisible to us.[180] (emphasis added)

Psychedelics are a consciousness portal to the immaterial realm—but are not necessarily a safe one. Strassman offered concerning the spirit molecule:

> It pulls us into worlds known only to itself. We need to hold on tight, and we must be prepared, for spiritual realms include both heaven and hell, both fantasy and nightmare. While the spirit molecule's role may seem angelic, there is no guarantee it will not take us to the demonic.[181]

In fact, it explains the biblical prohibitions against sorcery just as well as the most educated Christian apologetic.

The great danger is that the subject is in the hands of an unknown intelligence. The Bible warns that angelic appearances can be deceiving (2 Corinthians 11:14). Paranormal authors Brad and Sherry Steiger offer the "thesis that the aliens, angels, spirit guides, demons, and gods or goddesses encountered by unaware, yet somehow receptive percipients may actually be the product of a multidimensional intelligence that masks itself in physical forms that are more acceptable to humans than its true image—if it does, indeed, have a perceivable form at all."[182] Apparently, there is some consensus that demons can shape-shift or transform their physical bodies.

It seems fair to argue that the Bible supports the possibility of travel to the spirit realms via altered states of consciousness. Examples include: Jacob's vision of the "gateway of God" seen during a dream; Ezekiel's vision of God's throne (Ezekiel 1); Isaiah's vision of the throneroom (Isaiah 1); Paul questioning whether he was out of his body (2 Corinthians 12); Peter's statement, "in a trance I saw a vision" (Acts 11:5); Paul writing, "I was in a trance" (Acts 22:17); and John's statement that he was "in the Spirit" (Revelation 1:10). God uses altered states, but it seems they are by His will rather than by the experiencers' will. Dreams, visions, trances, and out-of-body travel are all supported as real "portals" in Scripture, but the practice of inducing them via psychotropic substances, Eastern meditation techniques, or rituals is forbidden as sorcery.

The Babalon Workings

Now that we've briefed ourselves on the question of metaphysical portals, psychotropic drugs, and occult incantations employed to open them (as also verified by Scripture), it was into this pot-smoke-filled, heroin-induced, LSD-taking atmosphere of the ''40s-'70s that NASA Jet Propulsion Laboratory rocket scientist Jack Parsons and Scientology founder L. Ron Hubbard came up with the infamous "Babalon Working" that allegedly opened a gate that fueled the modern UFO era and maybe played a role in the birth of Hillary Clinton.

I say this with a strong emphasis on *maybe*.

Both Parsons and Hubbard were disciples of Aliester Crowley and practiced his teaching called Thelema as a philosophy defined by the maxim, "Do what thou wilt shall be the whole of the law." It comes from Crowley's *Book of the Law*, which can be connected to the "Spirit Cooking" ceremonies of the Podestas and Abramovic, which was channeled by an incorporeal demonic intelligence named Aiwass.[183] Thelema is a narcissistic ideology that undergirds several esoteric magic societies like the AA and the Ordo Templi Orientis that fundamentally oppose God's moral law. Satan targets sexuality because procreation is the human capability that comes closest to the divine. As a result, it's not too surprising that sexual perversion and "sex magick" are essential components of occult rituals. Parsons and Hubbard's "working" entailed all sorts of such aberrant sexual activity.

In Thelemic literature, Babalon has three conceptual aspects: 1) the Gateway to the City of the Pyramids, 2) the Scarlet Woman, and 3) the Great Mother.[184] She serves as a portal for sorcerers, but probably not in the way one might expect. An occult reference explains:

> Within the mystical system of Crowley, the adept reaches a final stage where he or she must cross the Abyss, that great wilderness of nothingness and dissolution. Choronzon is the dweller there, and his job is to trap the traveler in his meaningless world of illusion. However, Babalon is on just the other side, beckoning. If the adept gives himself to her—the symbol of this act is the pouring of the adept's blood into her graal—he becomes impregnated in her, then to be reborn as a master and a saint that dwells in the City of the Pyramids.[185]

In other words, the adept's great hope is reincarnation as a master and saint in the City of the Pyramids. It sounds promising to obtain an honorary position in an exotic location like Egypt, but, in reality, it only amounts to the same old "oneism." Rather than dwelling in a glamorous metropolis, the residents of the so-called city are disintegrated. According to Thelemapedia, "They have destroyed their earthly ego-identities, becoming nothing more than piles of dust (i.e. the remaining aspects of their True Selves without the self-sense of 'I')."[186] Monism offers no distinctions, no justice, no hope, and no love…nothing but dissolution and absorption into the meaningless whole. Occultism promises a beautiful city, but only delivers disintegration.

The second "scarlet woman" aspect of Babalon seemed to be not much more than an honorary title for Crowley's female sex-magick partners, of whom seven were given the title.[187] The third aspect "Great Mother" borrows from the book of Revelation's "MOTHER OF HARLOTS" imagery and is an important figure in Crowley's depraved, blasphemous, and pantheistic "Gnostic Mass."

Parsons and Hubbard's motive was largely self-gratification, but the Working explicitly stated the goal of transforming traditional values. The rituals were aimed at incarnating the archetypal divine feminine and changing culture through her influence. It is a matter of record that feminism and pantheistic monism were sowed into public consciousness from the ivory towers of academia shortly subsequent to Parsons' dark invocation:

The ultimate goal of these operations, carried out during February and March 1946, was to give birth to the magical being, or "moonchild," described in Crowley's works. Using the powerful energy of IX degree Sex Magick, the rites were intended to open a doorway through which the goddess Babalon herself might appear in human form.[188]

Parsons believed that he and Hubbard accomplished this task in a series of rituals culminating in 1946. Parsons' biography preserves a celebratory statement regarding her embodiment in the womb. In a fragment from his writings, Parsons, exhausted and exultant, declared his work a success. He believed that Babalon, in the manner of the Immaculate Conception, was due to be born to a woman somewhere on earth in nine months' time. "Babalon is incarnate upon the earth today, awaiting the proper hour for her manifestation," he wrote.[189]

Accordingly, one would expect a female child was to be born around 1947, and, indeed, such an influential feminist was delivered that year who may offer the most promise for identifying the fruit of Parsons' infamous ritual.[190] That would be none other than *Hillary Rodham Clinton*. Intriguingly, Parsons later referred again to "Babalon the Scarlet Woman" and this time by a particular name in his *Book of the Antichrist*. On October 31, 1948, a full sixty-nine years ago when the female child would have been only around one year of age, Parsons wrote that her spirit contacted him, calling itself "Hilarion," who, he said, would become an international public figure dedicated to bringing the work of the Antichrist to fruition.[191] Why is that important? Because the etymology of Hilarion is the arcane "Hillary."[192]

I asked myself: 1) how many internationally influential feminists were 2) born in 1947 who are 3) named "Hillary" and that 4) have the potential to become the leader of the most powerful nation on earth, which 5) was dedicated from its inception to the enthronement of Osiris-Apollo, who 6) the Bible recognizes as Antichrist and 7) a spirit calling itself "Hillary" made clear to Jack Parsons sixty-nine years ago it is dedicated to helping become king of the earth?

Can a mathematician please provide me the statistical probability of chance for this?

This came to my mind when reading the Wikileaks e-mail revelations and remembering how Hillary hinted "alien disclosure" would be made if she was elected president[193] and Abramovic, the Podestas and other close Hillary affiliates were manifest believers in the same UFOs and "contiguous aliens"[194] that Parsons and Hubbard sought (the Church of Scientology Hubbard started is based on an alien called "Xenu"),[195] as well as being practitioners of the same Crowley occultism that Parsons and Hubbard were devotees of, and it immediately seemed to me beyond probability of coincidence. Rather, I straightway thought in the days leading up to the presidential election that these modern Thelemists actually believed Hillary is—or could be—the incarnation of the archetype divine feminine, the Whore of Babylon, the "Hilarion" that is set to take the throne of the most powerful nation on earth to assist Antichrist in his bid to rule the entire world.

But, you may say, Hillary lost the election and that is the end of that. Right?

Ummm…not so fast. When America's next presidential election takes place in 2020, Hillary will be 72 years old as we enter that year. And the number 72—as all occultists and assuredly Abramovic and the Podestas know—is the highest number in satanism and archaic sorcery. It is the number of lead devils, according to *The Lesser Key of Solomon*, the number of evil disciples and accomplices of Set that enclosed the god Osiris (Apollo to the Greeks and the spirit that possesses Antichrist in the book of Revelation) in a coffin, the number of goetic demons, the age when Aliester Crowley died, and so on.

But this number has a very important wicked connection to US presidents past *and future* too, especially as it involves the coming of Antichrist and the Masonic prophecy on the Great Seal. In a section titled "The First American Osiris" from my book *Zenith 2016*, I explain:

> Through Masonic alchemistry, presidential *apotheosis*—that is, the leader of the United States (America's Pharaoh) being trans-formed into a god within the Capitol Dome/womb of Isis in sight of the Obelisk of Osiris (the Washington Monument to those whom Masons call "profane," the uninitiated)—actually began with America's first and most revered president, Master Freemason George Washington. In fact, Masons in attendance at Washington's funeral in 1799 cast sprigs of acacia "to symbol-ize both Osiris' resurrection and Washington's imminent resur-rection in the realm where Osiris presides."[196] According to this Masonic enchantment, Osiris (Horus) was rising within a new

president in DC as Washington took his role as Osiris of the underworld....

When visitors to Washington DC tour the Capitol, one of the unquestionable highlights is to visit the womb of Isis—the Capitol Dome—where, when peering upward from inside Isis' continuously pregnant belly, tourists can see hidden in plain sight Brumidi's 4,664-square-foot fresco, *The Apotheosis of George Washington*. The word "apotheosis" means to "deify" or to "become a god," and explains part of the reason US presidents, military commanders, and members of Congress lay in state in the Capitol Dome. The womb of Isis is where they go at death to magically reach apotheosis and transform into gods.

Those who believe the United States was founded on Christianity and visit the Capitol for the first time will be surprised by the stark contrast to historic Christian artwork of the ascension of Jesus Christ compared to the "heaven" George Washington rises into from within the energized Capitol Dome/womb of Isis. It is not occupied by angels, but with devils and pagan deities important to Masonic belief. These include Hermes, Neptune, Venus (Isis), Ceres, Minerva, and Vulcan (Satan), of course, the son of Jupiter and Juno to which human sacrifices are made and about whom Manly Hall said brings "the seething energies of Lucifer" into the Mason's hands.[197]

Beside those pagan gods which accompany Washington inside the Capitol Dome, the scene is rich with symbols analogous with ancient and modern magic, including the powerful trident—considered of the utmost importance for sorcery and indispensable to the efficacy of infernal rites—and the caduceus, tied to Apollo and Freemasonic Gnosticism in which Jesus was a myth based on Apollo's son, Asclepius, the god of medicine and healing whose snake-entwined staff remains a symbol of medicine today. Occult numerology associated with the legend of Isis and Osiris is also encoded throughout the painting, such as the thirteen maidens, the six scenes of pagan gods around the perimeter forming a hexagram, and the entire scene bounded by the powerful Pythagorian/Freemasonic "binding" utility—**seventy-two** five-pointed stars within circles [bold emphasis added].

Much has been written by historians within and without Masonry as to the relevance of the number seventy-two (72) and the alchemy related to it. In the Kabbalah, Freemasonry, and Jewish apocalyptic writings, the number equals the total of wings Enoch received when transformed into Metatron (3 Enoch 9:2). This plays an important role for the Brotherhood, as Metatron or "the angel in the whirlwind" was enabled as the guiding spirit over America during George W. Bush's administration for the purpose of directing the *future* and *fate* of the United States (as also prayed by Congressman Major R. Owens of New York before the House of Representatives on Wednesday, February 28, 2001).

But in the context of the Capitol Dome and the seventy-two stars that circle Washington's apotheosis in the womb of Isis, the significance of this symbolism is far more important. In sacred literature, including the Bible, stars are symbolic of angels, and within Masonic Gnosticism, seventy-two is the number of fallen angels or kosmokrators" (reflected in the seventy-two conspirators that controlled Osiris' life in Egyptian myth) that currently administer the affairs of earth. Experts in the study of the Divine Council believe that, beginning at the Tower of Babel, the world and its inhabitants were disinherited by the sovereign God of Israel and placed under the authority of seventy-two angels [some Bible versions say 70] which became corrupt and disloyal to God in their administration of those nations (Psalm 82). These beings quickly became worshipped on earth as gods following Babel, led by Nimrod/Gilgamesh/

Osiris/Apollo. Consistent with this tradition, the designers of the Capitol Dome, the Great Seal of the United States, and the Obelisk Washington Monument circled the *Apotheosis of Washington* with seventy-two pentagram stars, dedicated the Obelisk seventy-two years after the signing of the Declaration of Independence, and placed seventy-two stones on the Great Seal's uncapped pyramid, above which the eye of Horus/Osiris/Apollo stares. These three sets of seventy-two (72), combined with the imagery and occult numerology of the Osiris/Obelisk, the Isis/Dome, and the oracular Great Seal, are richly symbolic of the influence of Satan and his angels over the world (see Luke 4:5–6, 2 Corinthians 4:4, and Ephesians 6:12) with a prophecy toward Satan's final earthly empire—the coming *novus ordo seclorum*, or new golden pagan age [what Parsons in *The Book of the Antichrist* prophesied "Hilarion" will help establish].

In order for the "inevitable" worship of Osiris to be "reestablished" on earth, the seventy-two demons that govern the nations must be controlled, thus they are set in magical constraints on the Great Seal, the Washington Obelisk, and the pentagram circles around the *Apotheosis of Washington* to bind and force the desired effect.

In *The Secret Destiny of America*, Hall noted as well that the seventy-two stones of the pyramid on the Great Seal correspond to the seventy-two arrangements of the Tetragrammaton, or the four-lettered name of God in Hebrew. "These four letters can be combined in seventy-two combinations, resulting in what is called the Shemhamforesh, which represents, in turn, the laws, powers, and energies of Nature."[198] The idea that the mystical name of God could be invoked to bind or loose those supernatural agents (powers and energies of nature, as Hall called them) is meaningful creed within many occult tenets, including Kabbalah and Freemasonry. This is why the seventy-two stars are pentagram-shaped around the deified Freemason, George Washington. Medieval books of magic, or grimoires such as the Key of Solomon and the Lesser Key of Solomon not only identify the star systems Orion (Osiris) and Pleiades (Apollo) as the "home" of these powers, but applies great importance to the pentagram shape of the stars for binding and loosing their influence. Adept Rosicrucians and Freemasons have long used these magical texts—the Key of Solomon and the Lesser Key of Solomon—to do just that....

Unlike other grimoires including the sixteenth-century *Pseudomonarchia Daemonum* and the seventeenth-century *Lemegeton*, the Key of Solomon does not contain the "Diabolical Signature" of the devil or demons, which the Ars Goetia describes as numbering seventy-two and who were, according to legend, constrained to assist King Solomon after he bound them in a bronze vessel sealed by magic symbols. Such books routinely contain invocations and curses for summoning, binding, and loosing these demons in order to force them to do the conjurers will. Even members of the Church of Satan sign letters using the Shemhamforash, from the Hebrew name of God or Tetragrammaton, producing a blasphemous reinterpretation of the seventy-two entities.

Given these startling connections from *Zenith 2016*, I suggest you keep an eye on Hillary, who will be 72 years old in the leadup to the next presidential election in 2020 and whose 2016 campaign management included those who were familiar with and practiced the magic Parsons and Hubbard incorporated to produce the "Hilarion" incarnation from the Babalon Working.

Additionally, whereas numerous rabbis in Israel see Donald Trump as paving the way for Messiah, some of the same mystics have pointed out that the gematria (Hebrew numerology used by rabbis to decipher hidden revelations in the Bible) of all three parts of Hillary's name—Hillary (הילרי), Rodham (רודהם), and Clinton (קלינטון)—each equals the number 255. Why is that important to these Jewish spiritual leaders? Because "the word for a female from the nation of Amalek (עמלקיה) is also 255." Amalek is the archetypical evil—the spirit that the Babalon Working supposedly incarnated in 1947—"that Israel is commanded to oppose anywhere and at any time," they say, before adding, "The total of all three of [Hillary's] names is 765 (255 x 3), which is the same value as צרה עת ("time of terrible distress"). The term צרה עת comes from the book of Daniel 12:1, which describes the time when Michael, the guardian angel of Israel, will stand in defense of his people at the time of great tribulation.

On this point, William Branham, a prophecy preacher who at one time was America's most well-known evangelist, gave very specific prophecies that were published in 1933 concerning events that would transpire in the years leading to Antichrist. His predictions turned out to be surprisingly accurate. He foresaw Mussolini invading Ethiopia, America being drawn into a world war against Germany when it would be led by a man named Adolf Hitler, the growth of communism under Russia, egg-shaped cars driving themselves in a technological future age, and so on. But in his sixth and seventh visions, he beheld a woman in the United States "clothed in splendor, and great power was given to her. She was lovely of feature, but there was a hardness about her that defied description…. she was yet cruel, wicked and cunning. She dominated the land with her authority, and she had complete power over the people."

Following this came his seventh vision, in which he says a "voice bade him to look once more. As he turned and beheld, a great explosion rent the entire land, and left the land of America a smoldering, chaotic ruin. As far as the eye could see there was nothing but craters, smoking piles of debris, and no humanity in sight. The vision then faded away."[199]

Such an explosion can only describe an atomic bomb, which was not even tested until 1945, twelve years later.

If Branham foresaw this future scenario accurately, the rise of Hilarion in 2020 could quickly lead to the consummation of the deep occultism of the deep state.

chapter seven

The Secret Destiny of America?

On Wednesday November 30, 2016, pastors and members of Congress, including former 2016 presidential candidate, Republican Texas Senator Ted Cruz, met on Capitol Hill to pray. This wasn't your usual Congressional-Clergy Town Hall get-together organized by Wallbuilders and the Jefferson Gathering. It was a specific, down-on-your-knees moment to accomplish a single major task—to ask God to cut Satan's power from the US Capitol and to bring revival to the nation.

Dave Kistler of the North Carolina Pastors Network was in attendance and noted how US Senate Chaplain Barry Black preached and prophesied that a revival is coming to America and "will commence…in the halls of Congress." Dale Walker of the Tennessee Pastors Network, also in attendance, agreed with this prophecy.

"If God rules in the halls of legislation, it's the pulpit's benefit of being there, being on site and standing up and speaking the law of God to our elected leaders and praying for them," Walker said. "It's been the absence of the pulpits is the reason why Satan has ruled in the halls of legislation."

Kistler added that they were allowed to pray in the US Senate chamber as well as in the Kennedy Caucus Room in the Capitol.

"We got on our knees…and it sounded almost like a labor room as people were crying out to God for the revival that Chaplain Black believes is coming and that we believe is coming," Kistler explained.

"To do that in the Senate chamber was an absolutely astounding opportunity, and again it puts an exclamation point on the Senate chaplain's assessment that revival is on the way and may indeed begin in the halls of Congress."[200]

Three months after that prayer meeting at the Capitol, Christian author Lance Wallnau went on the *Jim Bakker Show* and said God used Donald Trump to deliver "the nation from the spirit of witchcraft in the Oval Office."

"The spirit of witchcraft was in the Oval Office, it was about to intensify to a higher-level demon principality, and God came along with a wrecking ball, shocked everyone, the church cried out for mercy and bam—God knocked that spirit out, and what you're looking at [in the current hard-left resistance] is the manifestation of an enraged demon through the populace," he added.[201]

I do not believe Lance is aware of the information I provided in the last few chapters concerning the Babalon Working and the "spirit of witchcraft" that thought it was about to take the throne in DC, but either way, I am certain he is right about outrage from a prince of darkness over recent supplications to God for this country. In fact, in February, during a waning crescent moon, the first of many of the devil's followers cast binding spells on President Trump to magically subvert his agenda. That event and several following have been covered in major media, from the *Boston Globe* and *Rolling Stone* to Breitbart and Reuters. As a reenergized spiritual movement, witchcraft, neo-paganism, and satanism have been experiencing a revolutionary (and I'm certain supernatural) energy that has allowed them capital to create a radical social presence in schools, on publicly owned lands, in courtrooms, and now in the political arena. Memes, the Internet, online discussion forums, experiential magic, and apathy in the local church have resulted in the emergence of occultism as the spirituality of choice by fashionable, trendy social warriors. Today's Millennial witches and satanists are tech savvy too, and have made access to archaic invocations like "chaos magic" readily available online to anybody of any age who cares to peruse the libraries (or "Liber," as Aliester Crowley would have called it) of forbidden knowledge so that they, too, can perform their own Babalon Workings. This catalyzing activism has resulted in so much public interest in "the craft" (defined by the Bible as "rebellion") that joining Mephistopheles to subdue a US president no longer seems surreal—at least not by Obama's agitators, whose hero Saul Alinsky dedicated his book *Rules for Radicals* to Lucifer, the original rebel. Even the *Los Angeles Times* invited Wiccan practitioner Diana Wagman to cast a spell on Trump and then followed by publishing her op-ed "I put a spell on you, Mr. President,"[202] which detailed how people can conjure entities and elements to resist those who dare call on the Christian God.

The Pew Research Center points to eight years of Obama as a big part of the fertilizer that grew this degree of hostility toward Christianity and general belief in God.[203] This naturally follows, as it was Obama himself who said in 2006 that "whatever we once were, we are no longer a Christian nation," and promised he would "fundamentally transform" America.[204]

Contrast that with another president—Donald Trump—who said in June 2017 while speaking at the Faith & Freedom Coalition conference in Washington that he will never let Christians down even though "we are under siege."[205]

Therein lies the contest, at least in the mind of the growing community of American witches and satanists. The enemy is not just the new president. Their mass rituals are intended to "Bind Donald Trump and *All Who Abet Him*."[206] It is a high-stakes battle and declaration of war against most of the readers of this book and for the future state of the union.

And make no mistake about this, either. Many of these people are more than tree-hugging old hippies dancing skyclad (nude) in moonlight or Millennials toting around chic little Gaia-worshipping paperbacks. Some are true believers in mixing politics with powerful supernaturalism, which they have sought out and that can, under the right circumstances, take on a social vivacity of its own.

From their most celebrated manuals (which I won't mention here because I don't want curious people seeking them out), practitioners of occultism agree that powerful nonhuman energies, including evil ones, can emanate from their symbols and incantations and can, once summoned, be released upon a gullible society to encourage a destructive collective group mind. As people pass these "thoughtforms" or memes from one to another and the ideas go viral, the power and reach of the entity spreads with it until it becomes an unimaginably destructive force. Writing about the Masonic involvement in the French Revolution, Gary Lachman makes an extraordinary and important observation about such immaterial destructive forces—which had unseen plans of their own—released as a result of occult politics:

> Cazotte himself was aware of the dangerous energies unleashed by the Revolution.... Although Cazotte didn't use the term, he would no doubt have agreed that, whatever started it, the Revolution soon took on a life of its own, coming under the power of an *egregore*, Greek for "watcher," a kind of immaterial entity that is created by and presides over a human activity or collective. According to the anonymous author of the fascinating *Meditations on the Tarot*, there are no "good" *egregores*, only "negative" ones.... True or not, *egregores* can nevertheless be "engendered by the collective will and imagination of nations." As Joscelyn Godwin points out, "an *egregore* is augmented by human belief, ritual and especially by sacrifice. If it is sufficiently nourished by such energies, the *egregore* can take on a life of its own and appear to be an independent, personal divinity, with a limited

power on behalf of its devotees and an unlimited appetite for their future devotion." If, as some esotericists believe, human conflicts are the result of spiritual forces for spiritual ends, and these forces are not all "good," then collective catastrophes like the French Revolution take on a different significance.[207]

Students of history have often looked with interest at the French Revolution and what dynamics caused it to result in the horror of death and torture under Robespierre compared to the Revolutionary War in America that resulted in unprecedented freedoms and monetary success. While citizens in America were rejoicing in newfound liberty, in Paris more than twenty thousand people were beheaded in the guillotines. The years following in France were marked by a reign of terror leading up to totalitarianism and Napolean (whose name means Apollo incarnate, the same spirit that will inhabit Antichrist, according to the book of Revelation). Why were the American and French Revolutions followed by such contrasting conclusions? The difference was that the American Revolution was fought on Christian principles, while the French Revolution—like many of the witches, satanists, and Obama agitators reflect currently—was anti-God. The egregore-forces behind the French Revolution were out to eliminate God and His followers as the enemies of France. They even placed a nude statue of a woman on the altar in the church at Notre Dame and proclaimed the God of Christianity dead. Soon thereafter, the French government collapsed.

Long before modern witches, the ancient world (especially among polytheistic faiths) held that the gods were often intimately involved in establishing the preeminence of kings, courts, and hierarchical systems of political power. This gave rise among pagans, popes, and monarchs to the "divine rights of kings" political philosophy and religious doctrine surrounding royalty and political legitimacy where the right to rule is derived directly from the will of the gods (or God). That spirit, too, it seems, has been resurrected alongside the Witches of Eastwick in the recreation of the Arch of Baal—the pagan archway that has been recently globetrotting the world to be erected at places wherever globalists and the world's New World Order elite gather, including in 2017 at the first-ever Cultural Summit of the powerful G7 nations that represent 64 percent of the world's net wealth (Canada, France, Germany, Italy, Japan, the United Kingdom, the United States, and the European Union).

"The structure is a reproduction of a Roman victory arch built in Palmyra, Syria at the end of the second century CE," reported Adam Eliyahu Berkowitz on May 29, 2017, for *Breaking Israel News*. "Originally it stood in front of a Roman temple where pagans worshiped the Mesopotamian god, Bel, also known as Ba'al, in a form of idol worship that figures prominently in the Bible. The original arch was destroyed by the Islamic State (ISIS) in 2015, but one year later, the Institute for Digital Archaeology used 3-D printing technology to reproduce a 20-foot full-scale replica"[208] for the United Nations.

Rabbi Jonathan Cahn was in New York when the Arch visited that city and has written how Baal also became the anti-God substitute for the God of Abraham, a false god of Hebrew apostasy in the Bible that led to their destruction. "Baal was their devil god. In fact the name for Satan, Beelzebul and Beelzebub, is derived from Baal.'"[209]

In the Old Testament, King Ahab and Queen Jezebel served as the leaders of the Northern Kingdom of Israel. During their reign, they imported Baal worship from the Sidonian Jezebel's homeland and built a house of worship for him in Samaria and erected Asherah poles in his honor for the people to worship. Children were sacrificed to Baal in some parts of the ancient world, and we are told in 1 Kings 16:33, "Ahab did more to provoke the LORD, the God of Israel, to anger than all the kings of Israel who were before him."

Today, the Arch of Baal is once again making the rounds as the herald of those who would be kings, and at least one rabbi believes it may be a sign of the metaphysical gateway Antichrist himself will soon walk through.[210] Another notable rabbi, Nir Ben Artzi, believes the timing of the recreated Arch and the emergence of modern witchcraft and black magic is not coincidental. It is an ancient spirit that has arrived to war against Donald Trump and the coming of Messiah, he says, to usurp God's rule[211] (by paving the way for an anti-Messiah).

This is exactly what some founding fathers dedicated America to accomplish.

Are you surprised by that statement?

The subject of the faith that this beautiful and successful country is built upon continues to remain a discussion brought up in many conversations across the world daily. The opinion that we came to our astounding fruition as a result of several forefathers whose legislative convictions were tempered in Yahweh and Yeshua is a common one. The impression that the very bricks laid upon our soil were dedicated to the Creator's will, provision, and consequent blessing is also a concept that hangs on our thoughts like a gentle reminder that we are *one nation under God*.

Truth is, although the roots of our foundation can certainly be traced to historical events preceding the American Revolution against British rule, hundreds of years before America's first birthday, certain secret societies and pagan religions graced our soils with their own brand of religion and eschatology. They were—and continue to be—the original deep-state, shadow-government influence that some believe to be the true power in Washington, DC.

By July 4, 1776—when the quills were dipped and ready for the signing of the Declaration of Independence—our leaders had already been affected by the sway of their paganism. In fact, with all the clamor created by war and promises of freedom, the underlining occultism that has been present since the beginning was at an all-time high as many voices were exhorting their own deities for blessing. The gods of old, had they ears to hear, would have taken in many prayers in those days...and Deism was the veil of choice under which these exhortations by dubious fraternity members were so frequently shrouded.

True Religion of Many of the Founding Fathers

Deism had become a trendy belief system on our land circa 1725, grew to dominance for many decades, and then finally declined in the early 1800s. Benjamin Franklin was born in 1706, so before his twentieth birthday, Deism would have been the new, fashionable, and intellectual faith for up-and-coming politicians. George Washington, John Adams, and Thomas Paine were born in the 1730s, followed by Thomas Jefferson, James Monroe, and James Madison in the '40s and '50s. These men established their education under the influence of major universities and Deist professors in preparation for US leadership; Washington was the exception, as his education was primarily through observation of aristocratic and wealthy dealings among the Virginia high class—most of which were openly Deist. Much documentation suggests that these men were all Deists as a result of cultural exposure during the Age of Reason (the Enlightenment era), but there are several choice documents and letters that suggest something far more bizarre than mere Deism was bubbling underneath the polished exterior for at least some of these men.

Thomas Paine

Thomas Paine is known for his heavy influence in the American Revolution. His tract *Common Sense*, according to historians, proved to inspire the writing of the Declaration of Independence. His *Crisis* pamphlets were read aloud during the wartime era by George Washington to the troops. The memory of this man's role in our country's freedom, as stated on his very gravestone, reads: "On this site was buried Thomas Paine, 1737–1809, Author of *Common Sense*, the pamphlet that stirred American colonies to independence. John Adams said: 'Without the pen of Paine, the sword of Washington would have been wielded in vain,' and 'History is to ascribe the American Revolution to Thomas

Paine.'" Paine's role as a founding father may be more overlooked than some, but it is certainly solid. So, was he a Christian?

Consider what he wrote in his *The Age of Reason; Being an Investigation of True and Fabulous Theology*:

> I do not believe in the creed professed by the Jewish church, by the Roman church, by the Greek church, by the Turkish church, by the Protestant church, nor by any church that I know of. My own mind is my own church.
>
> All national institutions of churches, whether Jewish, Christian or Turkish, appear to me no other than human inventions, set up to terrify and enslave mankind, and monopolize power and profit....
>
> Each of those churches show certain books, which they call revelation, or the word of God. The Jews say, that their word of God was given by God to Moses, face to face; the Christians say, that their word of God came by divine inspiration: and the Turks say, that their word of God (the Koran) was brought by an angel from Heaven. Each of those churches accuse the other of unbelief; and for my own part, I disbelieve them all....
>
> When Moses told the children of Israel that he received the two tables of the commandments from the hands of God, they were not obliged to believe him, because they had no other authority for it than his telling them so; and I have no other authority for it than some historian telling me so. The commandments carry no internal evidence of divinity with them; they contain some good moral precepts, such as any man qualified to be a lawgiver, or a legislator, could produce himself, without having recourse to supernatural intervention.[212]

This view is similar to those shared by others of the founding fathers. If one were to research these men at length, they would find that they all were quoted as having appreciated the morality upheld within Christianity. But men like Paine no more belonged to the Body of Christ in his appreciativeness toward it than a Christian would be a Buddhist based on his or her appreciation of philosophy. Paine went on to address quite openly the faults he found in such concepts as the virgin birth of Christ, His resurrection, and His ascension, accepting only the probability of His death on the cross as a finite human man who lived among the Jews at one point in history. His open refutation of Christianity's core doctrines goes much deeper still than this. Unabashedly, he writes that the Old Testament itself, and all the content therein, is "scarcely anything but a history of the grossest vices and a collection of the most paltry and contemptible tales."[213] Moving on to his personal grievances of the New Testament, Paine even postulates that the Holy Spirit's impregnation of Mary was equivalent to any other scandalous, premarital act between a male suitor and a betrothed woman when he says, "What is it the Testament teaches us?—to believe that the Almighty committed debauchery with a woman engaged to be married, and the belief of this debauchery is called faith."[214] His summary of this "blasphemously obscene" belief system is as follows:

It is not the existence, or non-existence, of the persons [Jesus, Mary, and Joseph] that I trouble myself about; it is the fable of Jesus Christ, as told in the New Testament, and the wild and visionary doctrine raised thereon, against which I contend. The story, taking it as it is told, is blasphemously obscene. It gives an account of a young woman engaged to be married, and while under this engagement she is, to speak plain language, debauched by a ghost, under the impious pretence (Luke, chap. i., ver. 35), that "the Holy Ghost shall come upon thee, and the power of the Highest shall overshadow thee." Notwithstanding which, Joseph afterward marries her, cohabits with her as his wife, and in his turn rivals the ghost. This is putting the story into intelligible language, and when told in this manner, there is not a priest but must be ashamed to own it.[215]

His final sentence here, in modern English, can be reworded: "Any priest or pastor willing to preach the heresy of Jesus Christ as the Son of God should be ashamed of himself."

Needless to say, Thomas Paine—the forefather to whom the victory of the American Revolution has been repeatedly bestowed upon—was not a Christian. He was a Deist, and a radical one. According to the textbook, *The Faiths of the Founding Fathers*, "Thomas Paine, [a member of the Deism] movement's *radical wing* viewed Christianity as a barrier to moral improvement and to social justice."[216]

Thomas Jefferson

Well-known founding father and celebrated signer of the Declaration, Thomas Jefferson, likewise had limited beliefs in Jesus Christ and His purpose upon the earth. Revelation 22:19 says, "And if any man shall take away from the words of the book of this prophecy, God shall take away his part out of the book of life, and out of the holy city, and from the things which are written in this book." Jefferson was not concerned about this severe threat or its eternal implications when he used a razor blade to maim the Holy Bible, cutting choice teachings from the four Gospels and gluing them into a more so-called enlightened document popularly known as the "Jefferson Bible" (formally known as *The Life and Morals of Jesus of Nazareth*). Jefferson's cuts removed all of Christ's miracles, all of His divinity as the Son, and most mention of the supernatural. The purpose of this, he says, was to purify Christ's role and teachings from what the "priests" had corrupted throughout time. In a letter written to John Adams in 1813, Jefferson explained:

In extracting the pure principles which he [Christ] taught, we should have to strip off the artificial vestments in which they have been muffled by priests, who have travestied them into various forms, as instruments of riches and power to themselves. We must dismiss the Platonists and Plotinists, the Stagyrites and Gamalielites, the Eclectics, the Gnostics and Scholastics, their essences and emanations, their logos and demiurges, aeons and daemons, male and female, with a long train of etc., etc., etc., or, shall I say at once, of nonsense. We must reduce our volume to the simple evangelists, select, even from them, the very words only of Jesus, paring off the amphibologisms into which they have been led, by forgetting often, or not understanding, what had fallen from him, by giving their own misconceptions as his dicta, and expressing unintelligibly for others what they had not understood themselves. There will be found remaining the most sublime and benevolent code of morals which has ever been offered to man. I have performed this operation for my own use, by cutting verse by verse out of the printed book, and arranging the matter which is evidently his, and which is as easily distinguishable as diamonds in a dunghill. The result is an 8vo [Latin *octavo*—meaning one eighth the length of the original printed format] of forty-six pages, of pure and unsophisticated doctrines.[217]

But Jefferson shredded the Bible apart to create this "improved" gospel—one spared of all the "dunghills" such as Christ's virgin birth and supernatural worth—without even the slightest inkling of fear that the "book of life" promise in Revelation would apply to his name. This is due to the fact that Jefferson didn't even begin to respect the book of Revelation to begin with, as he said to Alexander Smyth in a letter dated January 17, 1825: "It is between fifty and sixty years since I read it [the Book of Revelation] and I then considered it as merely the ravings of a maniac, no more worthy nor capable of explanation than the incoherences of our own nightly dreams."[218] This sentiment was penned a short number of years after he stated in his letter to William Short in 1819:

> But the greatest of all the Reformers of the depraved religion of his own country, was Jesus of Nazareth. Abstracting what is really his from the rubbish in which it is buried, easily distinguished by it's lustre from the dross of his biographers, and as separable from that as the diamond from the dung hill, we have the outlines of a system of the most sublime morality which has ever fallen from the lips of man: outlines which it is lamentable he did not live to fill up.[219]

Similar to his cutting apart of the New Testament, Jefferson believed that only parts of the Old Testament were of any value whatsoever. In a letter to Adams on January 24, 1814, he poses a question of the Ten Commandments' origin, saying that even though legend postulates they were written with the finger of God, we only have Moses' testimony to believe such a thing, and that we all have equal rights to doubt their authenticity. So, like Paine, Jefferson appreciated the morality as taught by a finite and human Jesus, but there exists plenty of evidence that Jefferson was no more a Christian man than any other Deist philosopher.

Benjamin Franklin

Another commonly known Deist, Benjamin Franklin, was a great supporter of freedom from England. It was through his career in printing early on that the writings of Thomas Paine found their way into the troops during war time and fed their hunger for a life outside England's dictatorial rule. But in addition to the wonderful deeds he carried out in the interest of our land of liberty and justice, Franklin was heavily involved in secret societies throughout our home region as well as France and England. In the scholarly journal article, "The Masonic Chronology of Benjamin Franklin," we read that "the Masonic career of Benjamin Franklin extends over a period of almost sixty years, during which time he was accorded the highest Masonic honors at home and abroad."[220]

Philadelphia's St. John's Masonic Lodge (the first Masonic building in America where Franklin penned the society's bylaws) awarded him with the title of Master Freemason during the same era he was elected Vénérable Maître W. M. (English "Worshipful Master") at the *Loge des IX Soeurs de Paris* ("Nine Sisters Lodge of Paris"; it was at this location he assisted in the initiation of famous French enlightenment writer François-Marie Arouet—a.k.a. "Voltaire"—in 1778 just months before Franklin officiated Voltaire's Masonic funeral amidst the brethren the same year). In the summer of 1734, he printed and published his *Mason Book*, which was the very first Masonic book printed in our country— and this act was carried out only a month after he had achieved the rank of "Grand Master of Pennsylvania."[221] (Later in 1749, he was appointed the "Provincial Grand Master of Pennsylvania by Thomas Oxnard of Boston."[222]) During his American administration, the State House (Independence Hall) was built, and he and the brethren of St. John's Lodge laid the cornerstone.[223] According to the recorded minutes in the proceedings of the Grand Masonic Lodge of the Crown & Anchor building of London in 1760, Franklin was listed as "Provincial Grand Master."[224] His death in 1790 is documented as passing "to the Grand Lodge beyond," and his tombstone in Christ Church Yard of Pennsylvania would be a sacred gathering site for future Masonic services held in his honor.[225]

Not only was Franklin a founding father of our country, he was a founding father of our country's Freemasonry roots. It's nearly unthinkable that we would have established such fervor for Freemasonry on our soil without him.

Yet, Franklin's personal dirty laundry list goes deep. In order to understand just how deep, we have to visit some facts about the "Hellfire

Club" of Sir Francis Dashwood. (It was men like Dashwood, along with their anything-goes lifestyles resulting in extreme corruption of character and terrible decision-making, who heralded from the enlightenment Age of Reason to which these founding fathers belonged.)

Dashwood was the founder of the "Order of the Friars of St. Francis of Wycombe," later appropriately coined the Hellfire Club. Several full-length films have been made on this subject. Membership to Dashwood's Hellfire Club (and many others like it during this time) was made up of some of the most prominent names in the British—and soon American—government, as well as jovial buddies from the upper-crust society. The club's first meeting was conducted on *Walpurgisnacht* (German "Walpurgis Night," so named after the venerated eighth-century abbess St. Walpurga), April 30, 1752. The alternate and popularly used title *Hexennacht* literally translates "Witch's Night." The Germanic origins trace to the night when witches gather on the Brocken, the pinnacle of the Harz Mountains in Northern Germany, to await the heralding springtime (though this evening is observed in several countries throughout the world not limited to Germany). The scene of witches and warlocks interacting with the devil on the Brocken for his favor has been revered over and over again through the play adaptation of Johann Wolfgang von Goethe's *Faust!*—and from many reports historically, those scenes are not entirely a work of fiction. Many documents attest to the wicked revelries that occur on *Walpurgisnacht*, including, but not limited to, fantastic orgies and demonic human or animal sacrifices to Satan as trade for his power and blessing.

Those who wish to fend off or scare away the witches partake in many protection rituals and customs (varying from country to country, but frequently involving bonfires in some way or other). Some tales involve a kind of unholy Passover event whereupon all stables and barns must be locked up with crosses on the doorposts alongside tacked sprigs of juniper and elder (sacred to pagan deities), and holy bells are placed around the necks of cows, lest the parading witches of Brocken capture the livestock and deliver them to their own horrific devices. Over the years, much like Halloween in the States, most of the original rituals and customs have been replaced with modern parties and fun bonfires where people by the score gather to drink beer, socialize, and eat fattening treats. But from one culture to another, today, the evening of *Walpurgisnacht* is an invitation for rebel youth to vandalize neighbors' property and wreak havoc throughout the area with a tongue-in-cheek blame placed on those wily Brocken witches of yesteryear.

In 1752, it was no coincidence that Sir Francis Dashwood chose to launch his Hellfire Club on a date well known for sexual orgies, fiery sacrifices, and deals with the devil. Much like some of the acts carried out by revelers who observe *Walpurgisnacht*, Dashwood organized his club to partake in debauchery fitting the motto in stained glass above the grand entrance of one of his later meeting sites—*Fais ce que tu voudras* ("Do what you will" or "Do what thou wilt")—essentially encouraging all members to drink deeply from the cup of wantonness and shameless iniquity for the duration of their gathering. (This motto was interestingly adopted later as a lifestyle mantra by Aleister Crowley, a Rosicrucian and 33rd-Degree Freemason, also popularly known as "the wickedest man in the world.")

Once the meetings were established in the Medmenham Abbey, décor was raised within depicting phallic artwork and structures, as well as mythological imagery. Caves underground at the site were also decorated accordingly. These caves are known as the "Hellfire Caves," and they still exist to this day. Although merriment was conducted in the main hall, when the men wished to indulge in gaieties so immoral that it would have jeopardized their standing as upright politicians and "Christian" aristocrats, the parties were taken underground. Women prostitutes dressed as nuns would attend and offer their "holy services" to the present "monks," and the orgies would begin.

Not limited to mere orgies and drunkenness were these meetings, however. Blatant blasphemy and mock religious rituals for the appeasement of pagan deities was the norm. (More than one of the movies made about this club of men involves mock human sacrifices, one of which in 1961 depicted the act taking place under a Baphomet symbol.) It is said that Dashwood used a sacred Eucharist cup to pour anointings upon pagan altars and deity effigies. Among the long list of gods who were given unspeakably sickening "offerings" and sacrifices (more than merely the Eucharist-cup example just given, but far too vile to give in full detail here) were Dionysus, Venus, Bacchus, Priapus, Daphne, and Flora. There are rumors in heavy circulation that Black Masses and satanic rituals took place regularly. Evidence that the "monks" were summoning the devil is not hard to find…

A story is told of an evening wherein English journalist and politician John Wilkes fastened a pull-string through a loop connected to a trunk with a monkey (dressed as a devil or demon) trapped inside. He waited for the right moment to pull the string and release the animal with the other members of the brotherhood present as a practical joke. It went as well as he could have hoped, as the primate instantly flew out of his prison and clung to John Montagu, 4th Earl of Sandwich, another of the brethren. But it is Lord Sandwich's response to the sudden appearance of the "devil"—a response the brethren thought was hilarious but which we find disturbingly revealing of the club's underlying nature— that is relevant to our reflection here:

> At the chosen moment, Wilkes pulled the cord and out popped the wretched animal which leapt on to the shoulders of Lord Sandwich, who, feeling the shock and seeing the animal grinning horribly at him concluded that *the Devil had obeyed his summons* in good earnest and had come to carry him bodily away. The harder he tried to shake off the poor creature the tighter it clung, whilst Sandwich cried out: "Spare me gracious Devil: spare a wretch who never was sincerely your servant. I sinned only from vanity of being in the fashion; thou knowest I

never have been half so wicked as I pretended: never have been able to commit the thousandth part of *the vices which I have boasted of*…leave me therefore and *go to those who are more truly devoted to your service.*"[226]

According to this oh-so-comical narrative, it wasn't at all uncommon that these "monks" of the Hellfire brethren would get together and "summon the devil"—or at least, as Lord Sandwich admitted, "boast" about doing so. What is perhaps more enlightening is the fact that Sandwich, when he believed he had finally succeeded in summoning the devil who was now appearing for his dues, pleaded with the perceived apparition that he be spared, as he wasn't as "truly devoted" to Satan as the rest of the Hellfire Club members. If, by his own admission, Sandwich was not as devoted as the others despite his direct summoning of the devil and the other "vices" he spoke of, what in the world were these other men doing that could possibly be so much worse as to prove their "true devotion"? It leaves much darkness to the imagination…

Later, when the club was dying off, it was documented that John Tucker—Hellfire Club "monk" and Member of Parliament for Weymouth, Massachusetts—was shocked to see the club's disassembling. The description of this moment is also telling: "'I was last Sunday at Medmenham and to my amazement found the Chapter Room stripped naked.' Evidently, Sir Francis had decided that the time had come to *remove all traces of incriminating evidence of the Club's existence*, including even the prints of the heads of kings and nuns and the pegs for the clothes with the brothers' names above."[227]

Such hiding of "incriminating evidence" was the way of the brethren from the beginning, as all nefarious secret societies charge its members with vows of the utmost secrecy, and this one was no different. The fact, then, that Benjamin Franklin's visits to this club and participation in its revelries remains an ongoing rumor with much supporting proof is unsettling. Many historians, books, and articles, as well as exposés produced by such sources as the History Channel specials on the secret societies of the founding fathers, go as far as calling him an official "member," whereas countless others simply say that he was a frequenter of the monks' establishment and would have—at the very least—been an eyewitness to the acts carried out in the club. What we know for certain, however, is that he was there, on the grounds of the Hellfire Club, on several occasions, *during* the debauchery. A letter to a friend back home in Philadelphia makes this fact irrefutable. Dashwood held the office of Joint Postmasters General in Great Britain from 1766 to 1781, the year of his death. Franklin was Deputy Postmaster General in America during this revolutionary period, so Dashwood was Franklin's superior officer. It is a historic fact that their working together made the two men close friends, and Franklin was often invited for visits to Dashwood's estate in West Wycombe.

Since the secretary of the Hell-Fire Club burned the club's records the day before [Dashwood's] death, there is no absolute proof that Franklin (or anyone else for that matter) was a member [outside of admission by documented correspondence that is]. But we do know that he made constant visits to West Wycombe and in July 1772 made a special trip from London to spend sixteen days with Sir Francis. We also know that there was a meeting of the club during this period and there seems to be no reason why Franklin should have gone to Wycombe at this special time unless he was a member. *Only club members were allowed at Wycombe during meetings.* Franklin did go into the caves, and only club members (except for servants and the "nuns") were allowed past the iron gate. Franklin wrote to a friend in Philadelphia: "The exquisite sense of classical design, charmingly reproduced by the Lord le Despencer [Dashwood] at West Wycombe, whimsical and puzzling as it may sometimes be in its imagery, is as evident *below the earth* as above it." This ["below the earth" reference] can refer only to the [Hellfire Club] caves.[228]

And if Franklin were present, as the evidence is clear he was, common sense begs the questions: Would a secret society as despicably wicked as the Hellfire Club allow such a renowned figure into their midst if his only purpose there was to observe? Would that not be a threat to them if such a noteworthy man as Benjamin Franklin was calmly sitting nearby, sipping wine and taking mental notes about their orgies, pagan offerings, and mock human sacrifices? By the very nature of his refusal to participate, he would have been making a statement that he found their behaviors a moral contradiction to their office, would he not? Therefore, through the most rudimentary of kindergarten logic, wouldn't he be a tattle-tale risk?

One does not have to be an expert in the field of research regarding secret societies to know that bystanders (translation: eyewitnesses) would not be allowed on the premises during such horrific events unless they, too, had been initiated into the society and held full participation in its ceremonies. All signs point to the facts that Franklin was a member of the Hellfire Club (as hundreds of sources convincingly portray) and that he would have taken part in their rituals, including mock sacrifices.

That makes this next bit about him even more unscrupulous.

In early 1998, about *two hundred years* after Franklin's death, conservation work began on 36 Craven Street in London at the "Benjamin Franklin House" where he lived off and on between 1757 and 1775. When Jim Field of the renovation crew discovered the first of a collection of more than 1,200 animal and human bones in the basement under the floor of the Seminar Room (including enough skeletons for four whole adults and six whole children, but accumulatively, the bones were from at least fifteen people), an abrupt halt was brought to the conservation plans until a brief investigation could bring answers as to the nature of their concealment. *Sunday Times* ran the story, and an excerpt from this article states: "Initial estimates are that the bones are about *two hundred years old* [dating them to approximately the last decade of Franklin's life] and were buried at the time Franklin was living in the house, which was his home from 1757 to 1762 and from 1764 to 1775. Most of the bones show signs of having been dissected, sawn or cut. One skull has been drilled with several holes."[229] After careful analysis and much documentation, it has been proven indisputably that the bones were buried while Franklin was living there.

The most popular explanation for the discovery by those who wish to exonerate Franklin from any dubious activity is the idea that the bones were obtained for study by Dr. William Hewson—a pioneer of hematology (the study of blood and blood disease)—who ran an anatomy school within Franklin's home. Hewson, the story goes, conducted experiments on human cadavers to provide the medical community with beneficial research. It wasn't until 1832 that such experimentation for the betterment of all mankind was made legal due to resistance from religious groups, so Hewson had to hide all traces of his work. The likeliest of all assumptions then, if this version of the story is true, is that Hewson obtained the cadavers from "the resurrectionists" body snatchers who provided fresh bodies in the middle of night via the Thames River and then disposed of them via burial in Franklin's basement.

However, some of the bones were from animals, and many of the bones had been blackened by fire. If Hewson's practice centered on animals occasionally, which is not unheard of for anatomical/medical experimentation, that part could be explained. What cannot be explained is why these bones would have been charred, as if by fiery sacrifice.

Understandably, between the close association of Franklin with the Hellfire Club and the burned bones buried beneath his house, many have come forward with theories that Franklin was far more involved with satanic rituals than he wanted the world to know about. Some postulate that the bodies arrived dead and were thereafter dissected and offered ceremoniously to pagan deities in that classic Dashwood flair; others suggest an even more frightening concept that Franklin was America's first serial killer who followed through with real human sacrifices and thereafter had the bodies of his victims transported to Dr.

Hewson so that if the evidence were ever found, Franklin would be able to skirt the blame on the noble cause of future medical ingenuity. Had Franklin's reputation never initially been linked with visitations to the Hellfire Club and the darker sects openly connected to Freemasonry, these theories would sound conspiratorial and juvenile. Once the trail of questionable details is linked, however, such a notion is much less far-fetched.

But whatever the reason—anatomy school, human sacrifice, or posthumous offerings to the gods—at the very least, we know Franklin was not the "Christian founding father" he has so many times been remembered to be, and he said as much in a letter to Yale University's president, Ezra Stiles:

> As to Jesus of Nazareth, my Opinion of whom you particularly desire, I think the System of Morals and his Religion, as he left them to us, the best the world ever saw or is likely to see; but I apprehend it has received various corrupt changes, and I have, with most of the present Dissenters in England, some Doubts as to his divinity.[230]

Once again, we have a fellow "appreciator" of Jesus of Nazareth and the morals He spoke of, but Franklin was not by any stretch of the imagination a Christian man.

John Adams

Franklin's close associate John Adams gave a similar response when asked about his convictions of the Holy Bible and its central character in a letter to Thomas Jefferson dated September 3, 1816:

> I almost shudder at the thought of alluding to the most fatal example of the abuses of grief which the history of mankind has

preserved—the Cross. Consider what calamities that engine of grief has produced![231]

To refer to the Gospels and the cross upon which Christ hung for the covering of humanity's sins as an "engine of grief" is all the evidence we need from John Adams to move right along to the next on the list, knowing that Adams, too, was no Christian.

George Washington

Of course, the name many have been waiting for is the most celebrated founding father in US history: George Washington. Washington, like the others, appreciated the morality that Christ preached, but he, too, was a Deist—*and* a Freemason of the highest rank as of August 4, 1753, at the Masonic Lodge No. 4 in Fredericksburg, Virginia. We need not look far to find convincing proof that Washington's associates already knew he was not a Christian in the traditional sense, as the country continues to claim.

Bishop James White, personal pastor to Washington for more than two decades, gave testimony that although our first president attended church regularly for religious cameos, Washington never gave anyone any reason to believe it was out of sincere conviction any more than it would have been to satisfy the expectations of his country's Christian citizens. White said, "I do not believe that any degree of recollection will bring to my mind any fact which would prove General Washington to have been a believer in the Christian revelation."[232] White's assistant, Reverend James Abercrombie, held the same opinion, and when questioned, his plain response was, "Sir, Washington was a Deist."[233]

Thomas Jefferson, in his journal entry on February 1, 1800, recalled a day when Washington had cleverly outmaneuvered a group of persistent clergymen who asked Washington outright whether he was going to proclaim or deny the Christian faith during his farewell address as president. Their inquiry came as a result of Washington's continually avoiding the issue while in office. They had it in mind to put him on the spot and force an answer for the clarification of the American people. Jefferson writes:

> [T]he old fox was too cunning for them. He answered every article in their address particularly except that, which he passed over without notice.... I know that Gouverneur Morris, who pretended to be in his secrets and believed himself to be so, has often told me that General Washington believed no more in the system [Christianity] than he did.[234]

At least another fifty equivalent examples could be given that strengthen the existent doubts of Washington's Christianity. Although it has been documented scores of times that he found the moral fibers of Christianity a benefit to mankind (are we all seeing the pattern here?), and he said so often, no personal writings or quote of his can irrefutably prove that he was a Christian. *Many* documents and quotes *can* be found that prove at least his personal clergy believed he was not, and only acted as if he was so the question of his faith would not become a stumbling block to his reputation and legacy as first president of this "Christian" nation.

With these names addressed, one could continue to expound upon this list and include hundreds of others whose roles in the early-development phases of our country were crucial. Sadly, a heavy number of these names would also fall into the category of Freemason or Deist, and often simultaneously. Suffice it to say that our government was *not*, as so many still think, founded by devout followers of Christ. Some might say, and for good reason, that it was the opposite.

This opinion could easily be born out of a deeper understanding of Masonic and Freemasonic roots.

Seventh-Century Rosicrucianism and the Ancient and Mystical Order Rosae Crucis

At the start of our overview on the faith of the founding fathers, the point was made that people too often begin their research into the subject from the American Revolution and forward, inadvertently missing the paganism that had long been established on our soil before the United States of America was conceived. The same can be said of the research into Masonry and Freemasonry. So many books, articles, and documentaries (as well as Internet sites dedicated to the subject) begin the dig around the apron of George Washington or the geographical pentagram of DC, since the purposes of those works are to address the occultism that pervades our young America. This paves way for the errant concept that if Freemasonry has any kind of religious slant—Christian, pagan, satanic, etc.—it would have been born around the late 1700s. Therefore, when Freemasonic religions in the US are considered, the religions of our US founding fathers are immediately married to the conclusions (which is faulty). For instance, one might say, "Freemasonry could not have been built upon [this or that] religion, because that's not the religion Washington and his men belonged to. By process of elimination then, we can safely assume that at worst, the Freemasonic rituals were harmless, creative, Deistic simulations."

Though such reasoning seems logical, it limits the conclusion to the timeline of the men (and women) who supervised America's birth, and not to the origins (and influences therein) of the Freemasonic Order—which is *ancient*. It is surprising to observe how few people are aware how far back the rabbit hole of Masonry and Freemasonry travels.

First, it is important to refute a popular assumption that there were only a few Freemasonic leaders active at the time of the American Revolution, and that the importance of this is trivial to our nation's formation. Although a few sources claim the United States of America was only marginally connected to Masonic influence, they are becoming a minority.

Nancy Pelosi, at the first session of the 110th Congress on January 5, 2007, delivered House Resolution 33, which was a commemoration of the past "*thousands* of Freemasons in every State in the Nation and honoring them for their many contributions to the Nation throughout its history." Two items on the agenda read, "Freemasons, *whose long lineage extends back to before the Nation's founding*" and "the Founding Fathers of this great Nation and signers of the Constitution, *most of whom were Freemasons.*"[235] Perhaps she was referring to the well-known early brethren of the Craft: Washington, Monroe, Jackson, Polk, Buchanan, A. Johnson, Garfield, McKinley, T. Roosevelt, Taft, Harding, F. Roosevelt, Truman, L. B. Johnson, Ford, Franklin, Revere, Burke, and Hancock. Perhaps she was referring to John Adams, Alexander Hamilton, Thomas Jefferson, and numerous others who were accounted friends of the brotherhood. Regardless of who she may have had in mind at the time of her address, it is the result of much public display just like this that the issue has mostly been dropped and acknowledgment of significant Masonic sway at the nation's onset has been accepted.

Occult expert Manly P. Hall of Freemasonic infamy wrote: "Was Francis Bacon's vision of the 'New Atlantis' a prophetic dream of the great civilization, which was so soon to rise upon the soil of the New World? It cannot be doubted that the secret societies…conspired to establish [such] upon the American continent." Hall continued that historical incidents in the early development of the United States clearly bore "the influence of that secret body, which has so long guided the destinies of peoples and religions. By them nations are created as vehicles for the promulgation of ideals, and while nations are true to these ideals they survive; when they vary from them, they vanish like the Atlantis of old which had ceased to 'know the gods.'"[236]

To the few remaining sources that postulate Masonry was a Christian endeavor until it was sullied by occultists like Albert Pike, consider what Pelosi said about Masonry "extend[ing] back to *before* the Nation's founding."

Prior to Washington, the first Grand Master of the American Masonic Order is largely considered to be Sir Francis Bacon of the Baconian "New Atlantis" dream (which we will discuss shortly) circa 1620. And *his* primary influence according to most historians? Rosicrucianism: a seventh-century European cultural movement syncretizing Kabbalism, Christianity, and Hermeticism toward the goal of spiritual reformation among man.

Kabbalism—although the meaning of the word *kabbalah* translates "tradition" (of the Hebrews)—can in no way be compared to orthodox Judaism. The precise meaning of its practice varies from each adherent to the next, depending on their own cultural application of its teachings (kind of how Christianity's convictions and teachings vary from one denomination to the other, all based on the Cross of Calvary, yet rendering religious practices that at times can be polar opposites of each other). Origins trace to orally passed traditions from the ancient rabbis of Moses' time and evolves into differentiating convictions as later generations made modifications. However, as it relates to Rosicrucianism in the seventeenth century just prior to the Deistic Age of Reason, the core doctrine is that of a Western esoteric and occultic nature drawing its insights from none other than theosophical mysticism. Many have summarized Kabbalism as the early Jews' own Mystery Religion.

Hermeticism (also called Hermetism) is both philosophical and religious, stemming primarily from the sacred Egyptian-Greek *Hermetic Corpus* wisdom texts, frequently dated to approximately AD 100–300 (although almost just as often, they are dated to Pharaonic Egypt by others, though these dating methods are highly scrutinized). These texts were written as a conversation between a teacher by the name of Hermes Trismegistus (literally, "thrice-greatest Hermes") and a disciple seeking enlightenment. Discussions between these two characters falls deeply into reflections on the cosmos, divinity, unlocking spiritual rebirth through the power of the mind, alchemical achievements (cloaked in metaphor), and vehement defense of pagan rituals and veneration of sacred imagery. Although, like Kabbalism, Hermeticism has evolved greatly over time—both due to divergent applications of the doctrine as well as significant mistranslations of the original writings—it almost always insists throughout all its variations that it is the supreme *Prisca theologia* (Latin "old theology"; the belief in one single and infinitely true theology found in *all* religions of the world as bestowed upon mankind by God [or "the gods" in some cases] from the beginning). By the fourteenth century (heading into the Renaissance), Hermeticism proved to be a profoundly dominating authority on alchemy and magic, inspiring countless authors in subsequent centuries (Sir Thomas Browne, Giordano Bruno, and Pico della Mirandola, to name a few) who rose to stardom with their own canons of enlightenment and spiritual human transcendence via these methods.

But if the seventeenth-century Rosicrucianism is the forerunner of American Masonry through personalities like the credited first Grand Master Sir Francis Bacon, then what is the forerunner of Rosicrucianism? Let's trace this back even farther to the Ancient and Mystical Order Rosae Crucis (represented today by AMORC, the organization claiming to be the highest authority of the ancient Order; *Rosae Crucis* translates "Rose Cross"). The cross symbol is contemporarily associated to the death of Christ, but the Order Rosae Crucis predates Christianity, so according to the official AMORC organization today, at the time the earliest symbols were drawn, the cross was a representation of the shape of the human body (consider da Vinci's "Vitruvian Man"). The rose, according to the same source, "represents the individual's unfolding consciousness."[237] Their site goes on to say quite openly:

The Rosicrucian movement, of which the Rosicrucian Order, AMORC, is the most prominent modern representative, has its roots in the mystery traditions, philosophy, and *myths of ancient*

Egypt dating back to approximately 1500 BCE. In antiquity the word "mystery" referred to a special gnosis, a *secret wisdom.* Thousands of years ago in ancient Egypt select bodies or schools were formed to explore the mysteries of life and *learn the secrets of this hidden wisdom.* Only sincere students, displaying a desire for knowledge and meeting certain tests were considered worthy of being inducted into these mysteries. Over the course of centuries these mystery schools added an initiatory dimension to the knowledge they transmitted.[238]

Now, if this source is true, we're finally getting somewhere. It appears that the earliest forms of today's Freemasonic fraternities, albeit by a different name, were established in ancient Egyptian and pagan mysticism. The site goes on to share some interestingly familiar details regarding the Order's ceremonious operations:

It is further traditionally related that the Order's first member-students met in *secluded chambers in magnificent old temples,* where, as candidates, they were *initiated into the great mysteries.* [Sound familiar?] Their mystical studies then assumed a more closed character and were held exclusively in temples which had been built for that purpose [a "Grand Lodge" of its day]. Rosicrucian tradition relates that the great pyramids of Giza were most sacred in the eyes of initiates. Contrary to what historians affirm, our tradition relates that the Giza pyramids were not built to be the tombs of pharaohs, but *were actually places of study and mystical initiation.* The mystery schools, over centuries of time, gradually evolved into great centers of learning, attracting students from throughout the known world.[239]

According to AMORC, the first school of the Order was launched by Pharaoh Thutmose III. A short number of years later, Pharaoh

Amenhotep IV (later Akhnaton) became a celebrated initiate and established worship of the sun (or solar disk, "Aton"). Following this, famous Greek and Roman philosophers (such as Thales, Pythagoras, and Plotinus), "journeyed to Egypt and were initiated into the mystery schools. They then brought their advanced learning and wisdom to the Western world. Their experiences are the first records of what eventually grew and blossomed into the Rosicrucian Order."[240]

As with any religions involving varying sects, denominations, orders, organizations, divisions, and so on, the Rosicrucian Order has always varied in its practices from discipleship group to discipleship group. Whereas there were certainly individuals drawn into the practice of the ancient Order Rosae Crucis and the latter Rosicrucian Order who sought only the "unfolding consciousness" enlightenment promised (approaching it from an intellectual-growth angle), a great number of leaders took it well beyond that and into spiritually perverse acts of regularly communing with demons and Satan. According to standard Christian theology, this is always the natural result of clandestine fellowships that concentrate upon enlightenment through exhortation to pagan deities, spiritism, clairvoyance, ESP, and so on via communication with the spiritual realm—that which is unsanctioned and unprotected by the blood of Christ—whether the worshiper intended it or not. It remains to be an invitation for demonic influences to mimic the pursued entities, and once they respond (as history has shown they *do*), the worshipper believes contact with the deity has been made and "enlightenment" was achieved.

Sir Francis Bacon, whom we have already expressed herein to be the accredited first American Freemason and "New Atlantis" dreamer, was close associate to John Dee. Dee was Queen Elizabeth I's personal advisor. As a celebrated mathematician, astronomer, astrologer, occult philosopher, Hermetic philosopher, divinest, alchemist, sorcerer, and crystal-gazer, Dee's authority of the relationship between science and magic was strong in an age when the rest of the surrounding world could not reasonably deny supernatural activity, but was excited to find explanation of the supernatural through newfound, Age-of-Reason methodologies. Dee stood as one of the most educated and scholarly men of his day. (In fact, the European "Age of Discovery/Exploration" is in part attributed to Dee's work in space navigation; he would go on to instruct some of England's most intense early "voyages of discovery." One of the many links between Dee and the Rosicrucian Order is his famous illustration of the *Monas Hieroglyphica*—a glyph showing the relationship between the moon, sun, elements, and fire—which was said to have been a partial inspiration to the *Chymical Wedding of Christian Rosenkreutz* pamphlet.)

Though Dee is a name well remembered for his contributions to the space and science communities of his era, it's not a secret that he religiously communed with demons—as well as with what he believed to be "angels"—as a means of uncovering the *Prisca theologia*. He believed that one universal language unlocked the secrets of creation, and that mankind had, at one point, been at perfect peace amidst his human brothers and sisters. Who better to ask for these secrets than angels and demons?

Ian Taylor, author of *In the Minds of Men: Darwin and the New World Order*, said during an interview:

[This is why] the Rosicrucians had to be a secret society. Their object was to discover God's truths *after* Him. But some of their methodologies were bordering on witchcraft.... They claimed that they could communicate with angels and demons. Well, in the first place, the Scripture tells you not to do it. But their idea was that if you could do that, surely those creatures, the angels and the demons, they know a lot of things that we don't know. After all, they've been around since time immemorial, and they are familiar with Heaven itself, so surely they can tell us many secrets. Well the Church...would take a dim view of that and [the Rosicrucians] could be put to death for that sort of thing.[241]

Chris Pinto's documentary *Secret Mysteries* goes on to say:

Dee was imprisoned under suspicion of sorcery: an accusation that would follow him throughout his life—and one that seems not unfounded, considering his system of magic is still practiced by many occultists to this day.… In his quest for knowledge, Dee tapped into the powers of the beyond, hoping to learn secrets from the spirit realm…but not everyone saw Dee's dabbling as communicating with angels of *God*. Dee once wrote that he was looked upon as a "companion of hellhounds," a "caller" and a "conjurer" of "wicked and damned spirits." Yet, like Bacon, he practiced much of his craft in secret as an active member of the Rosicrucians in England. Some even credit Dee as founder of the Rosicrucian movement. As such, communing with angelic beings that provide scientific knowledge was a familiar practice.… The secret societies of the Elizabethan era were in danger, not for the knowledge they possessed, but [for] how they obtained it through occult practices of summoning spirits and conjuring demons. They were nevertheless determined to continue for the cause of science and learning.… In a diary entry of June eighth, 1584, Dee records a startling account, [saying] Jesus was not God, and that no prayers ought to be made to Him. [The diary entries] further claimed that sin does not exist, and that man's soul simply moves from one body to another… in reincarnation.[242]

As the Rosicrucians ebbed each day farther toward a universalized ideology of reincarnation (a concept that became paramount in American Freemasonry), Dee continued to meld science, mathematics, magic, and alchemy as he conducted magic ceremonies, gazed into his obsidian scrying mirror, and prayed for the "angels" to give him the answers to the world's most sought-after questions. His reputation as a sorcerer has remained so prominent throughout history that he became the infamous inspiration behind J. K. Rowling's mighty chief wizard Dumbledore of "Hogwarts School of Witchcraft and Wizardry" in the *Harry Potter* book series—the character described to look exactly how Dee appeared while in service to Mary I of England (known as "Bloody Mary" for her persecution of Christians).

Sir Bacon prized Dee's achievements and followed in his footsteps. (Bacon had communed and worshiped a demonic presence [he called her a "muse"] by the name of Pallas Athena, based upon an extremely powerful Greek goddess who "shook her spear" from anger in the presence of *ignorance*—which is pertinent to the Hiram Abiff legend, as we will discuss shortly.) Thus, that ancient Egyptian Order Rosae Crucis became, through the complicated relationship and resulting influences of Bacon and Dee, the newly established form of the secret Masonic/ Freemasonic society.

Take the Ancient and Mystical Order Rosae Crucis (itself proven to be modified throughout the ages by pharaohs and ancient philosphers) and add the syncretism inaugurated by Rosicrucianism (Kabbalism, Christianity, and Hermeticism) along with the crystal-gazing, demon-worship, and angel-prayers of the Bacon/Dee era. If we're not already drowning in a pool of esoteric mystery, *then* add the Deistic, Age-of-Reason enlightenment slant (birthed by some of the same personalities that participated in Hellfire Club, "Do-what-thou-wilt" orgies/drunkenness/ mock rituals), and we arrive at the onset of United States Freemasonry.

It's no wonder that so many find the beliefs and rituals of the Freemasons confusing and ambiguous. But, perhaps this is an appropriate time to remind the reader what Paul said in 1 Corinthians 10:20: "The things which the Gentiles sacrifice, they sacrifice to devils, and not to God: and I would not that ye should have fellowship with devils."

Was America dedicated to such a thing?

chapter eight

The Not-So-Hidden Agenda

B y default of the inclusion of the word "mason" in the terms "Masonry" and "Freemasonry," anyone can gather that the societies were formed in the Baconian era with an interest in major-city (or kingdom) architecture. A mason lays stones, so these fraternities are clearly about the mission of building. But if mere architecture was the only goal, what explanation might there be behind all the ancient orders of mysticism? This question might seem like one with an obvious answer to veterans of literature discussing the occultic symbolism of Washington, DC, but it is a question that must be asked for those readers who are only just joining the discussion. What were these secret builders up to, and why were their societies built upon the foundations of occultism?

Before we address these questions, please note that just as some followed the Rosicrucian Order to seek personal growth and not to pray to dark deities or practice alchemy, most men and women in Freemasonic circles today are morally upright people. They either do not know about the plans set by the men who have gone before and above them, or they believe it to all be rumors perpetuated by conspiratorial crazies and find themselves understandably exhausted by the stereotypes. Some of these very personalities have tossed all darker theories out, saying the equivalent to: "If you are not a Freemason, then I think it's ridiculous that you would talk about what we are really doing. I always hear from conspiracy theorists that I'm 'just not high enough to know what the higher degrees are up to,' but the accuser, himself, is not a Freemason, so he knows even less than I do about who we are and what we stand for. For once and for all, we are not doing [fill in the blank]." Because slight variations to this argument continue to appear, I feel it's time in the reflection to show what a Freemason *did* say on the subject—one who happens to be one of the most respected, learned, authoritative, and celebrated Freemasons of all time. Sovereign Grand Commander Albert Pike, in the Masonic handbook, *Morals and Dogma*, wrote:

> Masonry, like all the Religions, all the Mysteries, Hermetic, and Alchemy, *conceals its secrets from all* except the Adepts and Sages, or the Elect, and *uses false explanations and misinterpretations of its symbols to mislead* those who deserve only to be misled; to conceal the Truth, which it calls Light, from them, and to draw them away from it.[243]

It would be imprudent and inaccurate to suggest that every Freemason currently has, or has had in the past, a sinister scheme for America's future on their mind. For those Freemasons who are not yet in the upper levels, it is understandably frustrating that they keep being told by outsiders that they are in the dark about their own society. However, as Pike—one of the greatest spokesmen of Freemasonry in world history—just explained, that is precisely what is going on. All the lower-level Freemasons receive is "false explanations and misinterpretations" until they have proven themselves worthy of keeping secrets. By then, they have already agreed to a horrific end should they default on their promises of confidentiality.

There is simply too much occultic symbolism associated with Freemasonry for researchers to completely let go of the idea that both early and modern upper rungs of the society intend only to simulate harmless or entertaining social rituals. It remains a blatant and open fact that the architecture of our Capitol was built with unsettling imagery in its very stones—the nature of which is always pagan...*and frequently satanic.*

Consider what Chris Pinto, award-winning filmmaker of the *Secret Mysteries of America's Beginnings* series, said of the satanic roots of Masonry in the era leading up to the American Revolution in his preface to *Zenith 2016*:

> It is well known that [John] Dee was a sorcerer who summoned demonic spirits to obtain secret knowledge; a practice used by Rosicrucians (of whom Dee was the chief in England) for centuries. The root word for "demon" means "a knowing one." The Rosicrucians desired to know secrets of science (i.e., knowledge) and consulted demons to get information. [Sir Francis] Bacon also made contact with demonic spirits, including the goddess Pallas Athena, whom he claimed was his muse or inspiration. In time, Dee handed off the leadership of the Rosicrucian Society to Bacon, who would enfold the secrets of Rosicrucianism into the system of Freemasonry.
>
> Little wonder that Sir Francis Bacon would become the father of the modern scientific method, and that men like Benjamin Franklin and Thomas Jefferson would follow his example in their scientific endeavors. Franklin and Jefferson are both claimed by modern Rosicrucians as being of their order.
>
> Like the Gnostics, the Rosicrucians craved knowledge; it was this desire that led them to worship Lucifer. The secret orders regard Lucifer as the "angel of light" who, in the form of a serpent, bid mankind to partake of the "Tree of Knowledge of Good and Evil" so that their eyes would be open and they could become as gods. This is the inner doctrine of Rosicrucianism, Freemasonry, and all the secret orders—and always has been. In the nineteenth century, when Masons like Pike and Mackey

(along with leading occultists such as Eliphas Levi and Madame H. P. Blavatsky) [of whom we will later address] described this doctrine in their writings, they were only admitting in print what had been secretly known for centuries. The difference was that with the revolutionary movements, freedom of religion allowed them to publish such things without fear of persecution.[244]

This is an interesting trail of thought, for sure. However, Pinto did not limit his reflection of American Masonic origins to Dee and Bacon. He goes on to address the longstanding "secrets in stone" exercises put in place by earlier Masons in the interest of introducing syncretized symbolism in sacred places:

Centuries before all this, in 1492, Rosslyn Chapel was built by Scottish Freemasons. To this day, the chapel is considered a puzzle because it is filled with carvings and icons of [both] Christian and Pagan religions. Why? The reason is because Freemasons have always had the inner doctrine of amalgamating religious beliefs. Much of this can be traced back to the Knights Templar, who are said to have fled to Scotland when they were persecuted in Europe (circa 1307).... Furthermore, in the wake of the Scottish Jacobite rebellions of the early 1700s, many Scottish Masons and Rosicrucians fled to America, bringing their occult doctrines with them. One of their power centers was the Fredericksburg Lodge No. 4, whose members included George Washington, James Monroe, and eight of the Revolutionary War generals.[245]

Manly P. Hall, known as "Masonry's greatest philosopher" to his celebrators, once wrote a book called *The Secret Destiny of America*. Even the book's title holds an ominous insinuation. (That our country would have been born with a "secret destiny" is a concept we will visit at length throughout this work.) Hall confirms Pinto's assertion in his book with the following words regarding how early Freemasons "reclothed" their ideologies in "Christian phraseology" in order to flatter and deceive a land whose residents held Christian values dear prior to the Revolution:

> The rise of the Christian Church broke up the intellectual pattern of the classical pagan world. By persecution of this pattern's ideologies it drove the secret societies into greater secrecy; *the pagan intellectuals then reclothed their original ideas in a garment of Christian phraseology, but bestowed the keys of the symbolism only upon those duly initiated and bound to secrecy by their vows....*
>
> They signed each stone with the secret symbols of their cult, and into the intricate carvings of church and chapel they worked the old pagan figures and designs. Many guilds sprang up, binding skilled craftsmen in confraternities of arts and crafts and trades. Architecture remained the chosen instrument for the perpetuation of the Great Design....
>
> All the sciences contained brilliant far-seeing men who equally desired to contribute their part to the philosophic empire of the future. Secret societies were formed in their own professions, *using the emblems established in their arts to conceal their social aspirations.* Thus did the Alchemists come into being [including such men as Dee and Bacon], the mystic chemists seeking the elixir of life, the wise man's stone [of which Dee spent his entire life devotedly seeking], the universal medicine, and the agent for the transmutation of metals.[246]

So what began as a subtle syncretism of Christian symbolism alongside pagan symbolism became an outright *replacement* of pagan symbols over sacred Christian images by the time our capital was built. Pinto says as much: "The practice of carving their doctrines in stone continued in the new world with the building of Washington, DC. This is why one will find in our nation's capital countless images of gods and goddesses, along with zodiacs, the Washington Monument Obelisk, reflecting pools, and a whole cacophony of pagan imagery. *There are no monuments to Jesus Christ, the apostles, or anything having to do with the Christian faith.*"[247]

Who were the design engineers and builders of our nation's capital? That would be those men we outlined at the beginning of this study: the presidents, politicians, founding fathers, government associates, aristocratic elitists, and finally, those who "appreciated" the morality of Christ while flirting with "Hellfire Club" debauchery on the weekends. The architecture of our country is entirely pagan. Are we supposed to surmise that this was done by accident? That the builders who dedicated each stone of Washington, DC, to pagan gods made Jesus Christ the victim of unintentional oversight? That they intended to glorify the Man behind the morality they "appreciated," but they simply got busy and forgot? Or, can we prize common-sense logic well enough to conclude that our founding fathers and prominent American leaders deliberately and calculatedly dedicated our land to pagan gods for an underlying (and terrifying) purpose?

If the symbols embedded in our capital are allowed to speak for themselves, I believe we have a strong case for precisely that brand of conclusion. All the images are displayed out in the open for any visitor to view in person. The *intent* of the society's masterminds may be shrouded under layers of secrecy, but their artwork is blatantly public.

So, if the society does, in fact, have an agenda related to the dark etchings and monuments on our land, how have our citizens remained so unaware if the proof of it is not even remotely hidden?

The answer to that question may in part be due to the value Freemasons place on keeping a secret.

The Legend of Hiram Abiff / Vows of Silence

The tale of Hiram Abiff (also known as "the Widow's Son" and often-times recognized as King Hiram I of Tyre or Huram Abi, son of a widow from the tribe of Naphtali), is ritually reenacted amidst the brethren each time a Freemason reaches the Master level (or 3rd Degree). The story involves several variations throughout history, but a popular regal-ing of the central elements (*as known to the general public*) is as follows:

- Around a thousand years before Christ's birth, King Solomon appointed a master architect to oversee the building of the sacred Jerusalem Temple—the housing site, as designed by God directly, of the Ten Commandments tablets. This architect was named Hiram Abiff.
- Solomon shared God's divine and heavenly building design with Abiff, but swore him to secrecy. Abiff agreed to keep the design a secret at all costs, including at the threat of death.
- Three of Abiff's apprentice workers grew jealous of his position as master mason. They sought to gain access to the riddles of deific Masonry—believing that this would unlock secret knowl-edge of the universe (or in some variations "give them magical powers," "make them the greatest masons," etc.)—by repeatedly asking Abiff for the restricted access code. Abiff did not divulge the information, so a plan was set in motion to ambush him at the next opportunity. The three apprentices studied Abiff's schedule patterns and set the ambush plan in motion for mid-day, as each day at noon, Abiff walked away from the worksite to pray. (The popular version says he frequented the Holy of Holies in the depths of the Temple at this time.)
- Just after they were in position—one apprentice stationed at each of Abiff's three exits—Abiff headed to the eastern door

to leave. The first apprentice met him there and demanded the code. Abiff informed him that he would only be given the code after the Temple was completed and the apprentice had proved himself worthy of the secrets. Angered, the apprentice struck Abiff in the throat.

- Abiff fled, stumbling to the southern door, where he was met by the second apprentice demanding the same answer. Abiff refused again and was dealt a blow to the chest.

- Abiff fled once more to the western door, where the third apprentice repeated the demand. After a third refusal, he was finally killed with a strike to the forehead. Just before death, he is said to have cried out, "Who will help the widow's son?" (now rumored to be the Masonic cry for help from fellow brethren in the fraternity). His blood was shed entirely within the Temple walls.

- Abiff's body was taken outside and buried, where it was later discovered by Solomon and his men nearby an acacia tree. (Note the "acacia tree" for later.)

This is where the story has nearly uncountable variations of its ending, each involving many different aspects of burial, murder scandals with Solomon's name at the center, items of interest found at the exhumation of the body, the theory that the secrets of the building plans died with Abiff, etc.

Modern historians (and some Freemasons) suggest that the legend of Hiram Abiff originated the term "free mason": a mason who has a free mind, freedom of religion, freedom of speech, freedom to travel the world to his heart's desire, and so on—and that "free masons" always have three assailants (like the apprentices in the story): ignorance (which, as stated prior, was also the greatest enemy of Sir Bacon's goddess Pallas Athena), fanaticism, and tyranny. Other theories have surfaced proposing that the "free mason" was simply a mason who didn't belong to, or allow himself to be mandated by, a mason guild, or that the term distinguishes the "free masons" from the "cowans" (Scotland's rough, unhewn stone builders). (Also worthy of note: Today's Masonic lodges are built based on the biblical description of King Solomon's temple as a result of the legend.)

What remains for today's Masonic fraternities, however, is the heroism laced into the legend of Abiff. So dedicated was he to the concealment of the Masonic secrets that he willingly died protecting them—and his death was mercilessly violent. The greatest hero of any brethren, or so the story signifies, is one who can keep the knowledge of the secret mysteries of the builders and brethren restricted, even in the face of bloody death. This legendary "access code" (sometimes referred to as "password," "code word," "secret code," or "keyword") is said to be given to a Master Mason as a sign of accomplishment or recognition for their service to the society only after they have proved themselves a worthy Apprentice and Craftsman (the first two levels of Freemasonry). The secret code of the Master Mason is then bestowed upon them following the ritual of Hiram Abiff.

The initiation rite of the Master Mason has been revealed numerous times by former Freemasons. The rite varies slightly from testimony to testimony, but key essentials of the ritual remain solid. To begin, the ritual is always held confidentially in the presence of the brethren. The candidate swears an oath of secrecy, vowing never to expose anything that happens within those walls to another human being outside of them. They are made to agree that, should they default on this promise, they risk being killed in horrific and/or painful ways.

As Stanley Monteith of *Brotherhood of Darkness* says:

It's a secret society. It's *always* been a secret society. And to reveal anything about these secret societies ensures your death. And people have tried to expose Masonry, even to this very day, [they] risk their lives in doing it.... When you actually go into

Masonry in the first three degrees, you'll promise that if you ever reveal any of the secrets of Masonry in the first degree, you'll have your tongue cut out and you'll be buried in the sands of the sea up to the level of your neck [when the waters reach] low tide. At the second degree…they cut out your heart, and at the third degree, they're going to cut out your entrails and burn them.[248]

Sounds sensational, no? But one does not have to look far to see that horrific murder (and other crimes) are well associated with Freemasonry. Former Freemason Charles Finney, who went on to be an illustrious Presbyterian leader of the Second Great Awakening, had a great deal to say about his experiences in his work, *Why I Left Freemasonry*. Under his heading entitled "Features of an Anti-Christ," Finney remarks: "Freemasonry knows no mercy, and swears its candidates to avenge violations of Masonic obligations unto death," and, "The penalties of these oaths are barbarous, even savage."[249] Under his heading "Some Fair Conclusions," Finney lists five disturbing reasons *the Christian Church must sever all ties from Freemasonry*. The fifth item thereof is mind-boggling:

Fifth, can a man who has taken, and still adheres to, the oath of the Royal Arch Mason be trusted to public office [such as a president or politician]? He swears to espouse the cause of a companion of this Degree when involved in any difficulty, so far as to extricate him, whether he be right or wrong. *He swears to conceal his crimes*, MURDER AND TREASON NOT EXCEPTED [caps in original]. Is such a man bound by such an oath to be trusted with office? Ought he to be accepted as a witness or juror when another Freemason is a party in the case? Ought he to be trusted with the office of Judge, or Justice of the Peace, or as a Sheriff, Constable, Marshal or any other office?…

Is any man who is under a most solemn oath to kill all who violate any part of Masonic oaths, a fit person to be at large among men?[250]

Perhaps some have heard of the strange disappearance of Captain William Morgan in 1826. Supposedly, Morgan was abducted by Freemasons and murdered after he threatened to expose their secrets in a book he had written. He had been arrested and taken to jail for failure to pay a debt, and was subsequently released when a group of men came to his "rescue." Immediately after he left the jailhouse, he was forced into a nearby carriage and was never seen alive again. It has been presumed he was murdered.

The account follows a complicated trail, and unfortunately, the story has been told with numerous variations depicting Morgan either as an innocent saint or disloyal buffoon, depending on the speaker. If the tale is divulged from the lips of a Freemason, Morgan was a drunken gambler and traitor, and after he was "escorted" to the carriage, he was thereafter given money in exchange for his own disappearance. Brotherhood members have throughout the years repeatedly come forward to admit that "misguided" members of the secret Order were definitely guilty of abducting Morgan (the trial evidence agrees), but that he agreed to make himself scarce in trade for the money and thereafter went on to live a peaceful life in Canada. However, there appear to be many plot-holes in this ending:

- First, numerous eyewitnesses (including bystanders and unbiased staff of the jailhouse) testified in the trial after Morgan's disappearance that he was forced into the carriage, all the while crying, "Murder! Murder!"
- Second, it is a fact that after the abduction—whether he went willingly or was abducted by force—Morgan was taken to Fort

Niagra on the Canadian shoreline and confined there. When an unidentified body washed up near that shore and was taken to Morgan's wife for identification, she didn't hesitate to confirm that the body was that of her husband.

- Third, the Freemason publications that asserted Morgan had been seen in foreign parts of the world appointed in dignified offices were largely dismissed as false rumors, as they were written without consideration of his middle age, lack of foreign language skills, and lack of education (education that would have been needed in order for him to have been appointed as a dignified official anywhere, including in his native land, let alone in a foreign country where years of expensive training would have been needed to establish him in such positions as they claimed).

- Fourth, all who came forward with the claim that they had seen and/or spoken to Morgan after his disappearance either belonged to the fraternity, or were well enough associated with the fraternity to give a biased testimony (whether that as a favor or from intimidation).

- Fifth, if the "gone to Canada" story Freemasons so staunchly adhere to is true, what purpose would that ultimately achieve, anyway? The book was already at the publishers, and Morgan's *Illustrations of Freemasonry* did, in fact, get published following his disappearance. The damage from the leak had already been dealt, and there was no "silencing" anyone by convincing them to leave the country, so that would have been a pointless way for the Brotherhood to clean up the mess Morgan made. An act of revenge upon the Freemasonic tattle-tale is the only logical reasoning behind this.

In the convoluted aftermath of the abduction, Dr. J. W. S. Mitchell, writer of the *History of Free-masonry, and Masonic Digest*, reflected the raging sentiment of the public when he wrote, "That William Morgan was murdered, we sincerely believe, and that one or more masons were concerned, and participated in the hellish deed, we have no reason to doubt."[251]

But the tale of Captain William Morgan, and the assertions by former Freemason Charles Finney, are only but two examples in a very, *very* long line of conspiracies attached to the Freemason's oaths. Countless other testimonies have referred to blood oaths of horrific repercussion, including throats being slit, eyeballs pierced, tongues torn out, feet flayed, bodies hacked into pieces, and so on, if a Freemason were to give up the wrong information.

But back to our reflection upon the modern-day rituals…

Once the oath of secrecy has been taken aloud during the candidate's ceremony, a reenactment of Hiram Abiff's death is carried out from beginning to end, including the ritualized mock-blows of the apprentices to the candidate/initiate. At this, the initiate dramatizes falling down dead. Two among the brotherhood stage an attempt to resurrect the body, but the efforts are unsuccessful. A third fellow succeeds in the mock-resurrection, and the initiate is "reborn" (reincarnated or resurrected Rosicrucian-style) into the role of Master Mason.

For the initiate, this dramatization is an honor of the highest measure, as it represents allegiance to the bond of brotherhood and the integrity of a promise kept. Those who have gone on to describe the importance of the ritual to the outside have said the act represents the Masons' need to mature in the natural world, whilst ensuring their spiritual maturity in preparation for the next life.

However, once Freemasonic symbolism (on display unabashedly throughout our nation's capital) is taken into consideration and paired with the character of Abiff, the *true* meaning of this ritual stands out as far more sinister than mere celebration of integrity. (I tend to prize common sense a little too often for the word "integrity" to be associated with any ritual promising an unworthy candidate's future disembowelment, as Monteith highlighted, but as this piece is written to provide information to the readers and not to share personal opinions, I will end that thread here.) Might Abiff represent someone or something other than the hero-builder of Solomon's day?

To answer this, we need to take a closer look at the Egyptian god Osiris: the highly praised judge of Rosicrucianists. As I explained so recently in *Unearthing the Lost World of the Cloudeaters*:

Osiris was the rebirth and regeneration god of Egypt who married his sister, Isis. Osiris' brother, Set (or "Seth"), wished to overthrow the throne for himself. He and seventy-two fellow conspirators (note this number, as it is important numerology we will discuss later) tricked Osiris into climbing inside a golden chest. Once inside, Set nailed the chest closed and had it thrown into the Nile River where it floated down the current and snagged in…an acacia tree, which was holding up the roof of a Phoenician coast palace in Byblos. Isis was heartbroken over the loss and searched the Nile for her husband. When she found him, he was drowned, but she took his body back home to care for it. Seth waited for Isis to momentarily leave the body, abducted his brother's remains a second time, chopped it into fourteen pieces, and threw those, also, into the Nile. Again Isis fled to the Nile in search of her husband's pieces, and found thirteen. The missing body part was, as you have probably guessed, his male reproductive organ. According to the myth, the organ had been swallowed by a medjed (also known as the "elephantfish" for its elephant trunk-like mouth)—a fish worshiped at Oxyrhynchus in ancient Egyptian religions.… Using a golden obelisk for the reproductive organ, Isis pieced Osiris back together and performed a ritual to impregnate herself. The son born of this unholy union was Horus—a reincarnation of the literal Osiris, whom she'd lost. Essentially, then, through the posthumous sex-magic ritual performed between Isis and the dead body of her husband, she is now mother to her own husband through Horus—the tutelary guardian god of the sky who watches over the world through the "eye of Horus."[252]

Apart from the fact that there are obvious parallels between the tales of Osiris and Hiram Abiff (both were victims of a violent murder by "brothers"; both burials involving references to an acacia tree; both deaths involve the loss of something grievously important [phallus; secret word or building plans]; both were eventually reborn [resurrected/reincarnated]; and several others depending on the versions told), many respected experts of Freemasonry (including respected Freemason authorities) have bluntly linked Osiris and Abiff.

Azariah T. C. Pierson wrote in *Traditions of Freemasonry*, "The legend and traditions of 'Hiram *Abif*…form the consummation of the connecting links between Freemasonry and the Ancient Mysteries."[253] Later in the same work, Pierson said, "We readily recognize in Hiram Abif the Osiris of the Egyptians."[254] Thirty-third-Degree Freemason and author Daniel Sickels of *The Freemason's Guide* came to the same conclusion, referring to the rite as "thoroughly Egyptian."[255] He goes on to say, "Osiris and the Tyrian Architect [which is Hiram Abiff, said in some associations to have been the king of Tyre] are one and the same…. In Egyptian Freemasonry, Osiris was the type of Beauty, Goodness, Order, and Truth. So, in the Temple-myth, the Tyrian [Abiff] is the symbol of Beauty and Order, and of that Creative Art which is ever ready to size the Ideal, and incarnate it in material forms."[256] Albert Mackey, in *The Lexicon of Freemasonry*, attested that the legend of Abiff was also "thoroughly Egyptian, and is closely allied to the Supreme Rite of the Isianic Mysteries"[257] (the "Supreme Rite" being the highest degree; the "Isianic Mysteries" was Mackey's reference to the mystery religion of Osiris and Isis). It appears clear then, through both obvious parallels as well as by Freemasonic admission and expertise, that the ritual of Hiram Abiff is none other than the ritualistic reenactment of Osiris and his sister/wife, Isis.

So what of it? Why do we care that the Freemasons are commemorating an ancient Egyptian god through the pseudo-hero Abiff? In the light of all they *could* be doing (Hellfire Club mock human sacrifices, charred bones in Franklin's basement, and disappearing captains come to mind...) why do we fear such playacting? There are all kinds of religions and clubs out there that participate in odd events. What is it about this one in particular that we find so concerning?

It all travels back to that ancient Rosae Crucis, Rosicrucian, Masonic/Freemasonic, agenda.

The "Magnetic" Link

By now, almost everyone in the country has seen the aerial shots of the pentagram in Washington, DC. As tools like Google Earth have provided instantaneous access to anyone on the globe wishing to see it for themselves, nobody can say it doesn't exist. Many choose to say it was a fluke accident, but that theory falls flat when the pentagram design is compared to all the other pagan images and monuments in and around it. Their claim might be that the design doesn't form a true pentagram since Rhode Island Avenue doesn't connect entirely to the rest of the shape as the classic symbol would. Several times, Freemasons have used this reasoning to point to the "accidental" architecture with comments such as, "Oh please! It's not even a *true* pentagram!"

However, that is easily explained by Manly P. Hall in *The Secret Teachings of All Ages*, and it, too, is intentional. Immediately under his heading "THE PENTAGRAM," Hall sheds some light on what the pentagram actually means, and why it frequently appears in black magic *without* a complete connection:

> In symbolism, an inverted figure [like the upside-down star] *always signifies a perverted power. The average person does not even suspect the*

occult properties of emblematic pentacles. On this subject the great Paracelsus has written: "No doubt many will scoff at the seals, their characters and their uses, which are described in these books, because it seems incredible to them that metals and characters which are dead [such as monuments, domes, seals, dollar bills, statues, architectural design of a city, and any other inanimate object] should have any power and effect. Yet no one has ever proved that the metals and also the characters as we know them are dead, for the salts, sulphur, and quintessences of metals are the highest preservatives of human life and are far superior to all other simples."[258]

This proves to us today that, even if the mainstream public does not believe inanimate objects have power—if we don't buy into that "life power" of "salts, sulpher, and quintessences of metals"— there are those who *do* believe in their living power and plan to see it carried into the fruition of its intended design. Such an undertaking in a major city would need to be completed by men of power. Who do we think of when we consider the most powerful men in the world? Perhaps the elected leaders of the most powerful country in the world who belong to equally powerful secret fraternities?

The black magician cannot use the symbols of white magic without bringing down upon himself the forces of white magic, which would be fatal to his schemes. He must therefore distort [or turn upside down, in the case of the pentagram] the hierograms so that they typify the occult fact that he himself is distorting the principles for which the symbols stand. Black magic is not a fundamental art; it is the misuse of an art. Therefore it has no symbols of its own. It merely takes the emblematic figures of white magic, and by inverting and reversing them signifies that it is left-handed.[259]

When viewing the map of our beloved Washington, DC, pentagram, the lowermost point of the inverted star begins at the back of the Oval Office and stretches out to a precise and perfectly executed design, *except* for the Rhode Island Avenue disconnect…which, as stated, was intentional. This would position the marker of the symbol to point straight at the home of our presidents, the first of which was Freemason George Washington.

A good instance of this practice is found in the pentagram, or five-pointed star, made of five connected lines. This figure is the time-honored symbol of the magical arts, and signifies the five properties of the Great Magical Agent, the five senses of man, the *five elements of nature*, the five extremities of the human body. *By means of the pentagram within his own soul, man not only may master and govern all creatures inferior to himself, but may demand consideration at the hands of those superior to himself.*

The pentagram is used extensively in black magic, but when so used its form *always differs* in one of three ways: *The star may be broken at one point by not permitting the converging lines to touch*; it may be inverted by having one point down and two up; or it may be distorted by having the points of varying lengths. When used in black magic, the pentagram is called the "sign of the cloven hoof," or the *footprint of the Devil*. The star with two points upward is also called the "Goat of Mendes," because the inverted star is the same shape as a goat's head [or Baphomet].[260]

This "Great Magical Agent" encapsulating the "five elements of nature" Hall referred to is recognized by several other names, most notably of which is the "Grand Telesma," thus coined by Hermes Trismegistus of the sacred *Hermetic Corpus* texts addressed earlier. Additional (and quite telling) information on this subject comes from renowned scholarly mystic Arthur Edward Waite.

Waite was a Freemason anda member of the Hermetic Order of the Golden Dawn, as well as the founder of the Fellowship of the Rosy Cross established in 1915. He wrote several acclaimed books, including

The Real History of the Rosicrucians, and was the cocreator of the Rider-Waite Tarot deck (the most popular Tarot deck in use within English-speaking countries today). In his book, *The Mysteries of Magic*, we read under article "IV.—The Great Magic Agent, or The Mysteries of the Astral Light" in the "Doctrines of Occult Force" section:

> There exists a force in Nature which is far more powerful than steam, by means of which a single man, who can master it and knows how to direct it, *might throw the world into confusion and transform its face.* It is diffused through infinity; it is the substance of heaven and earth, for it is either fixed or volatile according to its degrees of polarization. It was termed by Hermes Trismegistus the Grand Telesma.… It is substance and motion at one and the same time; it is a fluid and a perpetual vibration. The inherent force by which it is put into activity is called magnetism.… [A telling moment for sure… Magnetism is the drawing force of one object to another. Consider, then, what these occult builders might be interested in "drawing toward" Washington, DC…] The will of intelligent beings acts directly on this light, and, by means thereof, upon all nature, which is made subject to the modifications of intelligence.[261]

Let's stop and take a look at the enormous implications of that last sentence: We humans, the "intelligent beings," Waite says, when imposing our "will" upon "all nature" through the Grand Telesma or Astral Light, can manipulate the very laws of nature (thus creating a supernatural effect). In case it may be assumed that I have misinterpreted or misquoted this fantastical line of thought, on page 73 of this same work, Waite says, "The Great Magic Agent has…properties, [which, when] directed by the will of man, can modify all phases of Nature."[262] Perhaps put even more simply and adjusting this reflection to Freemasonic agenda: According to master occultists, humans can control the forces of nature and therefore impose their will upon others existing within it (in this case, American citizens) through the power of the Great Magical Agent/Grand Telesma—the symbol of which, according to these same occult masters, is the pentagram. The "inherent force" behind the pentagram, as Waite explained, is "magnetism," which serves to pull or draw something toward something else.

He goes on to explain that although the chemistry side of these forces had not yet been mastered (at the time of his writing), there would be a day when "the coming synthesis of chemistry will probably lead our physicists to a knowledge of the universal agent, and then what will hinder them from determining the strength, number, and direction of its magnets? A complete revolution of science will follow, and we shall return to the transcendent magic of the Chaldeans [Babylonians]."[263] And I would add: What would hinder them from determining Washington, DC, as the location of the magnetic pull?

But of course, to direct the forces of the Great Magical Agent to their proper location, one would need to place a design over the receiving end to establish occult connection. What better design to choose than the "time-honored [pentagram] symbol" Hall spoke of, which "signifies the five properties of the Great Magical Agent"? But wait… We *already have* that very symbol, stationed in Washington, DC, as a receptacle. And it's left open on Rhode Island Avenue, just as Hall discussed, for the "footprint of the Devil."

Let's see what else Waite has to say about the Great Magical Agent:

This force was known to the ancients; it consists of a universal agent having equilibrium for its supreme law, while its direction depends immediately on the Great Arcanum of transcendent magic. By the direction of this agent we can change the very order of the seasons, produce in the night the phenomena of day, correspond instantaneously from one end of the earth to the other, discern, like Apollonius, what is taking place at the

Antipodes, heal or hurt at a distance, and endow human speech with a universal reverberation and success. The Gnostics represented it as the burning body of the Holy Ghost, and this it was which was adored in the secret rites of the Sabbath or the Temple *under the symbolic figure of Baphomet* [the pentagram], or of the Androgyne Goat of Mendes [again, the pentagram].

This ambient and all-penetrating fluid, this ray detached from the sun's splendour, and fixed by the weight of the atmosphere and by the power of central attraction, this body of the Holy Ghost, which we call the Astral Light and the Universal Agent, this electro-magnetic ether, this vital and illuminous caloric, *is represented on ancient monuments by the girdle of Isis.*[264]

Wait, what? Isis? There are ancient monuments of Isis that represent the power of this Great Magical Agent? The same Isis who impregnated herself upon her dead husband's corpse through sex magic?

Oh, but that it would stop at only "ancient" monuments and memorials... Regrettably, however, there is more to Isis than her commemoration through archaic Egyptian effigies. I'm sure by now that many readers have heard about the obelisk/dome alignment just outside the Whitehouse... But again, for those of you who are just joining the discussion, let us consider Isis/Osiris/Horus and the magnetic pull of the Great Magical Agent toward our capital's "footprint of the Devil" pentagram.

The Great Magical Agent as a Means of Impregnation

When touring Washington, DC, or the Vatican, visitors are generally unaware of what it is they're looking at. Right there, displayed in front of any and all, is an ancient, talismanic diagram revolving around Isis, Osiris, and Horus, and this diagram includes the "magical" functions to bring these deities out from where they currently reside.

Similarly, in St. Peter's Square, the Vatican's esteemed courtyard, there is an oval-shaped ground design with lines tracing a cross with an obelisk at the center. The red granite obelisk, which stands forty meters tall, was carved by the Egyptians in the thirteenth century BC. In AD 37—only a few years after the death, resurrection, and ascension of Christ—Roman Emperor Caligula had the structure moved to the central spina of the *Circus Gai et Neronis* ("Circus of Nero" and frequently now "Circus of Caligula"). In 1586, Pope Sixtus V ordered the engineer and architect Domenico Fontana to once again uproot and transport the obelisk to its current location at the Vatican. The task took over four months, and utilized nine hundred laborers, one hundred forty horses, and seventy winches.

An aerial shot of this attraction shows what is known as a "Sun Wheel," with the varying lines forming "rays" that travel out from the center, wherein lies the obelisk—the placement of which in relation to the sun design is no accident. And note that although the line patterns are different, there is a similar design around the Washington Monument. It's clearly a sun-shaped layout, but instead of that "power-going-out" style, it has a "power-going-in" archetypal eclipse or lens-flare style. Due to the intentional similarity of these structured arrangements, the US has been referred to as the "Mirror Vatican." Our forefathers initially named our capital city "Rome."

The word "obelisk," when researched, typically leads to dead ends, save for a description of what it looks like and how it's built. In fact, it wasn't until the early 1900s that the symbolism behind the obelisk was more accessible to the modern, public world thanks to the exposure by the Encyclopedia Americana Corporation (and others). According to their findings (written in 1919):

The Obelisk represents the Sun. The ancient Egyptians were sun-worshippers: they regarded the great luminary as the creator of the universe, the maker of all gods above and below, and even as the author of himself. The sun as *Ra*, the great god of the Egyptians, was represented upon monuments by the solar disc. In time several other names and attributes were applied to him. The rising sun was called *Har-em-khu*, "Horus on the horizon." During his daily course he was *Ra*, "the life-giver," representing day, light, etc. The setting sun, the symbol of night, darkness, and death, was worshipped as *Tum* or *Temu*. When the number of deities in the Egyptian pantheon multiplied, *Ra* appeared upon the monuments and in the papyri under different forms and names, and is represented alike by animate and inanimate objects. The two most striking and characteristic monuments which represented him on earth were the obelisk and the pyramid. The obelisk, symbolical of light and life, represented his daily course; the pyramid, symbolical of darkness and death, the setting sun.

Ra was praised as "the Double Obelisk" and the "Double Sphinx" deity…. The double sphinx is the symbol of his early rising, and is called *Har-em-khu*, and according to the "Book of Dead" (q.v.) is the symbol of resurrection. The obelisk is the technical figure of one ray or pencil of light emanating from the sun.

The material chosen for the obelisk was generally red granite, or syenite—a few, however, being of hard sandstone. The former was procured from the granite quarries at Syene (the modern Assouan). Red granite, some Egyptologists think, was chosen for two reasons: First, as being the most durable material, fitly representing the eternal sun. Secondly, on account of its red hue, suggesting the color of the solar disc at his rising and setting.

There were many obelisks throughout Egypt, but *An*, the city of the Sun (Heb., *On*; Greek, *Heliopolis*, the Beth-shemesh of the Bible), was the centre of sun worship and undoubtedly contained several obelisks [including the one now standing in the Vatican's St. Peter's Square].[265]

In addition to the obelisk's association with being at the center of sun worship is the direct correlation of its shape to that of the male reproductive organ. The origin of the word "obelisk," as far back as most etymology dictionaries can trace, is the Greek *obelischos*, "small spit, obelisk, leg of a compass," which is diminutive of *obelos*, "pointed pillar, needle."[266] This explanation, however, is limited by a modernized description of its shape alone, and only dates back to (at the very earliest) the first Greeks circa 1900–1600 BC. The Greeks who assigned the sound of *o-bel-isk* to their developing language would have had a reason to name this pillar by the meaning the early inhabitants of that culture had assigned to it.

It is a well-known fact that "the original Egyptian obelisks were quite seriously conceived as phalli."[267] In fact, occult researcher/writer Charles Berger takes it one step further when he states, "*All* pillars or columns [in ancient cultures] originally had a phallic significance, and were therefore considered sacred."[268]

For some, the following explanation of etymology will be obvious, but I have observed in my experience that many readers don't truly consider etymology, and many others don't even know what it is. For this reason, I will explain the process.

Etymology is the study of how a word was originally formed. The word "Internet," as one example, is a modern word. There is no ancient word belonging to what we today know as the World Wide Web because it didn't exist in the ancient world. When we say "Internet," people know we are describing "a vast computer network linking smaller computer networks worldwide…[through the use of] the same set of communications protocols,"[269] or more simply, that thing we log on to over the computer at night to check e-mail. So, when we say "Internet," everyone knows what we're describing and what the word means in the same way many know that an obelisk is a "pointed pillar." However, the word "Internet" is a compound word made up of: 1) the prefix "inter-," meaning "'between,' 'among,' 'in the midst of,' 'mutually,' 'reciprocally,' 'together,' [and] 'during,'"[270] and 2) "net(work)," meaning "a netlike combination of filaments, lines, veins, passages, or the like."[271] Our culture has taken one prefix that means mutual, active cooperation between two or more sources and combined it with a word that describes a linking-up of pathways. This is how etymology works.

Fortunately, "Internet" is such a young word that we have no problem locating the etymological origins of it; unfortunately, "obelisk" is such an ancient word that many have a hard time locating the etymological origins of it. By the time "Internet" was a word, we had established worldwide communication, so the word is the same in many foreign languages, despite slight variations of accent marks, dialect, pronunciation, and so on, and generally everyone is capable of understanding the prefix "inter-" alongside the noun "net" because they are words our modern world is familiar with. When "obelisk" was formed as a word, there was limited communication between one region and another, so one has to look back to that one specific region of the earliest of languages to figure out what "o" and "bel" and "isk" would mean to them when put together.

Herodotus, the Greek traveler, is largely attributed as the writer who named the object as he documented the cultures he visited and the structures he observed. As such, he would have had the opportunity to look up at an edifice and call it by what it meant to the people of those lands but within his own language. In Greek, *o* is a prefix that frequently associates with "seed," *bel* means "lord" or "master," and *isk* is a suffix meaning "small." So the story goes that Herodotus was wandering about the civilizations of the ancient world, had prior familiarity with the concept that the structure was phallic to the original Egyptian carvers, and called it, essentially, "a smaller representation of the master's." If the *o* did mean to Herodotus (if he is, in fact, the coiner of the word) what it meant in other words with *o* as a prefix associating with "seed," then we arrive at: "a smaller representation of the master's seed [and by extension, his male reproductive organ]."

Which "master" would this refer to? That's where we get into the simpler etymology of the word *bel* to the first Greeks. "Belzebub" is Old English, based on Greek, which came from the original Hebrew for the Philistine god worshipped at Ekron, "*ba'al-z'bub*" (Hebrew; 2 Kings 1:2) and the Babylonian "sun god" or Baal, the "lord of the flies" when used by itself. Today, Christians have heard the name "Baalzebub" (more often "Beelzebub") and hear it as another name for Satan, but they very rarely understand that, to the ancients, "Baal" was a prefix/title the Hebrews assigned to the foreign little-g "gods" that were worshipped by neighboring territories. (Consider as examples *Baal-berith,* who was the "the covenant lord" of the Shechemites and *Baal-peor,* who was the "lord of the opening" over the Moabites and Midianites.) This renders our previous conclusion to read "a smaller representation of Baal's seed," or, more truncated, "the shaft of Baal."

From Cathy Burns' *Masonic and Occult Symbols Illustrated,* we read:

> The obelisk is a long pointed four-sided shaft, the uppermost portion of which forms a pyramid. The word "obelisk" literally means "Baal's Shaft" or Baal's organ of reproduction. This should be especially shocking when we realize that we have a gigantic obelisk in our nation's capital known as the Washington Monument.[272]

(To remind the reader of at least one thing Baal meant to the Egyptians, as well as to earlier chapters in this book, where cannibalism was connected to the arrival of giants and/or those cultures that worshipped the demon gods of the giants that migrated across the ancient world including the Americas: *Cahna-Bal* means "priest of Baal." It is from this that we derive the English word "cannibal," a person who consumes the flesh and blood of another human, based on the same rituals the priests of Baal carried out in honor of their god. Baal was highly associated with cannibalism in Jeremiah 19. Note that through the Roman Catholic doctrine of the Eucharist, it is believed that consumption of bread and wine at communion is to partake of the actual, literal flesh and blood of Jesus Christ. I direct no personal attack upon those who are sincerely visiting the Lord's Table to draw closer to Him within the Catholic faith. However, many reputable Christian scholars have pointed out that the Catholic Eucharist is a reenactment of the ritualistic flesh-eating by the Baal priests, and I doubt many sincere Catholics are aware of this.)

So far, we have the Sun Wheel at the Vatican and the "eclipse" or "lens flare" sun pattern at the Washington Monument to signify sun worship—*both* with a structure that meant "Baal's phallus" at the center. Now let's consider the shape and location of the domes.

Ancient pagan religions viewed an altar as symbolic of the female body. The Egyptian and Babylonian temples were built with strategic placement so that the shrine and the entrance of the temple faced in the same direction of the sun's rising in summer. On one day per year, the sun would hover directly above the erect obelisk ("charging it," so to speak), and as the sun went down, the shadow of the obelisk stretched along the courtyard and into the entrance of the temple and forward into the "dome." If the place of worship was designed as symbolic of the female body, and the dome is built in the shape of a pregnant belly, then it doesn't take rocket science to see that this was a representative "impregnating" of Baal's seed directly into the temple of the people.

The primeval concept, then, was designed in antiquity for the express purpose of regeneration, resurrection, and apotheosis, for deity incarnation from the underworld to earth's surface through union of the respective figures—the dome (ancient structural representation of the womb of Isis) and the obelisk (ancient representation of the erect male phallus of Baal—and *Osiris*—which we will discuss shortly).

The question should then be asked: Why do the world's most powerful government on earth (the US) and the world's most politically influential Church on earth (with headquarters at the Vatican) have these symbolic impregnation schematics built upon their ground, and what are they expecting this to accomplish?

Digging a little deeper into the theology behind all of this, one should remember that both the apostle Paul's writings and the book of Revelation pointed to the eschatological marriage between the political and religious authorities (the Antichrist and the False Prophet) at the return of Osiris/Apollo.

According to the official building records of both locations, the dome/obelisk design was adapted from the Roman Pantheon, which was the circular, domed rotunda "dedicated to all gods," and directed by Thomas Jefferson. The US Capitol building is also historically based on pagan Masonic temple themes. Jefferson wrote a letter to the architect behind the project, Benjamin LaTrobe, referring to the design as "the first temple dedicated to…embellishing with Athenian taste the course of a nation looking far beyond the range of Athenian destinies."[273] The "Athenian" empire was first known as "Osiria," the kingdom of Osiris. In 1833, Massachusetts Representative Rufus Choate agreed with Jefferson's esoteric affiliation, writing, "We have built no national temples but the Capitol."[274] William Henry and Mark Gray, in their book, *Freedom's Gate: Lost Symbols in the U.S. Capitol*, add that, "The U.S. Capitol has numerous architectural and other features that unquestionably identify it with ancient temples."[275] After listing various features to make their case that the US Capitol building is a "religious temple"—including housing the image of a deified being, heavenly beings, gods, symbols, inscriptions, sacred geometry, columns, prayers, and orientation to the sun—they conclude:

> The designers of the city of Washington DC oriented it to the Sun—especially the rising Sun on June 21 and December 21. The measurements for this orientation were made from the location of the center of the Dome of the U.S. Capitol, rendering it a "solar temple." Its alignment and encoded numerology point to the Sun as well as the stars. A golden circle on the Rotunda story and a white star in the Crypt marks this spot…. It is clear

that the builders viewed the Capitol as America's sole temple: a solemn...Solar Temple to be exact.[276]

Prophetic and supernatural alchemy. Again, this notion sounds sensational. However, the rabbit trail of proofs continues. Inasmuch as the obelisk was seen as the "shaft of Baal," it was also the "shaft of Osiris."

The legendary ritual for reincarnating Osiris (which, as we have discussed, is the ritual performed by Freemasons at each Master Mason ceremony) formed the core of Egyptian cosmology and was fantastically venerated on the most imposing scale throughout all of Egypt by towering obelisks (representing the phallus of Osiris) and domes (representing the pregnant belly of Isis) including at Karnak where the upright obelisks were "vitalized" or "stimulated" from the energy of the masturbatory sun-god Ra (mentioned prior) shining down upon them.

There is historical evidence that this elaborate myth and its rituals may have been based originally on real characters and events. It is noteworthy that in 1998, former secretary general of Egypt's Supreme Council of Antiquities, Zahi Hawass, claimed to have found the burial tomb of the god Osiris (Apollo/Nimrod) at the Giza Plateau. In the article, "Sandpit of Royalty," from the newspaper *Extra Bladet* (Copenhagen), January 31, 1999, Hawass was quoted saying:

I have found a shaft, going twenty-nine meters vertically down into the ground, exactly halfway between the Chefren Pyramid and the Sphinx. At the bottom, which was filled with water, we have found a burial chamber with four pillars. In the middle is a large granite sarcophagus, which I expect to be the grave of Osiris, the god.... I have been digging in Egypt's sand for more than thirty years, and up to date this is the most exciting discovery I have made.... We found the shaft in November and began pumping up the water recently. So several years will pass before we have finished investigating the find.[277]

As far as we know, this discovery did not ultimately provide the physical remains of the deified person. But what it did illustrate is that at least some very powerful Egyptologists believe Osiris was a historical figure, and that his body was stored somewhere at or near the Great Pyramid. Manly P. Hall, who knew that the Masonic legend of Hiram Abiff was a thinly veiled prophecy of the resurrection of Osiris, may have understood what Zahi Hawass was looking for, and why. Consider that he wrote in *The Secret Teachings of All Ages*: "The Dying God [Osiris] shall rise again! The secret room in the House of the Hidden Places shall be rediscovered. The Pyramid again shall stand as the ideal emblem of… resurrection, and regeneration."[278]

Some ancient Egyptian cultures held their own reenactments of the Osiris/Isis reincarnation ritual, in which the spirit of Osiris would be "raised" into a newly reigning pharaoh. When this occurred, theocratic statesmanship and the ultimate political authority was given to that leader. (This is later reflected in the political and religious doctrine of royal and political legitimacy or "the divine right of kings," who supposedly derived their right to rule from the will of God, with the exception of, in some countries, the king is subject to the Church and the pope.) The insinuation of this rite, among other meanings, was that the pharaoh's authority was as the son of the sun god, Ra, and as the incarnation of the falcon-headed and all-seeing god Horus until the pharaoh's death—whereupon he would become Osiris, the divine judge over the underworld. The pharaoh's son and predecessor on earth, then, became the newly anointed manifestation of Horus. Within this worldview, every generation of pharaohs would supply their gods with a human spokesperson who carried out their will, as well as ensuring that the earthly leadership would be divinely appointed at all times.

Yet the observant reader may wonder, "Was there something more to the pharaoh's deification than faith in ritual magic?" The cult center of Amun-Ra at Thebes may hold the answer, as it was the site of the largest religious structure ever built—the temple of Amun-Ra at Karnak—and the location of many extraordinary mysterious rites.

As I've written before, the great temple, with its one hundred miles of walls and gardens, was the place where each pharaoh reconciled his divinity in the company of Amun-Ra during the festival of Opet. The festival was held at the temple of Luxor and included a procession of gods carried on barges up the Nile River from Karnak to the temple. The royal family accompanied the gods on boats while the Egyptian laity walked along the shore, calling aloud and making requests of the gods. Once at Luxor, the pharaoh and his entourage entered the holy of holies, where the ceremony to raise the spirit of Osiris into the king was performed and pharaoh was transmogrified into a living deity (a repeat coronation, so to speak). Outside, large groups of dancers and musicians waited anxiously. When the king emerged as the "born-again" Osiris, the crowd erupted in gaiety. From that day forward, the pharaoh was considered to be the son and spiritual incarnation of the Supreme Deity. (The all-seeing eye of Horus/Apollo/Osiris above the unfinished pyramid on the Great Seal represents this event.)

Modern people, especially in America, may view the symbols used in this magic—the dome representing the habitually pregnant belly of Isis, and the obelisk, representing the erect phallus of Osiris—as profane or pornographic. But they were in fact ritualized fertility objects, which the ancients believed could produce tangible reactions, properties, or "manifestations" within the material world. The obelisk and dome as imitations of the deities' male and female reproductive organs could, through government representation, invoke into existence the being or beings symbolized by them. This is why, inside the temple or dome, temple prostitutes representing the human manifestation of the goddess were also available for ritual sex as a form of imitative magic. These prostitutes usually began their services to the goddess as children, and were deflowered at a very young age by a priest or, like Isis' choice piece, by a modeled obelisk of Osiris' phallus. Sometimes these prostitutes were chosen, on the basis of their beauty, as the sexual mates of sacred temple bulls that were considered the incarnation of Osiris. In other places, such as at Mendes, temple prostitutes were offered in coitus to divine goats. Through such imitative sex, the dome and obelisk became "energy receivers," capable of assimilating Ra's essence from the rays of the sun, which in turn drew forth the "seed" of the underworld Osiris. The seed of the dead deity would, according to the supernaturalism, transmit upward (through the portal) from out of the underworld through the base (testes) of the obelisk and magically emit from the tower's head into the womb (dome) of Isis, where incarnation into the sitting pharaoh/king/president would occur (during what Freemasons also call *the raising of Osiris ceremony*). In this way, Osiris could be habitually "born again" or reincarnated as Horus and constantly direct the spiritual destiny of the nation.

This metaphysical phenomenon, which originated with Nimrod/Semiramis and was central to numerous other ancient cultures, was especially developed in Egypt, where Nimrod/Semiramis were known as Osiris/Isis (and in Ezekiel chapter 8 the children of Israel set up the obelisk ["image of jealousy," verse 5] facing the entry of their Temple—just as the dome faces the obelisk in Washington, DC, and in the Vatican City—and were condemned by God for worshipping the Sun [Ra] while weeping for Osiris [Tammuz]). The familiar Masonic figure of the point within a circle is the symbol of this union between Ra, Osiris, and Isis. The "point" represents Osiris' phallus in the center of the circle or womb of Isis, which in turn is enlivened by the sun rays from Ra—just as is represented today at the Vatican, where the Egyptian obelisk of Osiris sits within a circle, and in Washington, DC, where the obelisk sits within the eclipse/lens flare oval—situated so as to be the first thing the sun (Ra) strikes as it rises over the capital city and which, when viewed from overhead, forms the magical point within a circle known as a *circumpunct*. The sorcery is further amplified, according to ancient occultic beliefs, by the presence of the Reflecting Pool in DC, which serves as a mirror to Heaven and "transferring point" for spirits and energies.

And just what is it the spirits see when they look downward on the Reflecting Pool in Washington? They find a city dedicated to and built in honor of the legendary deities Isis and Osiris, complete with the thirteen gathered pieces of Osiris (America's original thirteen colonies); the required obelisk known as the Washington Monument; the Capitol dome (of Isis) for impregnation and incarnation of deity into each pharaoh (president). And, last but not least, they observe official government buildings erected to face their respective counterparts and whose cornerstones—including the US Capitol dome—were dedicated during astrological alignments related to the zodiacal constellation Virgo (Isis), as required for the magic to occur.

And, one should note, lest this all seem nothing more than myth and fantasy, the magicians in Egypt were able to duplicate many of the supernatural acts that God performed at the hand of Moses during the Exodus.

Since Waite's analysis was so useful to us in understanding the importance of the magnetism at play behind the pentagram of DC and the beliefs of the occultists who designed it in yesteryear and those who believe in it yet today, let's see what he has to say about the relationship between the "Great Magical Agent," the sun, and the creation of a life.

> The soul of the earth is a permanent glance from the sun which the earth conceives and conserves by impregnation....for the atmosphere is the recipient, and, as it were, the crucible [receptacle] of the solar rays, by means of which there is produced that living image of the sun *which penetrates,* vivifies, and fructifies the entire earth, *determining all that is brought forth on its surface* by its continual currents and emanations, which are analogous to those of the sun itself. [More simply, it is the power of the sun's rays that determine what is "brought forth" on the earth, including all life, which Waite subsequently clarifies.]
>
> The Astral Light, being the instrument of life, naturally collects at living centres; it cleaves to the kernel of planets as to the

heart of man (and by the heart we understand, in magic, the great sympathetic), but *it identifies itself with the individual life of the existence in which it animates.* [So far, we see that it both "determines"—or chooses—*and* "animates" life in accordance to where it "collects." Think "magnetism"…] Thus it is terrestrial in its connection with the earth, and exclusively human in its connection with man.… The settlement and polarization of light about a centre produces a living being; it attracts all the matter necessary to protect and preserve it…[and] it is the first physical manifestation of the Divine Breath.…

The Astral Light was the instrument of the omnipotence of Adam.…

The Astral Light is the key of all dominion, the secret of all powers, the universal glass of visions, the bond of sympathies, the source of love, prophecy, and glory, the instrument of thaumaturgic art and divination. *To know how to master this agent so as to profit by and to direct its currents is to accomplish the magnum opus, to be master of the world, and the depository even of the power of God.*[279]

"Master of the world"? Men who "direct" the sun can be *masters of the world?* Now, not only have we established that the sun "determines" and "animates" life through its rays and currents, according to this celebrated scholar of mysticism, mere men can control it? They can be masters of the world? They can be "depositories even of the power of God"? Sounds more like "playing God" to me. But who could these men be whom Waite is referring to? Could he have been talking about the brethren he met with as a Freemason? He immediately goes on to say:

The absolute secret of this direction *has been possessed by certain men and can yet be recovered*—it is the Great Magic Arcanum; it depends on an incommunicable axiom, and on an instrument which is the great and unique Athanor of the Hermatists of the highest grade. *All magic science consists in the knowledge of this secret.* To know it and to dare make use of it is human omnipotence; to reveal it to an outsider is to lose it; to reveal it to a disciple is to abdicate in favour of such disciple, who, from that moment, has the right of life and death over his initiator, and will certainly kill him for fear of dying himself.[280]

Let's pretend for a moment that we weren't completely and unanimously distracted by Waite's mini-speech about the right of life and death and killing and dying, and focus instead on the group he's describing. Waite, himself, was a Freemason, and throughout much of his work, he refers to secrets shared between "disciples" and "initiators" of that very Order. Who else would he be talking about here? He clearly stated that "certain men" have in the past "possessed" the ability to direct the Astral Light (sun)—and that this art "can yet be recovered." *If* the redirection of the sun by man can "determine" and "animate" life through mystical impregnation via polarized vibrations/rays collecting at "centres" and so forth; and *if* the men chosen for such a task are the "disciples" and "initiators" of the Brotherhood Waite belonged to (Freemasons); and *if* Freemasons have so much of their occultic practices tied into Abiff/Osiris/Horus-type resurrections and reincarnations; and *if* there are magnetic "centres" drawing the power behind this potential animation of a new, reincarnated/resurrected lifeform to the "Devil's footprint" of Washington, DC...then what in the otherworld would they be trying to bring to life?

Follow this incredibly complicated thread as I simplify it to the best of my ability:

1. Isis is connected to the power of the Agent through monuments. She was the very sister/wife of Osiris, who impregnated herself through her dead husband's corpse in order to birth Horus, who was really Osiris reincarnated into a new body.

223

2. Horus-with-the-spirit-of-Osiris was gifted with the "Al-Seeing Eye," which is the symbol on our Great Seal of the United States, our dollar bill, and in countless places all over Washington, DC.

3. Osiris/Horus was/is openly recognized by the greatest Freemasons in history as the true identity of Hiram Abiff. These same Freemasons ritualize Hiram Abiff in their Master Mason ceremonies as a way of cementing the integrity of secrecy.

4. Hiram Abiff died protecting secret words and building plans of a *temple* dedicated to worship. These building plans had a purpose and order from a supernatural world (heaven) and Deity (God). As William Henry and Mark Gray pointed out in their work, *Freedom's Gate*, "It is clear that the builders viewed the Capitol as America's sole *temple*."[281] The building plans of our capital have now been shown to connect through Freemasonry to a purpose and order from a supernatural world (black magic of the open "footprint of the Devil" pentagram) and deities (Isis, Osiris, Horus, and all those other deities worshiped throughout time since the Ancient and Mysterious Order of the Rosae Crucis—but *never* Jesus Christ or Yahweh).

5. The Freemasonic structures just mentioned—those that have been put into place since the leadership of our first Freemasonic president—have the power (occultists believe) to direct *something* through the force of magnetism to the center of its representational symbol (the pentagram)…and with the shaft of Baal/Osiris and the ever-pregnant belly of Isis, along with the regenerative rays of the Astral Light, that *something* is no longer a something, but a *someone*.

A *someone* who will be risen upon the "Devil's footprint."

I will remind the reader at this very sensitive conjuncture of study that it doesn't matter if the mainstream believes any of this; it matters if *they* do. The Freemasons aren't just made up of a few groups of misguided teenagers conducting naïve rituals while playing Dungeons and Dragons in a basement somewhere. We are talking about a citadel of politically and socially powerful and nefarious schemers who have been planning something very dark since the time of Moses, when they were known by another name. And although many involved in Freemasonry are simply normal people with normal lives, *many* are not. If or when those of the Craft feel the time has come to conduct whatever life-breathing ceremonies they have organized, the most radical adherents of Freemasonry will pull from the depths of any and all dark spiritual conduits to see it finally, after thousands and thousands of years, come to pass. The Bible lists Satan as the "god of this world" (2 Corinthians 4:4), and his power throughout the ages has been very real.

I will now take a moment to ask the unsettling question that has been abundantly implied but remains to be asked directly: Was the United States designated to generate or "birth" the Antichrist?

Could it be that all these symbols and monuments and domes, etc., actually mean more than an "accidental oversight"? Considering all the mathematical and architectural planning that went into its construction, I think the answer is obvious. But don't take my word for it. There are plenty of other sources that suggest this very reality.

I might remind you that Manly P. Hall said:

> The rise of the Christian Church broke up the intellectual pattern of the classical pagan world. By persecution of this pattern's ideologies it drove the secret societies into greater secrecy; the pagan intellectuals then reclothed their original ideas in a garment of Christian phraseology, but bestowed the keys of the symbolism only upon those duly initiated and bound to secrecy by their vows.[282]

Gary Lachman, in his book, *Politics and the Occult*, describes in detail how Washington, DC, was laid out according to the precepts of sacred geometry "associated with Freemasonry."[283]

George W. Bush, forty-third president of the United States, in his 2005 Inaugural Address, said, "When our Founders declared a new order of the ages…they were acting on an ancient hope that is meant to be fulfilled."[284]

On that, was *Time* magazine sending a secret message to Freemasons everywhere when it portrayed Donald Trump as a danger to the ancient, occult scheme when in March 2017 it chose to depict his war on Washington in this way?[285]

chapter nine

The Great Seal Prophecy of America's Coming Grey Champion

n *The Secret Teachings for All Ages*, celebrated 33rd-Degree Freemason Manly P. Hall said:

> Not only were many of the founders of the United States Government Masons, but they received aid from a secret and august body existing in Europe, which helped them to establish this country for a peculiar and particular purpose known only to the initiated few. The Great Seal is the signature of this exalted body—unseen and for the most part unknown—and the unfinished pyramid upon its reverse side is a trestleboard setting forth symbolically *the task to the accomplishment of which the United States Government was dedicated from the day of its inception.*[286]

Hall spoke of many things regarding the Freemasonic symbolism of our capital city, but by *far* the most powerful signature of intent by the society, as Hall just stated, is the Great Seal. He didn't even try to hide the fact that the Seal involves a "task"—a "peculiar and particular" one that our nation was "dedicated" to by our founding fathers from "inception"!

Hermes Trismegistus of the *Hermetic Corpus* wisdom texts prized by the Rosicrucians (and by extension, the Freemasons) regaled his disciple with a principle for the workings of the universe: "As Above, So Below." This code is so buried in esoteric mysticism today that you find it even modeled by "The Magician" in the tarot deck; one of his hands holds a wand toward Heaven, and the other points to the earth, signifying the magician's (and alchemist's) role in the metaphysical link between Heaven and earth—and this artwork is a direct result of the "As Above, So Below" maxim. Straight from Trismegistus' *Emerald Tablet* writing from the *Hermetica* is the explanation of this mystical connection:

That which is Below corresponds to that which is Above, and that which is Above corresponds to that which is Below, to accomplish the miracle of the One Thing. And just as all things have come from this One Thing, through the meditation of One Mind, so do all created things originate from this One Thing, through Transformation.[287]

To those who are understandably confused by this obscure and cryptic text and what this "One Thing" might be, consider what Nikki Scully writes about the Emerald Tablet in her book, *Alchemical Healing: A Guide to Spiritual, Physical, and Transformational Medicine*:

The basic tenets of alchemy are distilled in the Emerald Tablet, one of the most quoted and studied of the guiding treatises of alchemical lore…. The Tablet suggests that "that which is above is the same as that which is below: All that exists is of One Mind, or of One Thing, and they are the same." It is the goal of the alchemist to bring spirit and matter into alignment and harmony. Within that relationship rests the secret of creation, and with it our ability to co-create our own reality….

The language used to convey ancient and medieval alchemy

was purposely misleading, encoded in terms so difficult to understand that the majority of those who tried to decipher it were either led astray or forced to give up....

Throughout all the processes of alchemy, it is important to remember the teaching from the Emerald Tablet.... *What happens in the spirit world is a reflection of what happens in the physical world.*[288]

Simply put, what happens on this earth can be controlled, manipulated, redirected, or entirely *created* based on the powerful, metaphysical link between the unseen realm and the enlightened few (magicians, sorcerers, alchemists, master Freemasons, etc.). What happens below on our natural earth, according to this philosophy, can mirror that of the supernatural—and the ambitions of a new society (or New World Order) become tangible via this concentration. Such a "mirror" is openly displayed in the Great Seal. It does, as Hall signifies, "symbolically" relate the "task" to which our country was "dedicated." He made it clear, as did Nikki Scully, that these symbols and languages are "purposely misleading" to the general public.

It is perhaps no wonder, then, that the nation remains misled and that only students of archaic/esoteric symbolism would be able to decipher the true "peculiar and particular purpose" of the Seal's design. By allowing the imagery to appear nationalistic in its branding, the truth can be shrouded behind what the general public perceives as patriotic.

When digging through the piles of research available on the Great Seal since its conception in 1776 (approved in 1782), the following implications are offered:

The Obverse Side

The animal chosen to bear the US Coat of Arms (with thirteen stripes) is the American Bald Eagle, supposedly chosen "because of its long life, great strength and majestic looks, and also because it was then believed to exist only on this continent.... The eagle represents freedom. Living as he does on the tops of lofty mountains, amid the solitary grandeur of Nature, he has unlimited freedom, whether with strong pinions he sweeps into the valleys below, or upward into the boundless spaces beyond."[289]

However, as stately as this all sounds, it is common knowledge that the earlier sketches were of William Barton's "phoenix in a nest of flames." Of this, Manly Hall said, "Its selection would of course have been appropriate." He went on to say:

Among the ancients a fabulous bird called the Phoenix is described by early writers such as Clement, Herodotus, and Pliny; in size and shape it resembled the eagle.... The Phoenix, it was said, lives for 500 years, and at its death its body opens and the new born Phoenix emerges. Because of this symbolism, the Phoenix is generally regarded as representing immortality and resurrection.

All symbols have their origin in something tangible, and the Phoenix is one sign of the secret orders of the ancient world and of the initiate of those orders, for it was common to refer to one who had been accepted into the temples as a man twice-born, or re-born [think Horus/Osiris]. Wisdom confers a new life, and those who become wise [or enlightened] are born again.

The Phoenix symbol is important in another way, as an emblem among nearly all civilized nations of royalty, power, superiority, and immortality. The Phoenix of China is identical in meaning with the Phoenix of Egypt; and the Phoenix of the Greeks is the same as the Thunder Bird of the American Indians....

It is immediately evident that the bird on the original seal is not an eagle...but the Phoenix.... The beak is of a different shape, the neck is much longer, and the small tuft of hair at the back of the head leaves no doubt as to the artist's intention.[290]

So, as far as Hall was concerned, and as far as the historical evidence shows, the eagle was never an eagle, but a reincarnating bird held to high importance in Freemasonic mysticism.

However, there is yet another corresponding mythological link to the eagle as the representative phoenix. Several other birds could have been chosen to be the veiled phoenix if the artist was deliberate in shaping their lines, but in the family tree of the Roman pantheon, Jupiter (Zeus to the Greeks) was the father of Apollo, and his sacred animal was the eagle, who almost never leaves his side. When this very eagle was combined with a thunderbolt in its talons in artwork—a common occurrence on Greek and Roman coins—the eagle was to be considered Jupiter, himself, in animal form. Interestingly, in almost every single depiction of this state, the eagle has its wings outstretched in precisely the same stance as the Eagle of the Great Seal, and its head is always facing the same direction. The comparison of the two images is so striking that if one were to approach a person with no understanding of the identities or symbolism of either the Roman/Greek coins or the US Seal (or US history), he or she would understandably think the Roman/Greek coin was an antique coin of America's ancient past. The unbearded "underworld Jupiter"—also known as Veiove, Vetis, or Vejovis, depending on the region the myth hails from—is depicted with a cluster of arrows in his hand, just like the eagle of the Great Seal.

Thus, there is a distinct allegory existing that the eagle of the US might in fact be a stand-in for the father of the Apollo/Osiris/Horus, who will be reborn into this world through reincarnation/resurrection—and who will arrive to finally place the missing "apex stone" upon the unfinished pyramid (on the reverse side of the Seal) for the New Atlantis.

In the eagle's left talon are thirteen arrows, said to represent the thirteen original colonies; in its right talon is an olive branch (with thirteen leaves and thirteen olives, again for the thirteen original colonies), said to represent peace. The duality of the arrows and the olive branch signifies, or so we're told, that our nation desires peace however and whenever possible (which is why the eagle has its head turned to the peaceful side), but we are ready to bravely go to war if necessary to preserve our values.

Above the eagle's head is a "glory" with thirteen stars, and from its beak is an unraveled scroll with the words *E PLURIBUS UNUM*—which translates, "out of many, one" (alternatively, "one, out of many")—made up of thirteen letters. (The English translation, when including the comma, is also comprised of thirteen characters.) The phrase *E pluribus unum* is said to have strong ties to another by Greek philosopher Heraclitus, whose writings survive only in what is called "the Fragments." Fragment 10 reads, "The one is made up of all things, and all things issue from the one," which is strangely similar to the Hermetic "As Above, So Below" maxim adored by Freemasons: "And just as all things have come from this One Thing, through the meditation of One Mind, so do all created things originate from this One Thing."

And though it has been suggested that the "out of many, one" allusion refers to the comradery of a people coming together (or "becoming one") through the common interest of love, patriotism, national pride, and so on, a more precise translation of *that* archetypal union is already given in the Latin *unus fiat ex pluribus* (literally, "it is based on one of a number of," i.e., a goal or accomplishment that is based on the joining of a number together as one, united). But that did not equal thirteen letters, nor did it have ties to the "As Above, So Below" proverb. Thus, *E pluribus unum* was chosen deliberately in place of its more appropriate counterpart. However, whether the final terminology was selected because it fit the "thirteen" theme, or because it reflected the metaphysical and alchemical connotations of the *Hermetic Corpus*, the public views the "oneness" undertone and, without digging deeper, naturally associates it with patriotic dogmas of unity that have propelled our national "family" since the beginning.

But just as "one nation, under God" and "In God We Trust" are obviously intentionally ambiguous, the question is raised: To what central goal are we united "as one" anyway, and who precisely are the "we" in this equation? Is it all the citizens of America coming together for peace, liberty, and justice? Or is it the initiates of a darker Order coming together for a "peculiar and particular purpose" related to "devil's footprint" pentagrams and pagan monuments?

Also, might there be more to the numerology surrounding the eagle than just that persistent number thirteen (which we will discuss shortly)? In 1846, 33rd-Degree Freemason and noted author James David Carter wrote in *Freemasonry and United States Government*:

> Among those who helped design the Great Seal of the United States the following are known to have been Masons: Benjamin Franklin, Thomas Jefferson, William Churchill Houston, and William Barton.... [W]hen an informed Mason examines the Great Seal, here is what he sees:
>
> On the obverse is an eagle whose dexter wing has thirty-two feathers, the number of ordinary degrees in Scottish Rite Freemasonry. The sinister wing has thirty-three feathers, the additional feather corresponding to the Thirty-Third Degree of the same Rite conferred for outstanding Masonic service. The tail feathers number nine, the number of degrees in the Chapter, Council, and Commandery of the York Rite of Freemasonry.... The total number of feathers in the two wings is sixty-five which, by gematria, is the value of the Hebrew phrase *yam yawchod* (together in unity)....
>
> The glory above the eagle's head is divided into twenty-four equal parts and reminds the observer of the Mason's gauge which is also divided into twenty-four equal parts and is emblematic of the service he is obligated to perform. The five-pointed stars remind him of the Masonic Blazing Star and the five points of fellowship....

The gold, silver, and azure colors represent the sun, moon, and Worshipful Master, the first that rules the day, the second, the night, and the third, the lodge. While silver, connected with the letter Gimel or G and being surrounded on an azure ground by a golden glory, reminds the Mason of the letter G, a most conspicuous furnishing of a proper lodge room. The shield on the eagle's breast affirms by its colors, valor (red), purity (white), and justice (blue), and reminds the Mason of the cardinal virtues. The value of these colors, by gematria, is 103, the value of the phrase *ehben ha-Adam* (the stone of Adam) and suggests the perfect ashlar, or squared stone, of Freemasonry. One hundred and three is also the value of the noun *bonaim*, a Ranbbinical word signifying "builders, Masons." Thus the national colors spell out, by gematria, the name of the fraternity. The scroll in the eagle's beak, bearing the words *E Pluribus Unum*…reminds him also of the unity which has made brothers of many.[291]

It seems almost naïve to assume that the front side of the Seal is merely patriotic. Freemason handiwork is all over it. The reverse side appears to be even more blatant. Once again, we turn to Hall to point out the obvious: "But if this design on the obverse side of the seal is stamped with the signature of the Order…the design on the reverse is even more definitely related to the old Mysteries."[292]

The Reverse Side

Hall describes the reverse side:

Here is represented the great pyramid of Gizah, composed of 13 rows of masonry, showing 72 stones (the importance of this number and its connection to ancient and modern saboteurs and shadow government, deep-state occultists is reviewed elsewhere in this book). The pyramid is without a cap stone, and above its upper platform floats a triangle containing the All-Seeing Eye surrounded by rays of light.[293]

The "Eye of Providence" floating above the Great Pyramid is an interesting twist. In the Renaissance Era, well before our nation's founding, it began appearing as a symbol of the Christian Holy Trinity: three equal sides for the Father, Son, and Holy Spirit, with the all-seeing eye of God (the three Persons together as one) at the center, accompanied by "glory rays" issuing from the three sides. Many may find this similarity of the Christian symbol to the Eye of Horus concerning, but when looking into the origins of the Eye of Providence, it's nearly impossible to locate which religion or culture recorded it first, and it *certainly did not* mean the same thing to each culture/religion. Though it doesn't always appear exactly the same from rendering to rendering, the artwork of the Eye of Providence is prominent in ancient imagery all over the world. In Buddhism, it's the "Eye of the World"; in Vietnamese Caodism, it's the "Divine Eye of God"; in Hinduism, it's the third eye of Shiva and the destroyer of all evil and ignorance; in Middle-Eastern religions, it often appears in the palm of the hand and represents protection (and a comparable symbol appears in Judaism at times as the "Eye [or "Hand"] of Miriam"); and so on.

The designers of the Great Seal knew very well that by the time America was born, this all-seeing eye would be recognized generically as the Eye of Providence, and that Christians arriving to the new land of freedom would associate it to the Eye of the Trinity, so they proceeded with confidence that this "reclothing" would satisfy citizens of the nation for centuries to come. Evidently, their confidence was well placed, because at the time of this writing, the vast majority of Americans either have no idea what they're looking at on the Seal, or they believe it to be representation of the Trinity (or "Eye of God/Providence," generically). But if it was merely the Trinity they were pointing to, why would the all-seeing eye of Yahweh, Jesus, and the Holy Spirit be hovering above the Great Pyramid of Giza, Egypt, instead of the more obviously appropriate image of America? They just as easily could have placed the Eye over the flag or over a crowd of patriots.

Let's consider what one of the most famous occultists in world history has said on the matter. I will remind the reader that this Freemason, Aleister Crowley, was known as the "wickedest man in the world." From his writings, we read of a warped and therefore unholy trinity deriving from Egyptian theology:

Evolution (within human memory) shows three great steps: 1. the worship of the Mother, when the universe was conceived as simple nourishment drawn directly from her; 2. the worship of the Father, when the universe was imagined as catastrophic; 3. the worship of the Child, in which we come to perceive events as a continual growth partaking in its elements of both these methods.

Egyptian theology foresaw this progress of humanity and symbolized it in the triad of Isis, Osiris, [and] Horus....

[T]he residing officer of the temple (the earth) is Horus, the Crowned and Conquering Child. And again, Egyptology and psychology help us to understand what is implied, and what effect to expect, in the world of thought and action.[294]

Though Crowley was referring to his timelines of majestic Aeons (time periods revealed to him through an "intelligence entity" known as Aiwass during his search for enlightenment [much like John Dee and his search for enlightenment through communication with "angels"]), and not to the Great Seal symbolism specifically, the Egyptian triad or trinity of Isis/Osiris/Horus was one that had been deeply embedded in the esoteric Mysteries (translation: religion of the Freemasons) that the 33rd-degree Freemason Crowley celebrated and that Hall referred to prior.

Earlier, we used the following quote from Hall's *Secret Teachings of All Ages*:

> The black magician cannot use the symbols of white magic without bringing down upon himself the forces of white magic, which would be fatal to his schemes. He must therefore distort the hierograms so that they typify the occult fact that he himself is distorting the principles for which the symbols stand. Black magic is not a fundamental art; it is the misuse of an art. Therefore it has no symbols of its own. It merely takes the emblematic figures of white magic, and by inverting and reversing them signifies that it is left-handed.[295]

In the article, "The All-Seeing Eye: Sacred Origins of a Hijacked Symbol" by David Percival of *The Conscious Reporter*, we see that Hall was not the only one to point out that symbols can be either misused intentionally or combined with others to "hijack" its original purpose in trade for a veiled evil:

> Is the all-seeing eye a symbol of divine omniscience or sinister influence? Today it symbolises control and domination by a shadowy elite, but its original use was quite different....
>
> Today the all-seeing eye is more likely to be seen as an "Illuminati" symbol of control and surveillance by elites who to a large degree run the show on this planet at this time. This is because, over time, dark sinister forces have taken over esoteric symbols that for thousands of years were used to convey positive, helpful, uplifting spiritual messages and principles. The all-seeing eye is a prime example of *how spiritual symbols have been hijacked and inverted.*[296]

Again and again, we see the pattern of Freemasons "reclothing," "distorting," "warping," "inverting," and "hijacking" symbols to make them appear as one thing to the general public but point to that "peculiar and particular purpose" behind the veil. In this particular instance, to the early settlers of the newly born United States of America, the all-seeing eye of the Holy Trinity was placed above the Great Pyramid to "warp" it into the all-seeing eye of the unholy trinity: Isis, Osiris, and Horus. One might now wonder: "Why the Great Pyramid specifically?"

Hall had this to say about the Great Pyramid and its link to the Baconian "New Atlantis" (translation: New World Order) dream:

> The Pyramid of Gizah was believed by the ancient Egyptians to be the shrine tomb of the god Hermes, or Thot, the personification of Universal Wisdom.
>
> No trace has ever been found of the cap of the great pyramid. A flat platform about thirty feet square gives no indication that this part of the structure was ever otherwise finished; and this is appropriate, as the Pyramid represents human society itself, imperfect and incomplete. The structure's ascending converging angles and faces represent the common aspiration of humankind; above floats the symbol of the esoteric orders, the radiant triangle with its all-seeing eye....
>
> There is a legend that in the lost Atlantis stood a great university in which originated most of the arts and sciences of the present race. The University was in the form of an immense pyramid with many galleries and corridors, and on the top was an observatory for the study of the stars. This temple to the sciences in the old Atlantis is shadowed forth in the seal of the new Atlantis. Was it the society of the unknown philosophers who scaled the new nation with the eternal emblems, that all the nations might know the purpose for which the new country had been founded?...
>
> The combination of the Phoenix, the pyramid, and the all-seeing eye is more than chance or coincidence. There is nothing

about the early struggles of the colonists to suggest such a selection to farmers, shopkeepers, and country gentlemen. There is only one possible origin for these symbols, and that is the secret societies which came to this country 150 years before the Revolutionary War. Most of the patriots who achieved American independence belonged to these societies, and derived their inspiration, courage, and high purpose from the ancient teaching. There can be no question that the great seal was directly inspired by these orders of the human Quest, and that it set forth the purpose for this nation as that purpose was seen and known to the Founding Fathers.

The monogram of the new Atlantis reveals this continent as set apart for the accomplishment of the great work—here is to arise the pyramid of human aspiration, the school of the secret sciences.[297]

Hall didn't limit his reflections of the Great Pyramid in this one work. In his *Secret Teachings of all Ages*, he took it a step farther, explaining that *all:*

> …the Seven Wonders of the World, while apparently designed for divers reasons, were really monuments erected to perpetuate the arcana of the Mysteries. They were symbolic structures, placed in peculiar spots, and the real purpose of their erection can be sensed only by the initiated…. The Seven Wonders of the World were built by Widow's sons in honor of the seven planetary genii. Their secret symbolism is identical with that of the seven seals of Revelation and the seven churches of Asia.[298]

He goes on to say of the Great Pyramid particularly, "The Great Pyramid was supreme among the temples of the Mysteries…. *It was the tomb of Osiris*, and was believed to have been built by the gods themselves, and the architect may have been the immortal Hermes. It is the monument of Mercury, the messenger of the gods, and the universal symbol of wisdom and letters."[299] Earlier on in this same work, he explains:

W. Marsham Adams calls the Great Pyramid "the House of the Hidden Places"; such indeed it was, for it represented the inner sanctuary of pre-Egyptian wisdom. By the Egyptians the Great Pyramid was associated with Hermes, the god of wisdom and letters and the Divine Illuminator worshiped through the planet Mercury. Relating Hermes to the Pyramid emphasizes anew the fact that it was in reality the supreme temple of the Invisible and Supreme Deity. The Great Pyramid was…the first temple of the Mysteries, the first structure erected as a repository for those secret truths which are the certain foundation of all arts and sciences. It was the perfect emblem of the *microcosm* and the *macrocosm* and, according to the secret teachings, *the tomb of Osiris, the black god of the Nile.…*

Through the mystic passageways and chambers of the Great Pyramid passed the illumined of antiquity. They entered its portals as men; they came forth as gods. It was the place of the "second birth," the "womb of the Mysteries."[300]

Rhodes Scholar James H. Billington and Harvard Professor Charles Eliot Norton also recognized the occult symbolism of the Great Seal, saying that it "hardly" represented our country in any way other than an "emblem of a Masonic fraternity."[301]

The reverse side has two mottos, *Annuit coeptis* (also thirteen letters; Latin, literally "[he/she/it] favors our undertakings") and *Novus ordo seclorum* (Latin, "New Order of the Ages").

For *Annuit coeptis*, Charles Thompson, designer of the Great Seal's final version, condensed line 625 of book IX of Virgil's *Aeneid*, which reads, *Juppiter omnipotes, audacibus annue coeptis* ("All-powerful Jupiter favors [the] daring undertakings"), to *Annuit coeptis* ("He approves [our] undertakings"). The phrase *Novus ordo seclorum* ("a new order of the ages") was adapted in 1782 from inspiration Thompson found in a prophetic line in Virgil's Eclogue IV: *Magnus ab integro seclorum nascitur ordo* (Virgil's *Eclogue IV*, line 5), the interpretation of the original Latin being, "And the majestic roll of circling centuries begins anew." This phrase is from the Cumaean Sibyl (a pagan prophetess of Apollo, identified in the Bible as a demonic deceiver) and involves the future birth of a divine son, spawned of "a new breed of men sent down from heaven" when he receives "the life of gods, and sees Heroes with gods commingling."

The meaning of all three Latin phrases from both sides together, once the imageries are all compared to Freemasonic agenda, could read:

1. Osiris/Isis/Jupiter favors the undertakings (*Annuit coeptis*)
2. of the one Order who have together built the As Above, So Below schemata in the capital city (*E pluribus unum*)
3. to herald in the New World Order of the Ages through the divine son (Horus or false messiah) (*Novus ordo seclorum*).

But the trail goes even deeper than this.

Returning to what 33rd-Degree Freemason James David Carter wrote in 1864, we read of this reverse-side symbolism and numerology:

On the reverse, is the All Seeing Eye within a triangle surrounded by a golden glory. Besides the obvious Masonic significance of this design, it has a cabalistic value of seventy plus three plus two hundred, equaling two hundred and seventy-three which is the value of the phrase *ehben mosu habonim* (the stone which the builders refused) familiar to all Royal Arch Masons. It is also the value of the Hebrew proper noun Hiram Abiff, the architect of Solomon's Temple and the principal character of the legend used

241

in the Master Mason degree.… The triangle also represents the capstone of the unfinished pyramid and reminds the Mason of the immortality of the soul and that in eternity he will complete the capstone of his earthly labors according to the designs on the trestle-board of the Supreme Architect of the Universe. The unfinished pyramid cannot fail to remind him of the unfinished condition of the Temple when tragedy struck down its Masters architect.

The blaze of glory found on either side of the Great Seal cannot fail to remind the Mason of the Great Light in Masonry which is the rule and guide to faith and practice and without which no Masonic lodge can exist. It reminds him that only more light can dispel the pall of ignorance in which he stumbles until he enters tile Celestial Lodge where all light is given.[302]

Again, many believe that the "New World Order" occult links in the Great Seal (as well as capital city monuments and architecture) is all just part of a conspiracy theory. But even spokespersons of the Freemasonic Order itself are coming forward to openly admit there's more "plan" than there is "art" behind these designs. If we are to allow the repetitious symbolism to speak for itself, we arrive at this conclusion. When we allow the historically venerated Freemasons to speak for themselves, we again arrive at this conclusion. Where is the "hidden conspiracy" amidst all this proof? Can we even suggest that anything is even "hidden" by this point? It seems altogether quite transparently barefaced.

But why all these instances of thirteen? Did the designers of the Seal really want to give that much attention to the thirteen original colonies? Once or twice is understandable, but consider a bullet list of how many times this number appears on both sides:

- 13 leaves on the olive branch
- 13 berries on the olive branch

- 13 arrows
- 13 stripes on the coat of arms
- 13 stars in the "glory" (above the eagle's head)
- 13 letters in *E pluribus unum*
- 13 characters (including the comma) in "out of many, one" and "one, out of many"
- 13 letters in *Annuit Coeptis*
- 13 rows (or "steps") on the unfinished pyramid

A rudimentary search provides a lengthy list of superstitious connections to thirteen, many of which eventually trace back to the occult (if one is willing to dig that far back). Such a fear of this number exists that there is an actual, clinical phobia related to it. Triskaidekaphobia is derived from the Greek words *tris*, *kai*, *deka*, and *phobos*, translating literally to "three and ten morbid fear," or "a morbid fear of three plus ten." The following are only a few interesting connections to thirteen:

- Most Wiccan covens are made up of thirteen members.
- At the Last Supper, there were thirteen men (twelve disciples plus Christ). Judas Iscariot, Christ's betrayer, has been described as the thirteenth person to join the table just a short time before he committed the most heinous crime in all world history. (Since then, there has been an ongoing superstition of meal gatherings involving exactly thirteen people.)
- On Friday the 13th, in October of the year 1307, King Philip IV of France had the Knights Templar arrested, most of whom were either tortured or executed immediately afterward. (Many believe this was the origin of the "Friday the 13th" superstition that still haunts us today.)
- In Viking lore, the god Loki was the thirteenth in the order of the Norse pantheon. After his arranged murder of fellow god Balder, Loki was the thirteenth guest to appear at the funeral.

(Some have said this is the origin of the superstition that if thirteen people gather together, one will perish in the coming year.)

- Apollo 13 was launched at 13:13:00 central standard time, and the oxygen tank exploded on April 13, 1970.
- Early on in the development of our modern calendars, a year with thirteen full moons (which happens for approximately thirty-seven years out of a century) would throw off the balance of the scheduled church festivals, feasts, and events. As such, it was at the least considered an unlucky number and at times considered an ill omen.
- Many television shows and Hollywood films have plots surrounding the number thirteen in relation to the occult, paranormal activity, or supernatural phenomena (such as *13 Ghosts*, *The Thirteenth Floor*, *Friday the 13th*, and *Warehouse 13*, just to name a few).
- A surprising number of hotels and business centers have completely and superstitiously omitted the number thirteen from their flooring design, and as a result, the elevator buttons go straight from twelve to fourteen. (The same can be said for quite a few airlines as well; there is no "row 13.")
- The Republic of Ireland was so convinced that the superstitions surrounding thirteen would discourage people from buying cars in 2013 (as the first two numbers on the vehicle registration are the last two of the four-digit year; i.e., 2011 registered car would start with "11" etc.) that the Society of the Irish Motor Industry cleared it with the government to add an additional numeral representing the first or second half of the year ("131" for the first half of 2013; "132" for the latter half).

And the list goes on. For some strange reason, a lot of people fear the number thirteen. It also, however, plays an interesting role in a few numbers games. Just as quick examples: the simplest alphanumeric conversion table assigns a number to each letter from 1 to 26 (A=1, B=2, C=3, and so on). Some have pointed out that the values of USA (numbers 21, 19, and 1) can easily be toyed with to equate 13 ($2 \times 1 = 2 + 1 = 3 + 9 = 12 + 1 = 13$). Another is AOL (America Online), whose logo appears to be the eye of Horus/Osiris in a pyramid (numbers 1, 15, and 12), and people are quick to point out that equation of 13 as well ($1 + 15 = 16 - 1 = 15 - 2 = 13$). Most of this just seems silly (as superstitions often do), but there is even still more to consider. For instance, the Illuminati (a radical, internal sect of Freemasonry) has thirteen top "satanic bloodlines": Astor, Bundy, Collins, DuPont, Freeman, Kennedy, Li, Onassis, Reynolds, Rockefeller, Rothschild, Russell, and Van Duyn.

But according to esotericists like Hall, the extraordinary truth about the number thirteen so affixed to the Great Seal was a marker for those who understood it as a Masonic "power number," sacred to the moon and representative of the head of Isis, as well as the number of Osiris' remaining body parts Isis recovered along the Nile River (fourteen total; the male reproductive organ was never found, equaling thirteen). This is, of course, not even taking into consideration what numerology Bible scholars might reveal.

- There are thirteen famines recorded in Scripture, which, as we all know, are times of terrible hunger and destitution for people of a country/territory (Genesis 12:10, Genesis 26:1, Genesis 41:54, Ruth 1:1, 2 Samuel 21:1, 1 Kings 18:1, 2 Kings 4:38, 2 Kings 7:4, 2 Kings 25:3, Nehemiah 5:3, Jeremiah 14:1, Luke 15:14, and Acts 11:28). In these events, the people were freed and fed only by a power higher than themselves, which was the Christian God. Consider, then, the fact that in the end times, the "savior" of such destitution will be the Antichrist of a World Order—before he ushers in the great destruction.
- Revelation chapter *13* is likely the most important and descriptive chapter of any book in the entire Bible concerning the

Antichrist, but in addition to that—and bearing in mind all the metaphysical and alchemical links between the secretive Freemasons and the Hermetic "As Above, So Below" maxim—Revelation *13:13* just got very interesting: "And he [Antichrist; Beast] doeth great wonders, so that *he maketh fire come down from heaven* [as above] *on the earth* [so below] in the sight of men" (KJV, emphasis added).

- In Gematria—the Assyro-Babylonian-Greek alphanumeric code system frequently used in association to the Rosicrucians' beloved Kabbalah texts—the name "Satan" in both Hebrew and Greek are multiples of 13 (Hebrew 364, 13 x 28; Greek 2197, 13^3).

But perhaps the most intriguing connection to the number is what Ethelbert W. Bullinger disclosed in his book, *Number in Scripture*:

As to the significance of *thirteen*, all are aware that it has come down to us as a number of ill-omen. Many superstitions cluster around it, and various explanations are current concerning them.

Unfortunately, those who go backwards to find a reason seldom go back far enough. The popular explanations do not, so far as we are aware, go further back than the Apostles. But we must go back to *the first occurrence* of the number *thirteen* in order to discover the key to its significance. It occurs first in Genesis 14:4, where we read "*Twelve* years they served Chedorlaomer, and the *thirteenth* year they REBELLED."

Hence every occurrence of the number *thirteen*, and likewise of *every multiple* of it, stamps that with which it stands in connection with *rebellion, apostasy, defection, corruption, disintegration, revolution*, or some kindred idea.[303]

Perhaps even more interesting than everything discussed about the Great Seal so far, however, are the true colors that began to show in the 1930s and '40s when it was decided the Seal would be placed on the dollar bill…

Guru Letters and Great Seal Prophecies

Franklin D. Roosevelt—the thirty-second president of the US—decided to run for an unprecedented third term and chose as his running mate for the vice-presidency the secretary of agriculture, 32nd-Degree Freemason, and self-appointed "practical mystic" Henry Agard Wallace. Roosevelt saw in Wallace an avid supporter of the New Deal, but Wallace's appeal was such that he could flatter both upper crust businessmen and big-city unionists as well as the blue-collar citizens of the nation. Democratic National Committee Chairman Jim Farley did not approve of Roosevelt's choice for VP, and he said as much when he spoke to both Roosevelt and his first lady, Eleanor. Eleanor was a powerful voice in the government, heavily involved with civil rights activism. After Farley voiced his concerns about Wallace's liberalism and his dabbling into the deep realms of mysticism and the occult, Eleanor agreed with Farley and tried to encourage the president to move on to someone else. Roosevelt—a 32nd-Degree Mason and Knight of Pythias (Shriner) with an equal thirst for mysticism—defended Wallace, however, praising him for his ability to lead others to a greater enlightenment, and then followed up by composing a speech that firmly stated his acceptance for nomination would *only* come after the acceptance of Wallace as VP. Eleanor was the first woman to give a speech to the Democratic National Convention, in which she conceded and asked the rest of FDR's supporters to do likewise. Wallace, as a result, became the thirty-third vice president of the US.

But a White House inter-office memo had already begun to show the delegates by 1935 that these two men had a bizarre relationship centering on more than just politics and government, as Wallace wrote to FDR:

> I feel for a short time yet that we must deal with the "strong ones," the "turbulent ones," the "fervent ones," and perhaps even with a temporary resurgence, with the "flameless ones," who with the last dying gasp will strive to reanimate their dying giant "Capitalism." Mr. President, you can be the "flaming one," the one with an ever-upsurging spirit to lead into the time when the children of men can sing again.[304]

But such strange language haunted many of Wallace's writings, as he had been a devout follower of Roerich philosophy.

Roerich was a painter, writer, philosopher, theosophist, archeologist, enlightener, and a growing public figure known by his birth name Nikolai Konstantinovich Rerikh in Russia before he left in 1918. After a brief stop in Finland and Scandinavia, he and his wife Helena traveled onward to London in 1919, where they founded the Agni Yoga Society, a school of mysticism (referred to by Roerich and his wife as the "system of living ethics") syncretizing spirituality and art. Followers of the Roerich Agni Yoga Society tell how Roerich and his wife were given the secrets of their art by Master Morya, the guru of Helena Blavatsky, who was a founder of the Theosophical Society of New York in 1875. Roerich's oil paintings were extravagant, earning him grand social connections all across England including H. G. Wells and a notable Buddhist by the name of Christmas Humphreys. His work was so profoundly affecting that they have been repeatedly remembered as "hypnotic." (His stance on the preservation of culture and art during war became so powerful over time, that when the inter-American "Treaty on the Protection of Artistic and Scientific Institutions and Historic Monuments" was penned in 1935, it was quickly and appropriately coined the "Roerich Pact." Subsequently, for the same and related endeavors, Roerich was nominated several times for the Nobel Peace Prize.)

After making an impression throughout the States with his oil paintings, Roerich was invited to the Art Institute of Chicago by its director to tour the country. He accepted, arrived by boat in 1920, and remained on US soil for three years, during which time he again made remarkable social connections. They quickly established several private societies and institutions of learning, all of which focused on deeply theosophical mysticism. Discontent to stay put, Roerich and his wife continued to travel the world, making a huge impact on every culture they visited. His legacy was so vast that even a planet was named after him (the "4426 Roerich").

But perhaps the greatest thing the Roerichs would be remembered for was their work in spiritual masteries toward the common goal of a utopian world (a "New Atlantis") with ideal societies, the philosophies and plans of which they both openly attributed to deities and entities who were not of this world via the lessons of Madame Blavatsky's theosophical *Secret Doctrine*. His teachings are still to this day imparted all over the globe, and his paintings are still on display in many countries, including the Nicholas Roerich Museum in New York, where people travel immense distances to experience the pinnacle of spiritual pilgrimage.

Wallace was overtaken by Roerich's occult wisdom traditions and enlightenment trainings. Roerich's particular devotion to mysticism was, however, increasingly focused on apocalyptic themes surrounding the coming of a new earthly order, which struck a chord with Wallace in the states at the peak of his political influence. But just before the third-term campaign with FDR, the Republican Party campaign team got their hands on Wallace's "Dear Guru" letters that he had addressed to Roerich. In them, he repeatedly and lovingly referred to this new utopia filled with a special breed of people in a mythical kingdom of order (though it was not "mythical" in Wallace's opinion). The Roerich/

Blavatsky disciple brainstormed with his crew and counterattacked with a threat to expose Republican candidate Wendell Willkie's extramarital affair, and at least for a time, the Dear Guru letters were contained. They were publicized years later by opponent Westbrook Pegler when Wallace ran for president in the 1948 election, which is why the public has access to them today.

One such letter read in part:

> Long have I been aware of the occasional fragrance from that other world which is the real world. But now I must live in the outer world and at the same time make over my mind and body to serve as fit instruments for the Lord of Justice. The changes in awareness must come as a result of steady, earnest recollect-edness. I shall strive to grow as rapidly as possible.... Yes, the Chalice is filling.[305]

This is a startling thing for a man in Wallace's position to say, considering Blavatsky's book *Secret Doctrine* defined the Lord of Justice as Osiris. Reciting the credos adopted from the seventeenth chapter of the *Book of the Dead*, Blavatsky says:

> Thus, in the seventeenth chapter...one finds Osiris saying he is *Toum* (the creative force in nature, giving form to all Beings, spirits and men), self-generated and self-existent....
>
> He is the Fire and Water, *i.e.*, Noun the primordial parent, and he created the gods out of his limbs....
>
> He is the Law of existence and Being (v. 10), the *Bennoo* (or phoenix, the bird of resurrection in Eternity), in whom night follows the day, and day the night—an allusion to the periodi-cal cycles of cosmic resurrection and human re-incarnation; for what can this mean? "The wayfarer who crosses millions of years, in the name of One, and the great green (primordial water

or Chaos) the name of the other" (v. 17), one begetting millions of years in succession, the other engulfing them, to restore them back.

He speaks of the Seven Luminous ones who follow their Lord, who confers justice....

All this is now shown to have been the source and origin of Christian dogmas. That which the Jews had from Egypt, through Moses and other initiates, was confused and distorted enough in later days; and that which the Church got from both, is still more misinterpreted. [In case you missed it, Blavatsky just said that the Osiris/Horus/Isis theology was the true origin of Christianity!...]

Yet their system is now proven identical [by this, she means identical to her beloved ideologies drawn from Egyptian theology heralding Osiris as the true god and judge] in this special department of symbology—the key, namely, to the mysteries of astronomy as connected with those of generation and conception [the mystical impregnation through sun-rays alignments we've discussed prior]—with those ideas of ancient religions, the theology of which has developed the phallic element [monuments such as the belly of Osiris and the "shaft of Ba'al/Osiris" in Washington, DC]. The Jewish system of sacred measures applied to religious symbols is the same, so far as geometrical and numerical combinations go, as those of Chaldea, Greece, and Egypt, having been adopted by the Jews during the centuries of their slavery and captivity with those nations.[306]

Her comment about the "Seven Luminous Ones" is a direct reference to the seven stars that Wallace would later speak of and under which the United States would serve following the inauguration of the New World Order and the resurrection of Osiris/Apollo.

Wallace's words, "Yes, the Chalice is filling," refer to the teachings of Roerich regarding the "Chalice of Buddha" (sometimes known as "the Blessed One"). This sacred cup was, at least metaphorically, a container of knowledge and enlightenment offered to those who exalted the upcoming messianic savior, the identity of which—when considering Roerich, Blavatsky, Freemasonry, and the context Wallace adhered to—is Osiris/Apollo. When this figure arrives, Roerich taught, the chalice would be filled. Wallace's comment exposes how close he believed this day was.

But let us not forget that FDR was no stranger to this mysticism, and he, too, had an appreciation for the wisdom Roerich and Blavatsky brought to the world. In *American Dreamer: The Life and Times of Henry A. Wallace,* authors John C. Culver and John Hyde note:

> Roosevelt, perhaps influenced by his mother's enthusiasm for Eastern art and mysticism, took a personal interest in the Roerichs' causes. Roosevelt met Roerich at least once, met with Roerich's associates on several occasions, and between 1934 and 1936 personally corresponded with Helena Roerich several times. "Mr. President," she wrote in a typical letter, "Your message was transmitted to me. I am happy that your great heart has so beautifully accepted the Message and Your lightbearing mind was free from prejudice."
>
> Indeed, it was Roosevelt who suggested to Wallace that he read an allegory by Arthur Hopkins called *The Glory Road,* which served as the basis for the coded language in the guru letters.[307]

But is it possible that FDR and Wallace were merely playacting all this out of boredom? Did they really *believe* that a messianic deliverer—one other than Christ—was on his way to earth through modernized portals based upon ancient architecture and symbolism? It seems a little outrageous and sensational, does it not?

Let's continue sorting the pieces...

Before our current dollar-bill design known as a Federal Reserve Note, we had several other currency notes worth one dollar starting from the Greenback United States Notes during the American Civil War to the Silver Certificate, the back of which had almost no design but the words "ONE DOLLAR" under "UNITED STATES OF AMERICA." It was during FDR's leadership that the Great Seal was henceforth determined to be added to our most heavily handled and traded paper currency piece. (Almost half of all the government's cash printing covers the replacement of the worn dollar bill.) The decision to add the Great Seal to the note was made in the mid-1930s, around the time the two mystics FDR and Wallace were exchanging weird inter-office memos and getting caught up in Dear Guru letter scandals.

It's also interesting that, since then, the $5, $10, $20, $50, and $100 bank notes have all been dramatically changed from their original design, but the dollar bill has not been altered since the FDR/Wallace era. This means that every single currency design in circulation through the US Treasury has been updated *except* the dollar bill (and the nearly obsolete $2 note, which is scarcely seen due to the production hiccup it faced in the 1960s and '70s and is therefore not considered worthy of updating). Rest assured, this is not a simple oversight. In fact, the citizens of our country have been asking for quite some time now when the dollar bill will receive the makeover the rest of our bills have, but budget orders have been passed to explicitly prevent it. *The Atlantic* carried the story in an article, "One Is the Loneliest Dollar Bill":

Why hasn't George Washington gotten a makeover in 50 years? The vending machine lobby, of course....

For the last several years, budgets composed by the president [Obama at the time of this article] and Congress have included specific language preventing the Treasury Department from using its funds to redesign the $1 bill....

The Federal Reserve redesigns currency largely to prevent counterfeiting, and $1 bills are not a frequent target. Would-be criminals are more often lured by larger bills, according to information provided to the Fed by the Secret Service and other law-enforcement agencies.

The vending industry has argued that the costs of redesigning its machines to recognize the new bills would be prohibitive. The National Automatic Merchandising Association estimated in 2008 that 20 million Americans use one of the nation's 7 million vending machines every work day.

Those concerns were instrumental in the Bush administration's move to block the $1 bill from a makeover in the early 2000s.[308]

According to this article, it boils down to vending machines and counterfeiting. Actually, the explanation seems quite sound, and there may not be any immediate reason to believe that there's a big conspiracy behind why the US government doesn't see the makeover of the one-dollar note a priority.

However, our good friend "Logic" would like to know: If the vending machines require redesign in order to recognize updated currency, how was that *not* an issue with the $5, $10, and $20 bills when each of them were updated? We know the machines must have been reengineered, because the new notes are readily accepted.

Immediate incoming signal from our friend "Logic" again: If a "would-be criminal" is only interested in counterfeiting the larger bills, thereby deeming the one-dollar note a nonissue for redesign, why would those same criminals even mess with the $5 bills that *have* now been given a makeover to prevent counterfeits? There is still reason for preventative measures with five dollars, certainly, but by not updating the one-dollar note, the same criminal masterminds who were evidently making a killing by printing fake five-dollar notes (which seems a bit unrealistic in the first place) now simply buy more ink and print fake one-dollar notes. If a fortune can be made by making fake money in five-dollar increments, it can be done in one-dollar increments, or it probably won't be done at all in smaller bills. So, the counterfeiting explanation has holes.

Plus, there's an issue of national pride. If there was enough reason to bring all the currency we currently have in production up to a new par in design, isn't it kind of an eyesore that we wouldn't do the same thing for our *most-handled* bank note in the name of patriotic uniformity?

The reasons given in this article for the lack of interest shown in giving the dollar bill a facelift may very well be true, despite the arguments just listed for why those reasons are deficient, but those who approached the subject of the dollar-bill design with understanding of its mystical/alchemical/metaphysical/Freemasonic/"As Above, So Below" symbolism may be tempted, as I am, to ask: *Might there be a motive behind why certain government officials and lobbying groups don't want the dollar bill design to be tampered with?* Even calling together a redesign committee means submitting the one-dollar note under the authority and scrutinizing gaze of some who *may* wish to remove, alter, or at least make a lesser focus of such esoteric insignias.

Wallace and FDR wouldn't have allowed it…and my guess is they weren't alone in that staunch position.

Although Roosevelt would be the one to set in motion the push to place the Great Seal of the United States on the US one-dollar bill, Wallace claimed it was he who first brought the seal's oracular significance to Roosevelt, believing the symbolism of the emblems carried inference to Roosevelt's New Deal, and, more important, a Masonic prophecy toward a New World Order. Wallace describes the meeting he had with Roosevelt:

> Roosevelt as he looked at the colored reproduction of the Seal was first struck with the representation of the All-Seeing Eye—a

Masonic representation of the Great Architect of the Universe. Next, he was impressed with the idea that the foundation for the new order of the ages had been laid in 1776 but that it would be completed only under the eye of the Great Architect. Roosevelt, like myself, was a 32nd-degree Mason. He suggested that the Seal be put on the dollar bill…and took the matter up with the Secretary of the Treasury [also a Freemason]…. He brought it up in a Cabinet meeting and asked James Farley [Postmaster General and a Roman Catholic] if he thought the Catholics would have any objection to the "all-seeing Eye," which he as a Mason looked on as a Masonic symbol of Deity. Farley said, "No, there would be no objection."[309]

Common sense would say that if both the obverse and reverse sides of the Great Seal were to be placed on the back of the one-dollar bill, the obverse (front) of the Seal would go on the left, since that's the natural direction our eyes wander when first observing or revisiting a meaningful image. However, FDR inverted this natural order, and the reverse side of the Seal appears on the left.

Was this a coincidence? An accident or oversight?

Not exactly. The science behind why the eyes flicker to the left focal piece of an image is steeply complicated and we do not have space here to dig into the whys and wherefores of how it all works. But in America and other English-speaking countries, the human tendency to view from left to right is intensified by the fact that we read literature from left to right in our culture. In fact, this left-to-right fact is so commonly known amidst artists in the States that even some highly paid Hollywood actors/actresses have demanded that they stand only to the right of their costars in front of the cameras during filming so that when the movie is later projected on screen they will be standing on the left and, therefore, will be the focal point of the scene. One example of this is Geoffrey Rush, who played Captain Hector Barbossa in Disney's *Pirates of the Caribbean* series. In an article called "Geoffrey Rush's Left to Right Theory" from *The Daily Star*, we read of his demand to have his monkey ever perched on his left shoulder so as not to steal the left-most position in a scene once reversed on screen, followed by the result:

> We do spot Geoffrey first and find our eyes wandering back to him. How clever Geoffrey is to come to that conclusion and use it to his advantage. He even requested that when sharing the screen with his "more attractive" cast members, he be standing on the left [the audience's left, the cast members' right] as much as possible, especially when it was Kiera Knightly.[310]

Regardless of who between FDR and Wallace first perceived the seal's Masonic prophetic significance, surviving records clearly show that it was FDR (and in his own handwriting, no less) who instructed that the obverse side of the seal be placed on the right side of the back of the dollar, and the reverse side of the seal with the pyramid and all-seeing eye be put on the left so that it would be the first thing a person saw when reading the back of the dollar from left to right. Thus, most Americans "were left with the impression that the mysterious pyramid and its heralding of a 'new order' were the foremost symbols of the American republic,"[311] notes Mitch Horowitz in *Occult America*.

It is natural to thus assume Wallace and Roosevelt also pondered the eagle on the Great Seal with its thirty-two feathers on the right wing and thirty-three on the left, representing the 32nd and 33rd degrees of Freemasonry, because in addition to being 32nd-Degree Masons, Roosevelt was the thirty-second president and Wallace the thirty-third vice president, an especially remarkable numerological coincidence given that Roosevelt was succeeded by Harry Truman, the thirty-third president of the United States and a 33rd-Degree Freemason.

Additionally, in a 1991 hardcover book on American presidents by the Smithsonian Institution (the world's largest research complex, founded by Freemason James Smithson) titled *The Smithsonian Trea-sury: Presidents*, it says on page 72 (there is that number again) that when Franklin Roosevelt died during the closing days of World War II, the responsibility "to formulate policies for a new world order" fell to Free-mason Harry Truman.[312] A painting on the same page depicts Truman standing over four other Masons—Chairman of the Joint Chiefs of Staff Admiral William D. Leahy; Army Air Force General Henry H. Arnold; Army Chief of Staff George C. Marshall; and Navy Commander in Chief Ernest J. King—a fitting diagram, given that all this is depicted on page 72 of a Smithsonian work, an intriguing choice for a statement on the vision for a New World Order given what the number seventy-two means within Masonic gnosticism regarding the seventy-two fallen angels or *kosmokrators* that currently administer the affairs of earth and who are magically bound within the US Capitol dome to bring about a New World Order.

Wallace certainly would not have chalked up such a brand of numer-ology as a coincidence. It is glaringly apparent, based on all the available literature on Wallace that he believed the Great Seal was a representa-tion of a prophecy regarding the beginning of a whole new world, with America stationed as the political head of all nations. When this was accomplished, Wallace believed, the Grand Architect of the Universe would finally be able to descend upon the earth and the all-seeing eye would symbolically be once again put in its proper place as the "apex stone" atop the unfinished pyramid. And since the unfinished pyramid is associated to finite, unfinished, or "broken" humanity, this grand placement of the missing stone would naturally symbolize a new type of perfection (or a new breed of improved people).

But this kind of prophecy doesn't simply happen on its own. Wallace penned in 1934, "It will take a more definite recognition of the Grand Architect of the Universe before the apex stone is finally fitted into place and this nation in the full strength of its power is in position to assume leadership among the nations in inaugurating 'the New Order of the

Ages.'"[313] But by "a more definite recognition," Wallace did not mean that people would need to proselytize Freemasonry agendas or hand out brochures door to door. He was referring to "definite recognition" as an item or entity holding so much authority by its mere existence that it cannot be denied; it has everyone's attention upon arrival. Interesting, then, that he also believed in a legendary item of Roerich/Bacon/Freemasonry lore that promised to accomplish exactly that.

Have you as a reader ever taken the time to look at the aprons Freemasons wear? If not, a good example would be the apron of George Washington, himself, which can easily be found online. Toward the bottom, underneath the watchful and intense "Eye of Providence," is a coffin with a skull and crossbones. Wallace and FDR, as well as many other mystics, believe there's more to this little symbol than mere death. Much like the Hitlerian ideologies of the superior Aryan race, FDR and Wallace held high hopes for a new kingdom on earth—a New Atlantis, as Sir Francis Bacon dreamed. And within this Atlantian kingdom, a replacement people rule in harmony. As Chris Pinto explains in *Zenith 2016*, we've already fulfilled most of what Sir Bacon predicted as the New Atlantis:

> Clearly, there were those who understood that the development of the new world was inspired by Bacon and his occult philosophies. It was Bacon who said, "Knowledge is power," and the pursuit of knowledge through scientific discovery has guided the success of America. If one reads *The New Atlantis*, where Bacon describes a society with tall buildings, flying machines, weapons of mass destruction, health spas, the magnification of sound, and experiments with poisons on animals for the purpose of curing human beings, it becomes readily discernable that our country has followed his blueprint from the start....
>
> Bacon's *New Atlantis* has also been called *The Land of the Rosicrucians* (see *A New Light on Bacon's New Atlantis* by Mather

Walker), and that is exactly what America has become, thanks to the secret societies. The rise of paganism in our country is no accident; it was planned from the beginning.... America's great struggle—which is indeed the wound of the whole world—is not against terrorists, communists, or liberals, but is the spiritual war against the one true God, waged in the manifestation of this ancient pagan dream.[314]

What is left of the fulfilment? All signs point to that earthly "messiah" who will come to place the capstone on the pyramid of old, establishing under his reign that "peculiar and particular purpose" otherwise known as the official New Atlantis dream. A New World Order. The New Order of the Ages. An "ancient hope that is meant to be fulfilled," as President Bush said.

And with all the focus placed on phallic Osiris monuments impregnating Isis bellies via astrological metaphysics and mysticism under the watchful eye of the resurrected Osiris/Horus/Apollo, an earthly messiah such as the one Bacon, FDR, Wallace, and other high-degree Freemasons expect will obviously not be born of a regular woman. Just like the Freemasons' beloved phoenix bird and the Master Mason ceremonies of Hiram Abiff, it will be a repeat life, regenerated—possibly—from ancient DNA, or at least represented by an object of symbolic regeneration.

What, then, do we make of this coffin/casket that keeps popping up on those Freemason aprons and all this talk about the Great Pyramid on the US Seal being the "tomb of Osiris"? And did Wallace already make this connection? It appears he did. On March 12, 1933, Wallace wrote Roerich:

Dear Guru,

I have been thinking of you holding the casket—the sacred most precious casket. And I have thought of the New Country going forward to meet the seven stars [Blavatsky's "Seven Luminous Ones" that serve under "Osiris," the Lord of Justice, and under which the US would serve at the fulfillment of the Sibyl's *novus ordo seclorum* prophecy on the Great Seal] under the sign of the three stars [possibly the three belt stars of Orion, related in myth to Osiris]. And I have thought of the admonition "Await the Stone."

We await the Stone and we welcome you again to this glorious land of destiny, clouded though it may be with strange fumbling fears. Who shall hold up the compelling vision to those who wander in darkness? In answer to this question we again welcome you. To drive out depression. To drive out fear.... And so I await your convenience prepared to do what I am to do.[315]

Investigative mythologist William Henry says this letter from Wallace made it clear that FDR, Roerich, and Wallace "were in search of this Divine Child...and his secret...Stone...[and that] they awaited...in the 'New Country' [America as the New Atlantis]."[316]

Central to the fulfillment of this scheme was the "sacred casket" that Wallace mentioned in his letter to Roerich, considered in esoteric circles to be the same as the casket or "coffin" of Osiris, and the Chintamani "Stone" or magical meteorite and holy relic believed to have been left by "missionaries" to earth from the region of the star Sirius in the constellation Canis Major ("The Great Dog"). The "Stone" supposedly held properties that could give eternal life and was believed by devotees to be the true cup of Christ. This mythology is also connected with Shambhala (which Roerich was looking for), a legendary kingdom in Tibet where supposedly enlightened immortals secretly live and who currently are guiding human evolution toward a one-world order. In fact, a portion of the Chintamani Stone was reportedly carried by Roerich as an emissary in 1935 to the founders of the now-defunct League of Nations, whose goal also was to create a one-world order. Aleister Crowley also believed in this teaching, referring to the fulfilment of it as the "New Age of Horus," with obvious connotations to a savior child heralding from the rebirth of Osiris.

Recall what was shown earlier regarding the *Annuit coeptis* and *Novus ordo seclorum* mottoes originating from Virgil's *Aeneid* and *Eclogue IV*, and even farther back to the Cumaean Sibyl. It was this same divine son—spawned of "a new breed of men sent down from heaven" when he receives "the life of gods, and sees Heroes with gods commingling"— that FDR, Wallace, and Roerich were anticipating. According to the prophecy, this is Apollo, son of Jupiter (Zeus), who returns to earth through mystical "life" given to him from the gods when the deity Saturn returns to reign over the earth in a new, pagan Golden Age. The prophecy reads:

Now the last age by Cumae's Sibyl sung
Has come and gone, and the majestic roll
Of circling centuries begins anew:
Justice returns, returns old Saturn's reign,
With a new breed of men sent down from heaven.
Only do thou, at the boy's birth in whom
The iron shall cease, the golden race arise,
Befriend him, chaste Lucina; 'tis thine own
Apollo reigns....
He shall receive the life of gods, and see
Heroes with gods commingling, and himself
Be seen of them, and with his father's worth
Reign o'er a world....
Assume thy greatness, for the time draws nigh,
Dear child of gods, great progeny of Jove [Jupiter/Zeus]!
See how it totters—the world's orbed might,
Earth, and wide ocean, and the vault profound,
All, see, enraptured of the coming time![317]

Virgil and the Cumaean Sibyl's prophecy point to fulfilment occurring when the earth and its oceans are unsteady (a time like today). Then the divine son (Horus/Apollo reincarnated or resurrected), the pagan savior, will appear when "heroes" and "gods" are joined as one. To anyone who has researched what occurred in Genesis regarding the Watchers (fallen angels) taking unto themselves the "daughters of men" to create a hybrid human/angel known as the Nephilim, this kind of "joining" can only end in invoking the wrath of God upon the earth. (I will also note at this moment that I think the human/animal hybrid chimeras that the transhumanist scientists are creating right now are also of immense concern—which I have spoken of at length in previous books and audio CD sets.)

But this is where the true clarity comes in, as I've written elsewhere.

In ancient literature, Jupiter was the Roman replacement of Yahweh as the greatest of the gods—a "counter-Yahweh." His son Apollo is a replacement of Jesus—a "counter-Jesus." This Apollo comes to rule the final New World Order, when "Justice returns, returns old Saturn's [Satan's] reign." The ancient goddess Justice, who returns Satan's reign (*Saturnia regna*, the pagan Golden Ae), was known to the Egyptians as Ma'at and to the Greeks as Themis, while to the Romans she was Lustitia. Statues and reliefs of her adorn thousands of government buildings and courts around the world, especially in Washington, DC, as familiar Lady Justice, blindfolded and holding scales and a sword. She represents the enforcement of secular law and is, according to the Sibyl's conjure, the authority who will require global compliance to the zenith of Satan's dominion concurrent with the coming of Apollo. What's more, the Bible's accuracy concerning this subject is alarming, including the idea that "pagan justice" will require surrender to a satanic system in a final world order under the rule of Jupiter's son.

In the New Testament, the identity of the god Apollo, repeat-coded in the Great Seal of the United States as the Masonic "messiah" who returns to rule the earth, is the same spirit—verified by the *same name*—

that will inhabit the political leader of the end-times New World Order. According to key Bible prophecies, the Antichrist will be the progeny or incarnation of the ancient spirit, *Apollo*. Second Thessalonians 2:3 warns: "Let no man deceive you by any means: for that day shall not come, except there come a falling away first, and that man of sin be revealed, the son of *perdition* [*Apoleia*; Apollyon, Apollo]" (emphasis added). Numerous scholarly and classical works identify "Apollyon" as the god "Apollo"—the Greek deity "of death and pestilence," and Webster's Dictionary points out that "Apollyon" was a common variant of "Apollo" throughout history.

An example of this is found in the classical play by the ancient Greek playwright Aeschylus, *The Agamemnon of Aeschylus*, in which Cassandra repeats more than once, "Apollo, thou destroyer, O Apollo, Lord of fair streets, Apollyon to me."[318] Accordingly, the name "Apollo" turns up in ancient literature with the verb *apollymi* or *apollyo* ("destroy"), and scholars, including W. R. F. Browning, believe that the apostle Paul may have identified the god Apollo as the "spirit of Antichrist" operating behind the persecuting Roman emperor, Domitian, who wanted to be recognized as "Apollo incarnate" in his day. Such identifying of Apollo with despots and "the spirit of Antichrist" is consistent even in modern history. For instance, note how Napoleon's name literally translates to "the true Apollo."

Revelation 17:8 likewise ties the coming of Antichrist with Apollo, revealing that the Beast shall ascend from the bottomless pit and enter him:

> The Beast that thou sawest was, and is not; and shall ascend out of the Bottomless Pit, and go into *perdition* [*Apolia*, Apollo]: and they that dwell on the Earth shall wonder, whose names were not written in the Book of Life from the foundation of the world, when they behold the Beast that was, and is not, and yet is. (emphasis added)

Among other things, this means that the Great Seal of the United States is a prophecy, hidden in plain sight by the founding fathers and devotees of Bacon's New Atlantis for more than two hundred years, foretelling the return of a terrifying demonic god who seizes control of earth in the new order of the ages. This supernatural entity was known and feared in ancient times by different names: Apollo, Osiris, and even farther back as Nimrod, whom Masons consider to be the father of their institution.[319]

Given all that we have established above and in preceding chapters, America at a minimum faces two futures: One is imagined by original, deep state occultists and founding fathers who dedicated America to a "Secret Destiny" under a Grey Champion the Bible calls Antichrist; and a second, more hopeful, future in which revival and spiritual stirring erupt as it has in times past, giving rise to the next Great Awakening.

But, let's be honest. While social revival may be the antidote for spiritual decline, which in turn rejuvenates believers and can alter the course of society, we are at present not yet experiencing the kind of enduring, deeply felt revival that awakens the spirit to recognize personal failings and even national depravity. While I am heartened by the similarities between the Jesus People Awakening of the '60s and the antiestablishment trust in government that played a role in the recent Trump election, as well as figures that show the next generation of Americans (Gen Z) may be the most conservative since WWII and that Millennials are less likely to commit adultery than almost any generation before, other statistical evidence suggests that, overall, our culture may be getting worse. On our present course, the US could be headed, state by state, toward disintegration.

Recently, conservative filmmaker Dinesh D'Souza sent out an e-mail notification titled: "On The Brink of Losing America Forever."[320] It reminded me of an article by the late Jamie Buckingham, award-winning columnist who, in 1990, penned the prescient feature for *Charisma & Christian Life*, "Buckle Up for the 90s," in which he forewarned:

I do not expect the tide of evil and immorality in America to ebb. We are cycling, as cultures and civilizations have always cycled, and are now on the down side of glory. Our once great and godly nation, having crested the hill of God's grace, has begun a slow descent into the abyss of self-destruction.[321]

Was Buckingham then, and D'Souza now, correct in their assessments? Is America in the final stage of empire, readying for collapse? Are we, like the Babylonian King Belshazzer, living in revelry, extravagance, unrepentant and unashamed of openly defying God while utterly oblivious to our impending doom?

Daniel chapter 5 records how, at the height of his political and military power, the ancient king Belshazzer, drunk on alcohol and in the midst of an orgiastic festival, ordered the holy vessels that "his father Nebuchadnezzar had taken out of the temple which was in Jerusalem" be brought into the festival so that he, his princes, his wives, and his concubines, might drink out of them (Daniel 5:2). While he praised his pagan gods, his actions served to symbolically shake his fist at the God of Israel by defying the King of Kings in front of a thousand of his lords.

Then something unexpected happened. A ghostly hand appeared against a wall behind the candles and wrote, *Mene, Mene, Tekel, Upharsin,* which meant: *Mene,* "God has numbered the days of your kingdom and brought it to an end"; *Tekel,* "You have been weighed and found wanting"; and *Upharsin,* "the kingdom is divided and given to the Medes and Persians."

This judgment was immediate. "In that night was Belshazzar the king of the Chaldeans slain. And Darius the Median took the kingdom, being about threescore and two years old" (Daniel 5:30–31).

The lesson of this passage is self-evident and significant.

God Himself had raised up Belshazzer's father Nebuchadnezzar, and the son should have known not to toy with the Almighty. To do so is to summon catastrophe.

Do the same rules apply today? If people who preside over legislative bodies abandon the holy things of God—His words and values—do they thereby espouse a social system that invites disaster? Is there a cause-and-effect connection between supernatural abandonment and disintegration of society?

At a time when America is considered the only true remaining superpower, our technological advances have not led to greater appreciation and thankfulness to God. We, like Belshazzar, have responded to Heaven's blessings by giving over to hedonism, rebellion, and witchcraft aimed at sacred institutions, including the presidency of the United States.

Yet something more than just cultural cycles is at play here. Supernatural forces, at war for the future of mankind and attuned to the prophecy on the Great Seal of the United States, are working toward a fantastic end game.

We would do well to consider Paul's words to the ancient city of Corinth, a city known for its pride, ostentation, homosexuality, and lasciviousness (which not only was tolerated, but consecrated through the worship of Venus). The apostle informed the saints living there: "The god of this world [Satan] hath blinded the minds of them which believe not, lest the light of the glorious gospel of Christ, who is the image of God, should shine unto them" (2 Corinthians 4:4).

Archons ruling from the air above—and governments within—Corinth had blinded the minds of most of its citizens until the latter were incapable of perceiving their horrid sinful estate and need of Jesus Christ.

It's interesting that Paul would send this warning to Corinth—a Greek prototype of America's wealth, military strength, and great philosophical society. Outwardly, one would have thought these educated gnostics were well-equipped intellectually to at least partially understand the spiritual truths and social significance contained within the words of Christ. Yet, Paul said their minds had been blinded by the god of this world. Their superior human knowledge, though impressive to fellow intelligentsia, had not protected them from the subtle influences filling the atmosphere around them. Drunk on fleshly pleasure, they became a nation in decline and didn't even know it.

It is within this supernatural realm that unregenerate minds are organized. Under demonic influence, they are orchestrated within a great evil system (or empire) described in various scriptural passages as a satanic order. In more than thirty important biblical passages, the Greek New Testament employs the term *kosmos* to describe an invisible order or government made up of unredeemed men, separated from the mind of God, who are naturally hostile to the ways of Christ and part of a resisting system or federation under the entity Saul Alinsky dedicated his *Rules for Radicals,* too—Lucifer.

At Satan's impulse, archons command this invisible, geopolitical sphere, dominating *kosmokrators* who, in turn, command spirits of lesser rank until every level of earthly government can be touched by this influence.

In Ephesians 6:12, the apostle says that it is this influence, not flesh and blood, that is at odds with the welfare of the world. The primary enemy is not the men who govern or philosophize, but the unseen forces that may puppet them. With vivid testimony to this, Satan offered to our Lord all the power and glory of the governments of this world. Satan said:

> All this power [control] will I give thee, and the glory of them [earthy cities]: for that is delivered unto me [at the Fall of man and/or during the divine council separation of the nations]: and to whomsoever I will I give it. If thou therefore wilt worship me, all shall be thine. (Luke 4:6–7)

With that claim of ownership (which Jesus did not dispute), a picture emerged of a world system out of step with God—a fallen planet under Satan's dominion, a place in need of redemption. If we could see through the veil into this invisible world, we would see a dynamic reality alive with good against evil and where legions war for control and destiny of nations.

Can Christians in America today effectively respond to this reality? Is there yet time to turn the course of our "one nation under God," or have we so exposed ourselves to the designs of a "Secret Destiny" that it's too late to undo the plans of malicious men and spirits?

When Solomon stood before God and wondered what the people of Israel should do if ever they came under the judgment of God and suffered social demise, the Almighty provided an answer, spelled out in four biblical fundamentals:

1. They were to humble themselves.
2. They were to pray.
3. They were to seek His face.
4. They were to turn from their wickedness (2 Chronicles 7:14).

If Israel would do these things, God would hear their prayers, see their repentance, forgive their sins, and heal their land.

These principles are eternal. God is unchanging. Jesus is the same yesterday, today, and forever, and the Law of Precedence suggests what He has done for others He will do for us today.

With that in mind, I have asked SkyWatch TV investigator Allie Anderson to recapitulate the verse above in a final chapter. Before that, Derek Gilbert shares his thoughts on the dangers of Dominionism and what to expect in the economy moving forward in the Trump administration, followed finally by concluding thoughts from our old friend Gary Stearman in the afterword.

chapter ten

Was a Vote for Trump a Vote for Dominionism?

By Derek Gilbert

As a group, conservative Christians are probably among the most patriotic of Americans. The phrase "For God and Country" could have been developed by a marketing group specifically to target American evangelicals. Unfortunately, for some of us, the priority is not in that order.

We also tend to be politically active. It's safe to say Donald Trump wouldn't be the forty-fifth president of the United States without the support of evangelicals. More than 80 percent of white, born-again evangelicals voted for Mr. Trump in the last election, a bigger share of that demographic than Mitt Romney, John McCain, or George W. Bush received in the three previous elections. What was it about Donald Trump's message that resonated with conservative Christians—especially white evangelicals?

Maybe the better question is why so many fewer of them voted for Hillary Clinton in 2016 than for Barack Obama in 2008 and 2012. The trend for the Democratic Party candidate over the last three elections is 24 percent–2 percent–16 percent, which suggests that racism, contrary to the loudly proclaimed beliefs of liberals throughout the downright vicious campaign, was not a key factor for evangelical Trump supporters.

If it was, we should have seen Hillary's share of the demographic go up, not down. (And Barack Obama did better with white evangelicals than John Kerry in 2004.)

The key question for American Christians, though, is not how Donald Trump got elected, but how we respond to his election going forward.

If you believe in a biblical standard of morality, you're probably concerned about the direction of the country. The sense that our nation's moral compass has gone haywire had more to do with Mrs. Clinton's embarrassing showing with Christians than anything else. Democrats don't seem to understand that pushing a pro-immigration or pro-social-justice agenda is still a losing strategy in America (at least for now). What they've done, maybe accidentally, is transform themselves into the party of those who oppose the culture that made America the most powerful and prosperous nation on earth.

In other words, since most voters *like* it here, all things considered, running on a platform of tearing the place down is maybe not the best idea. America isn't perfect, but most of us aren't ready to flip over the game board.

Back to point: Christians in America can choose from three paths going forward: One, assume we've dodged a bullet and do nothing because Donald Trump will singlehandedly roll back the forces of moral decay. Two, take advantage of the Democratic meltdown, seize control of all three branches of government, and impose biblical morality on the nation. The third path, as you might guess, is the one I support. I'll get to that later. But you're smart enough to have figured out already that it's somewhere between the other two.

Let's start with the going-back-to-sleep option. That's a non-starter. The Church has been unconscious for too long. Yet, as tempting as it might be to impose Christian morality through political action, that's simply not going to work, either. Forcing others to follow a set of rules doesn't change hearts, and the last time I checked, changing hearts—i.e., making disciples of all nations—is our prime directive. At worst, trying to create a Christian theocracy by emphasizing politics over preaching could lay the groundwork for the prophesied future global government.

It's often said that you can't legislate morality. Now, you're smart enough to know that's only partly true. Violent behavior and criminal activity—murder, rape, robbery, fraud—can, in fact, be discouraged and punished through legislation. On a deeper level, though, the statement is accurate. God's standard of righteousness goes far beyond physical actions.

For example, Jesus made it clear that lusting after someone other than your spouse isn't *like* committing adultery, it *is* adultery. In the late 1990s, just as the Internet was becoming widely used, a news program asked the question: Is it really being unfaithful to your spouse to carry on a virtual relationship with someone else? As you might guess, many of the people polled said no, it wasn't really cheating if the relationship wasn't physical. But the true answer, based on Jesus' standard, is unquestionably yes. The desire is the sin, regardless of whether the act is physically consummated.

Behavior that violates God's standard of holiness begins with rejection of His authority. Skeptics deny His existence. Others, including many professing Christians, ignore the parts of Scripture they don't like. Either way, the result is the same: People give their personal moral compass authority over that of God. It amounts to creating a new god who looks like the face in the mirror.

Behavior can be shaped by laws, but our justice system can't get to the root of immorality, sin. The heart. Rejection of the authority of God and His Word. Yet, for many American evangelicals, the answer to our nation's moral malaise is political activism—taking back Congress (check), electing the right president (check), and putting the right justices on the Supreme Court (in progress). *That's* how Christ will restore righteousness to America!

Uh, no. We won't fix sin at the ballot box.

Being a good citizen and exercising your right to vote is important. But it's not as important as training up our children in the way they should go, teaching them *why* God's Word is authoritative so they're prepared for the tsunami of skepticism and abuse they'll face when they venture out into the world. Sadly, for a nominally Christian nation, we're not prepared for the job. According to surveys conducted by the Barna Group and others, an overwhelming majority of Americans, and even self-described "born-again" Christians, don't really believe in God as He is described in the Bible. It's easier to trust the political process than the Word of God when you're not sure that the Bible is, in fact, the Word of God.

That said, there is one group that believes it takes the Word of God *very* seriously. These Christians, mainly from charismatic churches, see the election of Donald Trump as a key battle in a war for political control of the earth.

I wish that was an exaggeration. You see, the problem is that they believe God is still speaking to prophets, and sometimes the words these alleged prophets hear don't exactly jive with the Bible. Unless God contradicts Himself, taking over the world is not part of the Great Commission.

This group is part of a movement that believes in a doctrine called Dominionism, or Kingdom Now theology. In a nutshell, Dominion theology is the belief that Christians must take over the world before Jesus Christ can return to establish His Kingdom on earth.

Many American Christians have never heard of Dominion theology. When it's defined for them, they assume that Dominionists are the lunatic fringe of the body of Christ. The odds are, however, that many conservative Christians are familiar with, and agree with, doctrines that originated with this so-called fringe.

You see, Dominionism exerts a surprising amount of influence on conservative politics in America. Mainstream evangelical pastors and teachers, perhaps unknowingly, are granting Dominionists legitimacy.

And it's a doctrine that could lead well-meaning Christians to welcome the Antichrist with open arms—assuming, of course, that we're still here when A. C. takes his turn on the world stage.

— —

Jesus referred to Satan as the "father of lies." To earn that title, the adversary has displayed a remarkable talent for wooing humans to join his rebellion against God with carefully crafted half-truths.

This worked especially well to corrupt what Christ's earliest followers called the Way. After several centuries of brutal oppression failed to stop the spread of the gospel, Satan changed tactics and attacked the faith from inside. Appealing to the human desire for security (and wealth and power) was a lot more effective than persecution.

From a doctrinal standpoint, one of the worst things that ever happened to Christianity was when the emperor Constantine legalized it. Less than a century later, Christianity was the law in the Roman empire, making it a path to wealth and political influence. The fallen couldn't smash the Church from the outside, so instead it induced it to rot from within by playing on human greed and ambition.

It can be difficult to convince fellow believers that Dominion theology is a threat. As noted above, conservative American Christians are generally patriotic, often to the point of conflating God and country. Any suggestion that we're confusing patriotism with faithfulness to God can be interpreted as un-American, anti-Christian, or both.

This places Christian opponents of Dominionism in an uncomfortable position. Most of the critics warning the world about Dominion theology are atheists or liberal Christians freaking out about a literal takeover of society by an oppressive Christian theocracy. (The fact that this is about as likely as a snow cone surviving a trip through the fires of Gehenna has somehow eluded these critics.)

So Christian anti-Dominionists, for lack of a better label, find themselves in partial agreement with people who have very different views of religion, morality, culture, and just about everything else. Trust me, that's weird.

Those same liberal critics are often unable (or unwilling) to distinguish between professing Christians who are sharply divided about what Christ wants them to do. As a result, Christians critical of Dominion theology can find themselves in a theological crossfire between those who believe Christ wants His followers to take over the earth and those who believe *all* Christians want to take over the earth.

— —

Drilling down into Dominion theology to establish clearly defined beliefs is difficult. There is no central authority issuing statements of doctrine and no formal hierarchy, so identifying exactly what Dominionists believe, to quote Hal Lindsey, is like trying to nail custard to the wall. In its mildest form, Dominionism is not incompatible with orthodox Christianity. It is possible to believe that salvation is by grace through faith in Jesus Christ, while at the same time believing that Christians should work for political power so we can put government to work extending the Kingdom of God.

Generally speaking, Dominionism holds that Christians, under the direction of modern-day apostles and prophets, will be the government of God on earth until His enemies, including death, are defeated.

The doctrines of Dominionists are hard to pin down because they believe God speaks to a new group of prophets raised up for the coming supernatural showdown with the forces of evil. The revelations coming from these prophets are interpreted and administered by a new generation of apostles, who have the authority of their first-century forebearers.

Think about that for a minute. The apostles wrote most of the New Testament—everything we know about the life, miracles, and teachings of Jesus Christ. And a new group has emerged since Y2K claiming the same authority over Christian doctrine as Peter, Paul, James, and John!

The basic premise of Dominion theology is that humans lost dominion over earth when the devil deceived Adam in the Garden of Eden. Our mission is to recover that lost dominion. The strategy that's been laid out for the end-times Church is to take back the seven "mountains" or "kingdoms" of society—social institutions like religion, government, family, education, business, the media, etc.

This Seven Mountains Mandate, or Seven Mountains Prophecy in some circles, is based on a dream shared in 1975 by the founders of two youth ministries that are still active and prominent today. This dream has been turned into the strategy for world domination. And while there's no doubt the world would be a better place if genuine Christians held sway over, say, media or the education system, the concept isn't based on Scripture.

What Dominionists have done is extended the mandate given to Adam in Genesis 1:28 from dominion over "the fish of the sea and over the birds of the sky and over every living thing that moves on the earth"—the animal kingdom—to dominion over *non-believing humans*.

Dominionist eschatology teaches that victory over the kingdoms of this world will be achieved by a select group of spiritually advanced "overcomers" with supernatural power. Some in the movement teach that this group will literally be the incarnate Christ—the "Many-Membered Man Child," a reference to Revelation 12.

> And there appeared a great wonder in heaven; a woman clothed with the sun, and the moon under her feet, and upon her head a crown of twelve stars: …And she brought forth a man child, who was to rule all nations with a rod of iron.[322]

These "overcomers" are called by various names: New Breed, Elijah Generation, Phinehas Priesthood, Forerunners, and others. Their successful war against those who reject the authority of God implies that they'll have control over the police and military. Only when the enemies of God have been defeated—made "a footstool" under Jesus' feet—can Christ return and reign on earth.

This view of eschatology has problems. We'll deal with them briefly; our purpose here is not to present a thorough critique of Dominion theology, but to show that it's an attractive deception to well-meaning American Christians who, concerned about the moral decay of our nation, turn to political action as their primary response.

Anger at the liberals' successful strategy of pushing their social agenda through the courts and alarm at the spread of violent Islam is powerful motivation for conservative Christians to get behind a political candidate who claims to share their views. It's no surprise that four out of five white evangelicals voted for Donald Trump. And the promise of a victorious Church that destroys the forces of evil is far more appealing than dispensational premillennial eschatology, which sees a steady decline in morality and godliness until the Antichrist arrives to establish his global government and persecute the faithful remnant.

Who in their right mind looks forward to their children or grandchildren suffering through that kind of a hellish world?

In contrast, Dominion theology offers a different vision of the end times—a "victorious eschatology" in which the Church isn't persecuted, it prospers, taking and holding ground from the forces of evil until they've been made a footstool beneath Jesus' feet—because He's stuck in Heaven until we do.

Again, I wish that was an exaggeration. But there are teachers promoting exactly that view of Psalm 110:1 ("The LORD says to my Lord: 'Sit at my right hand, until I make your enemies your footstool'"). This doctrine makes the Great Commission—making disciples, winning souls, getting people saved, however you want to phrase it—of secondary importance to literally taking over the world.

There are a couple of problems with that view. First, you may have noticed the capital "I" in that sentence: "until *I* make your enemies your footstool."

That "I" is Yahweh. God the Father. Not you, me, or anyone else in the Body of Christ. Oh, He works *through* us, but to make the timing of Christ's return entirely dependent on our actions is very close to heresy. And, as I mentioned earlier, it's hard to see how conquering the world pleases God, much less triggers the return of Christ, unless world dominion is achieved by the sudden, voluntary surrender of billions of new Christian converts.

It's safe to say that's highly unlikely.

The second problem is that this view of Psalm 110 ignores the fact that the enemies of God are *already* under Christ's feet.

> 19 [A]nd what is the immeasurable greatness of his power toward us who believe, according to the working of his great might
> 20 that he worked in Christ when he raised him from the dead and seated him at his right hand in the heavenly places,
> 21 far above all rule and authority and power and dominion, and above every name that is named, not only in this age but also in the one to come.
> 22 And he put all things under his feet and gave him as head over all things to the church,
> 23 which is his body, the fullness of him who fills all in all.[323]

> 7 You made him for a little while lower than the angels;
> you have crowned him with glory and honor,
> 8 putting everything in subjection under his feet.[324]

[24] Then comes the end, when he delivers the kingdom to God the Father after destroying every rule and every authority and power.

[25] For he must reign until he has put all his enemies under his feet.

[26] The last enemy to be destroyed is death.

[27] For "God has put all things in subjection under his feet."[325]

Worse, Dominionism ignores a good bit of Bible prophecy. If the Church emerges at the end of history as the big winner through its own strength, where do the Antichrist, the False Prophet, Gog of Magog, and the Battle of Armageddon fit into the timeline? Well, they don't. Somehow, Christians are supposed to take over the media, Hollywood, government schools, the global banking system, and the military of every nation on earth *not* willing to be ruled by a government of self-appointed apostles and prophets.

Now, I have no doubt that this could happen if God willed it to be so. But that's not what He told us is coming in the Bible.

In other words, the "victorious eschatology" of Dominionism requires a preterist, or at least partial preterist, view of Bible prophecy. That means explaining away all (or most) end-times prophecies in the Bible as already fulfilled rather than seeing them as future events. For example, the Antichrist may be identified as the Roman emperor Nero and the war of Gog and Magog described in Ezekiel 38 might have been the First Crusade.

This is a minority view among Christians, but then so is the belief in a premillennial, pretribulation rapture. Most Christians belong to denominations that are amillennial, meaning they don't believe Jesus will return to earth to rule for one thousand years. A preterist view is not as problematic for them as for those of us who believe Daniel, Ezekiel, Paul, Jesus, John, *et al.*, were talking about events that haven't happened yet.

But Dominionist eschatology also requires belief in a postmillennial return of Jesus, meaning that His return comes *after* Satan is bound in chains for a thousand years and then let loose. This is in direct contradiction of Revelation 20:4, which tells us that Christ reigns for a thousand years *before* Satan is released.

Why do Dominionists teach this? Because they need a timeline wherein Christians defeat the enemies of God while Jesus is still in Heaven. Without that, there's no rationale for teaching that we must conquer the world for Christ.

Not that there is one, anyway. Did Jesus ever command His followers to go forth and form political action committees? No, of course not.

Now, that's not to say that Christians should avoid politics. It's just a reminder that Jesus never told His followers that they should make world domination part of the plan. If it had been, He could have done it two thousand years ago and saved humanity a world of heartache and pain.

More to the point: If taking dominion of the earth by the followers of Christ is required before Jesus can return and establish His Kingdom here, then why did He die on the cross? Wasn't that enough to defeat sin and death?

The implication of Dominion theology is *no it wasn't*. Our victory over the Seven Mountains of Culture is required because Jesus can't leave the right hand of the Father until we take those hills. That is a slippery theological slope.

Here's the thing: The challenge put to us Christians was not to create the future we want, but to fulfill the Great Commission as the future unfolds. We are to make disciples of all nations, and that means transforming lives by changing one heart at a time, *not* by literally sticking the Christian flag in the nations themselves, as some Dominionist teachers assert. We are to preach the gospel and show the world what the love of Christ looks like. Imposing biblical standards on unbelievers is an awful lot like totalitarianism.

No, it *is* totalitarianism. At least one prominent New Apostle pub-licly admitted it, but he justified it as necessary until unbelievers learn how to behave under the new Christian regime.

Even if we believe it would be for their own good, think on this: If God saw fit to give all of us free will, which means the freedom to make stupid choices, what gives us the right to deny other humans that free-dom (other than preventing people from harming themselves or others)?

Dominion theology is a lure to draw Christians off task. It diverts our energy away from bringing converts into the Kingdom, which Jesus told us was not of this world, and channels it into an effort to build the Kingdom of God on earth. That's closer to the New Age than the gospel.

So, back to my original point: Where do American Christians go from here? Our calling is not to build a theocracy, but we can't withdraw from society and the political process, either. There are two sure paths to totalitarianism: One is to impose our standards on unbelievers through force. The other is to abandon the field to the Enemy and let the rebel-lious small-G gods and their human dupes run the planet. Either choice is unacceptable.

Here's an old-fashioned idea: Let's get back to our original mission. Live our faith and share the hope we have in Christ with our families, friends, colleagues, and coworkers. Vote for candidates who best rep-resent biblical ideals, but let's stop fooling ourselves into believing that a political party will bring Christian values back to America. The two major parties won't do it, and no so-called third party will ever have the clout to do it. The system is rigged. The proof is the continued oppo-sition of establishment Republicans to the president—the ones who openly said they'd vote for Hillary Clinton over Donald Trump.

Make no mistake: This isn't surrender, a despondent Christian throwing in the towel and giving up the fight. No, it's time for bold action—a passionate and prolonged response to the opportunity that's dropped into our laps last November. Yes, make your voice known. Yes, push back against the pagan forces of progressivism. But our focus needs to be on witnessing, changing hearts so that future generations reject the debauched moral standards of the rebel gods—without the need for a veto-proof majority in the Senate.

Too many of us—this author included—have been suckered into playing the wrong game. Americans love competition, and American politics is packaged by our media like sports entertainment. The news channels give us play-by-play and color commentary, interviewing the players, breaking down game film, and updating the score with every new poll.

Except that the game is fixed. Politics isn't football or basketball; it's pro wrestling. The red team and blue team go at it hammer and tongs in front of the cameras, then take turns buying drinks when the lights are off.

What evangelicals have in Donald Trump is not a political savior, but a man fighting a valiant holding action against a determined and ruthless enemy. The influence of his administration on federal regulations and the Supreme Court, especially if Trump wins a second term, buys conservative Christians precious time by slowing the pace of change on our culture.

But the Deep State hasn't given up trying to drive President Trump out of the White House. His election was so improbable that it's hard not to see the hand of God in it. But even assuming President Trump wins a second term, the political class will have a hand-picked candidate back in the Oval Office someday. And then the reprieve granted by the election of Donald Trump will end.

Christians must take advantage of this time to get busy doing what we were called to do—preach the gospel! Share the hope we have in Christ! If there is to be a revival, another Great Awakening in our lifetimes, it's not going to be through acts of Congress, executive orders, or rulings by the Supreme Court. It will be through changed hearts and renewed minds.

Imposing rules from the top down only works if the fear of disobedience outweighs the potential reward. America has been a relatively law-abiding, peaceful nation for most of its history—not through the power of government, but because most of us believe that someday our actions will be judged by the omnipotent, omniscient, and omnipresent Creator of all things. Without the fear of the Lord, which the Bible tells us is the beginning of wisdom, the only style of government that keeps order is a dictatorship.

That would still be true if the dictator was a Christian trying to impose biblical values on a nation of pagans. The decay in our culture is the result of people losing the fear of God. Yet the Enemy has convinced too many Christians that righteousness can be restored through a majority of electoral votes. And for a small but politically active minority, the goal of saving the world by taking it over has become a false gospel.

At best, Dominion theology is a distraction from our true purpose. At a minimum, it's unbiblical, bordering on heresy. At worst, it's a trap that will deceive Christians into building the foundation for the kingdom of the Antichrist. And if the faithful are still on earth when he arrives, it could be the deception that lures well-meaning believers into welcoming the Beast with open arms.

chapter eleven

Trumponomics—

Or, Why Donald J. Trump Will Not Save Your Bacon

By Derek Gilbert

Introduction

Donald Trump stirred up the emotions of many Americans during the 2016 presidential campaign. At first, the media treated his campaign as a great sideshow, an entertaining diversion from an otherwise uninspiring slate of candidates. (Please—another Clinton or Bush was the best we could come up with?) Reporters and editors are always hungry for headlines in the Internet age. News isn't driven by the print deadlines of big daily newspapers or the evening newscasts on ABC, CBS, and NBC. Thanks to social media, the time to break a story is always *now*, and citizen journalists can have as much impact on an election as "credentialed" reporters. Woodward and Bernstein have been made obsolete by Drudge and Assange.

The major media probably didn't take Donald Trump seriously in the early going. To be honest, I assumed—especially after his unorthodox speech to announce his candidacy—that Trump was campaigning just to get ratings for his reality show, *The Apprentice*. As the campaign progressed, however, it became obvious that he was serious about trying to win. And that's when the tone of the media's coverage of Donald

Trump shifted from "amused" to "offended." How dare this obnoxious megalomaniac challenge the accepted order?

But Donald Trump is a genius when it comes to tapping into the emotions of Middle America. And, from our perch in Flyoverland, it's clear that the American heartland is throw-the-bums-out furious with the political class in Washington, DC.

That feeling has been growing for a long time. In 2006, local officials with the Republican and Democratic parties admitted to me privately (during commercial breaks, with the microphones for my weekday afternoon radio talk show turned off) that their national leadership had lost touch with Main Street America.

This became painfully obvious after the financial crisis that began in 2006. (Historians say the Great Recession began in December 2007, but I can tell you from personal experience that the real estate bubble started to collapse eighteen months earlier.) Bailouts of Wall Street banks were very unpopular, but they were forced on the American public anyway. It was infuriating to realize that bankers had blown the life savings of hard-working Americans by gambling on shady financial instruments that even the chairman of the Federal Reserve Bank didn't understand. It was doubly infuriating when elected officials, instead of throwing the guilty parties in prison, threw them nearly $13 trillion more extracted from American taxpayers.

Yes, $13 *trillion*. In 2010, a team from Bloomberg News found that the "$700 billion [of the Toxic Asset Relief Program, or TARP] is just a small part of a much larger pool of money that has gone into propping up our nation's financial system. And most of that taxpayer money hasn't had much public scrutiny at all." The actual amount "lent, spent, or guaranteed" to prop up the banks was about $12.8 trillion.[326]

That, dear reader, was about 88 percent of the Gross Domestic Product of the United States in 2009, and more than four times greater than the entire federal budget that year. Is it any wonder Americans were ticked off?

The Tea Party tried to turn that frustration into a political movement. For a number of reasons, that movement fizzled after a brief burst of energy in 2010. Analyzing the whys and wherefores of the Tea Party's collapse is outside the scope of this chapter, but it was clear by 2016 that the movement had lost focus. The emotion was still there, though, and Trump harnessed it into a coalition that carried him to victory.

It's not a surprise, looking back. Washington elites followed the bank bailouts with government takeovers of insurance giant AIG, General Motors, and Chrysler, moves that were also opposed by most Americans. And then came the infamous bill that had to be passed so we could find out what was in it, according to then Speaker of the House Nancy Pelosi, the Affordable Care Act, better known as Obamacare. Over the opposition of a majority of voters, the biggest boondoggle in American history was pushed through Congress. Americans are only now, seven years after it passed, learning what happens when the government takes over a product or service that's better handled by the private sector. To give just one example, the system is so convoluted and unprofitable that most people in our home state of Missouri can buy health insurance from only one company, and twenty-five counties will be without Obamacare options altogether in 2018.

One insurance professional told me that while Obamacare has made it possible for many people who were previously uninsured to obtain coverage, it's also forced almost as many people out of the market who couldn't afford the cost of the new government-designed health plans. In our case, a plan similar to the one I had while working in the corporate world would have cost about $26,000 in premiums and deductibles before it paid out a dime. And that's for two relatively healthy nonsmokers with no preexisting conditions.

Our crime, of course, is being over 50 and earning a middle-class income. Being punished by your government for working hard is infuriating, especially when this happens while we're told we need to open our borders and extend government services to immigrants from nations with no shared history, culture, religion, or values. In the old days, the word for that was "invasion." (Ask Native Americans how well an open-borders immigration policy worked for them.)

The bottom line is this: Donald Trump has his flaws, but he recognized and capitalized on a development that's shaken the world's political class to its core: A large segment of the American public woke up and discovered that they're being marginalized in the country for which their ancestors bled and died.

So what did Donald Trump promise that resonated with voters? Most were aware of the "great, great wall" he said he'd build. But for most of us, the government's economic policies will have a more personal impact.

Lower taxes

Like Ronald Reagin in 1980, President Trump proposed a large tax cut to stimulate the economy. The outline of his plan, which underwent some revision during the campaign, was posted as a PDF document to the president's website.

To begin with, the plan would purportedly eliminate income taxes for seventy-three million American households. It then reduces both the number of income brackets and the rates at which those brackets are taxed, from the current seven-bracket system, taxed at 10 percent, 15 percent, 25 percent, 28 percent, 33 percent, 35 percent, and 39.6 percent, to three brackets taxed at 10 percent, 20 percent, and 25 percent. Married filers earning $50,000 or less would pay no income tax, and those within the 10 percent bracket (marrieds earning $50,001 through $100,000) would keep most of their current deductions.[327]

In addition, the alternative minimum and estate taxes would be eliminated, and the corporate tax rate would be slashed from 35 percent to 15 percent. Analysts at the Tax Policy Center calculated that these changes would result in $6.2 trillion in tax cuts over the next ten years. In Trump-speak, that's *yuge*! But who really benefits? And will the president's proposed changes ever become a reality?

The bigger question is whether the Trump tax cuts, assuming he can push them through Congress, will have the same impact as Reagan's. The top tax bracket when President Reagan took office was 70 percent. That confiscatory rate was no doubt politically popular. It's always easy to sell the public on a "soak-the-rich" policy, but the actual result is to drive wealth out of the country and/or into complicated tax shelters that hide income from the Internal Revenue Service.

Then there is the net effect of high taxes on corporate earnings. Taxes are a cost of doing business. When government increases that cost by raising tax rates, do businesses simply accept a lower profit margin? No, they do not. They raise prices on goods and services to generate extra income to cover the extra cost of the new tax rate. So a tax increase for ABC Widget Corp. results in a higher price per widget, which raises the cost of machines built with ABC widgets.

In turn, things produced by the machines built with ABC widgets—say, tin cans—now cost more. So a company that produces canned corn has a higher cost per can because of the increased tax on ABC Widget. It's likely that taxes on the companies that produced the canning machines, the tin, and the canning company increased, too, with corresponding price increases on their products.

Now, who really pays for this new "corporate tax?" YOU. When you buy a can of corn or a washing machine or a new car, *you* pay the tax *plus* a markup equal to the profit margin each company in the chain of production needs to make to stay in business.

Of course, you never hear that from politicians campaigning against evil, greedy corporations. Voters angry at preferential treatment for the wealthy are happy to support politicians who promise them free stuff paid for by corporate fat cats, blissfully ignorant of the fact that those corporate taxes pass through right back to them. No wonder American families feel like trying to get ahead financially is a never-ending race on a treadmill.

Recognizing this vicious cycle, President Trump has proposed to end the benefit to corporations for hiding wealth offshore with "a one-time deemed repatriation of corporate cash held overseas at a significantly discounted 10 percent tax rate, followed by an end to the deferral of taxes on corporate income earned abroad."[328] Presumably, keeping money in America where it's spent on wages and reinvested in business would strengthen the economy, thus generating more tax revenue for the government by expanding the tax base.

In theory, then, tax cuts should benefit consumers. We win if our income taxes are cut, and we win when so-called corporate taxes are cut. Will it work? The example of the Reagan years seems to indicate that it will.

Reagan's plan lowered the rate on the top income tax bracket from 70 percent to 28 percent and dropped the corporate tax rate from 48 percent to 34 percent. At the same time, President Reagan promised to shrink the government to cut spending, and to fight inflation by reducing the amount of money in circulation. Even though President Reagan backed off his steep income tax cuts somewhat, it was apparently effective. After years of stagflation—economic contraction coupled with double-digit inflation, something traditional economic theory says can't possibly happen—the economy began moving again.

However, it isn't clear whether the tax cuts or the monetary policy of the Federal Reserve Bank were responsible for jolting the economy back to life. Fed chair Paul Volcker had begun raising the fed funds rate aggressively in October of 1979 to fight inflation, ultimately pushing the rate up to 20 percent in 1981. It worked. Inflation, which had soared to 13.3 percent in 1979, was tamed, but at the cost of economic growth. Unemployment spiked to 10.8 percent, the worst stretch of unemployment in America until the fiscal crisis hit in 2009.

Volcker's economic shock treatment burned inflation out of the economy by making it too expensive to borrow money. Then, when rates were lowered in 1982— first to 15.0 percent and then 8.5 percent in December—it was like a jolt of adrenaline to the business community. The fed funds rate hasn't been above 9.75 percent since, except for six months in 1984 when it was pushed back to 11.75 percent.

Since 2007, however, the rate has been below 5.0 percent, and since mid-2008, it's been below 2.0 percent. In December of 2008, at the height of the subprime mortgage crisis, Fed chair Ben Bernanke dropped the fed funds rate to 0.25 percent to keep the economy from locking up. A rate that low is essentially zero in terms of real borrowing cost. And the rate stayed there for seven years with no measurable effect on the economy.

Oh, bankers did great. Wall Street enjoyed access to money it could borrow for free. But the point of that rate was to encourage banks to lend money to businesses and consumers, to stimulate economic activity in Flyoverland. Somehow, though, that money never made it to Main Street. This was also partly due to policy changes during the Reagan years.

Regulations on business were eased by the Reagan administration. While this lowered the cost of business for many American companies, some of those restrictions had been placed on banks after the Great Depression. Removing them gave banks the freedom to speculate on risky real estate deals. That contributed to the savings & loan crisis of 1989, a mess that killed half the nation's S&Ls and cost American taxpayers $132 billion to clean up.[329] (And twenty years later, bank speculation in risky investments backed by subprime mortgages touched off the Great Recession. We never learn, do we?)

So, the $64 trillion question is this: Are there enough bullets in Donald Trump's economic gun to make America great again? The tax rates can't be cut as deeply as they were during the Reagan years because they aren't as high. The Federal Reserve hasn't been able to stimulate borrowing and investment with a fed funds rate that was effectively zero for seven years.

But are the numbers telling us a true story?

America First

A key message of the Trump campaign was "America First." This simple phrase was reflected in Trump's public stance on everything from trade to border security. Of course, this horrified the major media, which is dominated by globalists.

In a broader sense, America First is a rejection of US economic policy, which in recent years has favored Wall Street over Main Street. Why? Because Wall Street doesn't really care what happens on Main Street anymore.

As I argued in the chapter I wrote for *When Once We Were a Nation*, American banks appear to be repeating a pattern established by British banks in the second half of the nineteenth century: Bankers are no longer interested in wealth creation. Their business is wealth manipulation:

Traditional banking—holding deposits and making loans—is simply not where the largest banks put their efforts anymore. Loans to businesses are just 11.5 percent of the balance sheets of Wall Street's Big Six (Bank of America, JPMorgan Chase, Wells Fargo, Citi, Morgan Stanley, and Goldman Sachs), and the federal government, through Fannie Mae and Freddie Mac, now own or guarantee 90 percent of new home mortgages. The local branch of BoA, Citi, JPMC, or Citi is there mainly to get the corporate office access to FDIC deposit insurance and the Federal Reserve Bank's "discount window," its program of low-interest loans to commercial banks.

Speculation is the name of the game. That's where real money is made. The value of the global market for financial derivatives is estimated at $553 trillion, and the five biggest Wall Street banks—those listed above, minus Wells Fargo—hold more than 90 percent of all derivatives contracts.

To give you an idea of how much money that is, the annual Gross Domestic Product of the United States is about $17 trillion. Global GDP in 2014 was estimated at $77 trillion.

Let that sink in. The biggest banks in America, which created an economic disaster that the American government has so far committed $12.8 trillion to delay, are holding contracts on speculative investments *worth six and a half times more than the annual economic output of the entire planet.*

How has this change in banking affected Main Street? It's been awesome! For bankers.

The Dow Jones Industrial Average has surged by nearly 70 percent since 2012. The S&P 500 is up more than 80 percent over the same period. But while indicators for Wall Street look great, real wages for American families have been flat since 1970. The bottom 90 percent of wage earners have seen their income decline about 1 percent.

The top 0.1 percent—about 150,000 of the wealthiest Americans—have enjoyed a 385 percent increase over the same period.[330]

Now, if President Trump insists that Wall Street get behind his plan to create jobs on Main Street, how much incentive do they have to change to go along? It appears they have about 553 trillion reasons not to.

Similarly, corporations have a lot less vested in the success of the United States economy now than they did during the Reagan years—or, more accurately, the success of manufacturing in the U.S.

It's not just money that's been moved offshore. Manufacturing and, in some cases (IT support, for example), services have been moved overseas where labor costs are lower. This offers a competitive advantage for corporations over their competitors, but communities can suffer. Unemployed people on Main Street can no longer buy what corporations are selling.

Times have changed. The American public is simply not as involved in the production of goods as it was twenty-five or fifty years go. The value of American citizens to the economy today is as consumers, a market for products. While manufacturing has maintained a steady share of real GDP since 1960, around 12 percent, the percentage of American workers in manufacturing jobs has dropped from nearly 25 percent in 1960 to less than 10 percent today.[331] So how have American consumers managed to maintain a 70 percent share of GDP as they've transitioned from manufacturing jobs to working as waiters? By borrowing more than we can pay off. Easy credit has allowed Americans to maintain an illusion of prosperity by selling ourselves into debt slavery through easily obtainable credit cards, student loans, and even subprime auto loans.

Think about that—banks have been lending money to people who shouldn't qualify for credit to inflate auto sales and generate more revenue streams for the bankers. Then, as with subprime mortgages in the 2000s, those dicey loans are packaged into financial instruments and sold to other bankers as investments!

Who would buy such so-called securities? Investors willing to gamble on high-risk investments for a high rate of return in an era of unnaturally low interest rates. And what happens when American car buyers start defaulting on those loans? Dominoes fall. See the subprime mortgage crisis of 2008–09 for a template of what to expect.

There are ominous signs that this is already happening. At this writing in the spring of 2017, US auto loan delinquencies have risen to their highest levels since just before the economic crisis in 2007.[332] In other words, events already in motion may torpedo any plans President Trump has for the American economy.

Nationalism

Donald Trump's patriotic streak may be genuine. And there is a place for it, especially when it comes to controlling our borders to keep out criminals, drug gangs, and potential terrorists. When it comes to jobs, however, the main benefit of an America First policy may be to reduce the number of illegal aliens in the workplace. It's estimated that about eight million illegals are in the American workforce, a number that's been stable since 2009. That's about 5 percent of the US civilian workforce.

As of this writing, the official unemployment rate in the U.S. was 4.4 percent, a ten-year low. The president's supporters have cheered the Trump Effect on the economy, and there is a sense of confidence that's been lacking since the subprime mortgage bubble collapsed ten years ago. However, it is the view of this author that the low unemployment rate is nothing more than evidence of the old saying, "Figures don't lie but liars can figure."

The method of calculating unemployment has changed since the Reagan era. In 1994, the Bureau of Labor Statistics redefined workers who have been out of work for more than a year as long-term "discouraged" workers—people who've given up trying to find a job—and those non-working people simply aren't counted as unemployed.

In fact, the headline number given to the press by the BLS doesn't include the unemployed who actively looked for work within the last year, but not within the last four weeks. Those "discouraged" workers are figured into the broader U-6 unemployment rate (which is 8.1 percent at this writing),[333] which typically runs about four or five percentage points higher than the official U-3 number. But that's not the one the press puts in the headlines.

It's hard to get a handle on how many people really fit the description of "long-term discouraged" workers, but we can accurately track the drop in the labor-force participation rate. Fifty years ago, the percentage of American adults in the workforce was just below 60 percent. That number began rising in 1969 and climbed steadily for the next thirty years. After peaking in 2000 at 67.3 percent and hitting a plateau around 66 percent for about a decade, labor-force participation began dropping in 2008 as the global financial crisis picked up momentum.

Even though the recovery from the Great Recession officially began in mid-2009, and the unemployment rate began dropping in the spring of 2010, the labor-force participation rate continued to fall. As of this writing, it is 62.9 percent, a number it first hit in April, 2014, which marked a forty-year low.[334]

What kind of economic recovery results in fewer people working?

Now, back to the issue of economic nationalism: This is an over-simplification, but in terms of raw numbers, removing undocumented workers from the workplace would theoretically eliminate unemployment overnight.

That will never happen, of course. Employers using undocumented workers may be doing so to avoid government-mandated costs associated with employees, health insurance being just one of them. Undocumented workers are also less likely to complain about things like working conditions, overtime, and so on.

People who reacted with horror to Donald Trump's statements about Mexico during the campaign are missing an important aspect of the president's approach to getting things done. He's a dealmaker. He didn't succeed in business by letting his adversaries know what he'd settle for with his first offer. Will Trump repatriate all eleven million unauthorized immigrants in the US? Will he insist that Mexico pay for the wall? Probably not. But by setting improbable goals as the bars against which deals are ultimately measured, he's likely to get a lot more than if he'd revealed what he'd settle for, much less kept his promises to what was politically correct. He's more likely to get what he wants and people on the other side of the table can claim victory for pushing him back from his "demands." That's what winning looks like.

The problem is that many American jobs lost over the last fifty years didn't go to undocumented workers. Instead, they've gone to places with cheaper labor, outsourced to places like Mexico and China. But a lot of those jobs have simply disappeared, taken over by computers and robots. That's the downside of automation—manufacturers don't need to send jobs overseas when Robbie the Robot can do the job here. While President Trump deserves credit for negotiating high-profile deals with manufacturers, notably Ford and Carrier, to bring jobs from foreign factories back to the US, they may be short-term victories. Manufacturers won't pay humans to do work that can be automated—at least until the government eliminates the cost benefit of robots by requiring companies to provide health insurance to "synthetic persons."

Kidding aside, watch closely what happens to the transportation industry in the next ten years. About 70 percent of the nation's freight by weight moves by truck. The industry employs about 3.5 million professional drivers who earn an average of $40,000–$45,000 a year. Drivers for a company like Walmart can earn upwards of $70,000 annually.[335]

Now, you didn't think all the news we've seen about self-driving vehicles lately is really about lowering costs for Uber and Lyft, did you? About $140 billion, give or take, is a lot of money spent on humans who can only drive eleven hours a day. Watch for over-the-road truckers to lose jobs to Otto Pilot soon. (Seriously, it's coming. In a first-of-its-kind, a truckload of beer was delivered from Fort Collins to Colorado Springs by Otto, an Uber startup, in the fall of 2016.)

In short, President Trump's plan to bring jobs back to the US may be hamstrung by technology. When artificial intelligence and robotics reach a point in the not-too-distant future when they can efficiently perform most of the jobs that required skilled human labor a generation ago, what will be left for us? Other than writing computer code, that is—and that's only until the AIs can do that, too.

Budget Cuts

President Trump's recently proposed budget immediately generated an explosion of rage from his opponents. It was described as "cruel," "extreme," "dead on arrival," and "a blueprint for a banana republic-style military dictatorship."

Wow! Who knew?

Well, that was no surprise. Politicians other than Donald Trump also know you don't show your hand as soon as you pick up your cards.

Still, the vitriol that greeted the president's budget from within the Republican Party, notably senators John McCain and Lindsay Graham, was unusual. Or it would be if this pattern hadn't become familiar over the last two years.

So what is the president's plan and how will it affect you and me? First of all, let's start by acknowledging that his budget will not become law. No budget put forward by a president becomes law in its original form. By the time Congress is done slicing and splicing, it will look very different.

In short, his proposed $4.1 trillion budget cuts from a number of entitlement and education programs while adding substantially to the military and border security, including the president's wall along the border with Mexico. Even Republicans in Congress get hives thinking about the backlash from voters resulting from cuts to Medicaid and SNAP (formerly food stamps), while the intelligentsia rant that the proposed elimination of funding for the National Endowment for the Arts, the National Endowment for the Humanities, and the Corporation for Public Broadcasting just prove what a troglodyte the president (and by extension, anyone who supported him) truly is.

Yes. Well. Somebody has to pay for all those programs that pay thinkers to think, and that's been a bit of a problem for us Americans over the last forty years. Federal budget deficits were relatively small until 1976. When the Reagan administration took over in 1981, it kicked deficit spending up a notch. Thanks to easy credit and an economy that boomed by confusing debt with wealth, the US actually ran budget surpluses from 1998 through 2001. But 9/11 gave politicians the cover needed to justify huge deficits again, this time to fight the global war on terror. And saving the too-big-too-fail banks responsible for crashing the economic bus in 2007 drove deficits into the Twilight Zone, exceeding

$1 trillion a year during Barack Obama's first term. So as of this writing, the official national debt of the United States is closing in on $20 trillion.

The truly frightening thing about the federal debt is that those numbers are calculated with accounting methods that would probably land you and me in prison. Former US Comptroller General David M. Walker says the nation's actual debt, figured with Generally Accepted Accounting Principles (GAAP), is much higher:

> If you end up adding to that $18.5 trillion the unfunded civilian and military pensions and retiree healthcare, the additional underfunding for Social Security, the additional underfunding for Medicare, various commitments and contingencies that the federal government has, the real number is about $65 trillion rather than $18 trillion, and it's growing automatically absent reforms.[336]

That $65 trillion is probably closer to $70 trillion now and growing. It's a ticking time bomb that can't be ignored much longer. As with the looming implosion of auto loan debt, possibly followed soon after by student loan debt, at some point the federal debt must be addressed. The problem is that a nation where citizens can vote themselves entitlements is not likely to show the self-control necessary to get out from under such a burden.

Here's the other thing to bear in mind when sifting through the hysteria: President Trump's budget doesn't actually reduce spending. It increases federal spending by 3.5 percent a year for the next ten years. The proposed cuts are just a small slice of the budget pie Trump hopes to bake. Sixty-five percent of the $49 trillion in the proposed budget goes to four programs: Interest on the debt, Social Security, Medicare, and Medicaid (which doesn't actually get cut in the budget; it would just grow at a slower rate than previously projected).

The president believes he can achieve a balanced budget by 2027 with a plan like this. Can it work? Gut reaction: No, because it will never pass Congress. Plus, it's based on an assumption of 3 percent annual GDP growth. The Congressional Budget Office is predicting 1.9 percent growth, while the Federal Reserve Bank expects just 1.8 percent.[337]

So the path to a balanced budget depends on our congressmen showing restraint, which is unlikely, and an unprecedented economic recovery, also unlikely. And then, if, through some miracle of finance, the country runs a budget surplus again someday, do you honestly think that surplus will be used to pay down the debt, or will our elected representatives invent new programs on which to spend that windfall?

Now, having said all that, it's worth asking another important question: Who (besides Mark Taylor, Mary Colbert, and Kim Clement) really thought Donald Trump would be the next president of the United States in June of 2015? If we've learned nothing from the last two years, it's that the experts keep getting it wrong when it comes to Donald J. Trump.

The Forces Aligned Against Donald Trump

We've also seen that President Trump faces opposition from within and without his own political party. He wasn't supposed to win. The political class vets the candidates for whom we vote, and Mr. Trump was not one of them. As former House Speaker Newt Gingrich told Bill O'Reilly on Fox News, Trump has thrown "the establishment wing of the party" into a panic:

He's an outsider. He's not them, he's not part of the club. He's uncontrollable. He hasn't been through the initiation rites. He doesn't belong to the secret society, and I think that they don't see him—they have no idea how to relate to him.[338]

Establishment Republicans have had time to get over their shock and now openly challenge the president on nearly everything. They openly opposed him during the campaign, some even publicly vowing to support Democrat Hillary Clinton. Presumably, Mrs. Clinton posed less of a threat to the Deep State's true agenda of endless war in pursuit of empire.

Democrats have also rejected cooperation with President Trump, but they've taken in to an entirely new level. Instead of leaving Washington, like nearly all previous former presidents, Barack and Michelle Obama have moved into an eight-bedroom, nine-and-a-half bath, 8,200 square-foot home in DC. The former president's consigliere, Valerie Jarrett, has moved in with the Obamas, a pretty strong hint that the Resist movement that sprang up overnight in response to the election of Donald Trump is at least being encouraged, if not directed, by the former president and his staff.

Globalists were aghast at the election of Donald Trump. His America First message is diametrically opposed to their goal of eliminating national borders, which are annoying obstacles to moving resources (money, raw materials, people) around the world to maximize profits. Trump's opposition to two signature programs of the global elite, the Trans-Pacific Partnership (TPP) and the Trans-Atlantic Trade and Investment Partnership (T-TIP) won him few friends among those who believe in removing barriers to trade across borders, like national governments.

One of the most alarming aspects of the TPP, which would have covered 40 percent of the world's economy and some 792 million people, was the creation of tribunals, is the Investor-State Dispute Settlement mechanism. The ISDS would have allowed corporations to sue governments for any lost profits resulting from a nation's regulations. Rulings of the tribunals would have superseded national law, and judges would be private attorneys who work in corporate law—people who depend on big corporations for their livelihood.[339] In other words, the judges would be foxes guarding the henhouse. (To be clear, you and I are the hens in this illustration.)

Forty percent of the global economy is a lot of money, roughly $30 trillion a year. That's a big pie even when thinly sliced. But on January 23, 2017, President Donald Trump issued an executive order directing the US trade representative to withdraw from the TPP, effectively killing it, at least for now.

You recall what the apostle Paul said about the love of money. Do you think that executive order made any potential enemies for the president?

Groups like the Council on Foreign Relations have exercised a cartel on foreign policy in the US for decades. They, along with allies in the media and Hollywood, have pushed the message that our "small world after all" must unite beneath a global authority of some kind to guarantee peace, prosperity, and equality for all. Our children and grandchildren have been positively soaking in this message from the time they entered school (unless they were blessed enough to be home-schooled).

Isn't it ironic that so-called progressives, the ones who want the fewest restraints on their personal behavior, are the ones most likely to support a one-world government telling them what to do?

At the core, this is what motivates most of the Never-Trump movement. Now, there are some people who simply can't support President Trump because of things he's done, or is alleged to have done, in his personal life. That's understandable. Mr. Trump hasn't exactly led a life that would be held up as a model for young Christian men.

But most of those who oppose Donald Trump are coming from a different place. They'd have no problem with his treatment of women if his positions on trade, immigration, and national defense weren't a clear and present danger to the hopes and dreams of the global elite. Nationalism, especially American nationalism, threatens their goal of a world united under a single leader. Anything that weakens the appeal of nationalism, from pro-UN propaganda fed to schoolchildren to immigration policies that welcome people with no desire to integrate into the dominant culture, serves the ends of globalists.

Now, this next bit may sound like a fringe conspiracy theory, but not if you view the world through a spiritual lens: The closest parallel to the ultimate goal of globalists is the desire of the first would-be emperor of the world, Nimrod.

As I wrote in my book *The Great Inception*, archaeologists have identified a period in the history of the ancient Near East called the Uruk Expansion. It stretches from about 4000 BC to around 3100 BC. This was a remarkable time during which a single Sumerian city-state, Uruk in what is now southeastern Iraq, dominated virtually the entire Fertile Crescent.

The Bible tells us that the beginning of Nimrod's kingdom was Babel and Erech. Erech is Uruk, a kingdom so important in its day that we still call that land by the same name—Iraq.

At its peak, Uruk's influence stretched from southeast Iraq to northwest Iran, southeast Turkey and northern Syria, which must have seemed like the entire civilized world at that time. Nimrod, assuming he was responsible for Uruk's expansionist policy, controlled more territory than Saddam Hussein and ruled before the first pharaoh established his dynasty in Egypt.

The point is this: Nimrod wanted to control the world on behalf of the entities he served. It was for them that he built the Tower of Babel (which I argue in *The Great Inception* was the E-abzu, the "House of the Abyss," at the ancient city of Eridu) to be the "abode of the gods."[340]

Today's globalists, whether they realize it or not, are pushing humanity back to Babel. And Donald J. Trump is throwing obstacles in their path. This makes him a target.

Conclusion

So, will Donald J. Trump make America great again? Maybe, in the short term. He has a huge challenge ahead. His tax plan may provide a stimulus to the economy by putting money back in the pockets of consumers and removing the incentive for corporations to send it out of the country. His budget proposals remove much of the incentive for workers to stay home and collect entitlements and it redirects those funds to infrastructure and the military (especially the military). And his America First approach to immigration and trade theoretically encourages employers to bring jobs back to the country and hire citizens.

But the impact of the Trump tax and economic plans aren't likely to have the effect of the changes implemented during the Reagan years. First, taxes aren't as steep as they were in 1980, so tax cuts will have less impact. Second, the Federal Reserve Bank has been pushing historically low interest rates for the better part of a decade with little effect on the economy, except perhaps to delay an inevitable contraction. Third, American corporations are far less committed to the American economy now than they were thirty years ago.

Finally, the federal debt has saddled American taxpayers with a burden that could strangle any budding economic boom. Even if the Trump budget brings America back to a balanced budget by 2027, that $70+ trillion debt is still out there racking up interest charges, a bill that amounts to more than half a million dollars per taxpayer.

Viewing this with a supernatural worldview, one sees a long game at work, one that mirrors the history of Sumer more five thousand years ago. As I argue in *The Great Inception*, the principalities and powers who are the true enemies of humanity are once again pushing us away from self-reliance toward dependence on government; away from an agrarian, rural society toward one organized around cities; and ultimately away from independent nation-states toward a world ruled by a king beholden to the lord of the Abyss.

Can Donald Trump turn the tide and change the course of history? That's a tall order for a mere mortal. He may be able to stem the tide for a while, but in the long term, Bible prophecy tells us that a global government will emerge. Christians must recognize the window of opportunity we've been given to prepare for rough sailing ahead and to carry out the Great Commission, making disciples of all nations while there is still time.

It is possible that the improbable, nearly miraculous election of Donald Trump was a gift from God specifically to give us time to complete the harvest before His judgment.

Some may feel I've painted too bleak a picture of the future. Fair enough. But it's only bleak for those who don't know Jesus Christ as their Lord and Savior. If you're already a member of the Body of Christ—well, you knew the job was dangerous when you took it. We were never promised an easy road. Compared to our brothers and sisters around the world and throughout history, American Christians have had a soft ride for the last four hundred years or so. Things are going to get bumpy in the years ahead. But as Jesus told the disciples, "In the world you will have tribulation. But take heart; I have overcome the world."

chapter twelve

If My People...

By Allie Anderson

O ver the last several years, there has been a shift in the traditional Church. Home churches are becoming more common. Self-proclaimed Christians are emerging everywhere, and conservatism is on the rise. Values once considered "old-fashioned" are making a comeback. And, surprisingly, much of this is taking place within the young generations.

An uprising is sweeping the land. The election of 2016 is a mere byproduct of a deeper undercurrent that has been building for some time. When Vice President-Elect Mike Pence took oath on Ronald Reagan's Bible, choosing the verse 2 Chronicles 7:14 to place his hand upon, this displayed an enormous shift from the priorities and convictions of the preceding years of administration. This should not be read into by the Church as some message that Pence and Trump are here to "save the day," and that we can sit down in our La-Z-Boys and go back to sleep, but rather a rallying cry that the day we have been praying for is on the horizon, and this is our moment in time.

The Scripture that Pence chose says:

If my people, which are called by my name, shall humble themselves, and pray, and seek my face, and turn from their wicked
ways; then will I hear from heaven, and will forgive their sin, and
will heal their land. (2 Chronicles 7:14)

It is quoted frequently, especially during political shifts such as election times—but what does it really say when we peel back the layers and
begin to investigate what it really entails? In order to answer this question, we must take it apart line by line and decipher its message. When it
is analyzed, the seeker finds that the message of this Scripture is innately
one of action—and for some people, therein lies the problem.

Many times in our society, when this Scripture is referenced, it is
applied to modern American politics. This is the first mistake people
make. Understand that this is not a Scripture that was spoken specifically and directly *to* America. It was written thousands of years before
America's birth. It was written to *God's people.* It transcends our American political system. The promise is actually much broader than the
scope often credited to it. When God spoke this to Abraham, He called
His people in the possessive. He was speaking of people who were *His,
who belonged to Him,* as though they were in the palm of His hand. The
promise in this passage has and will continue throughout time, unbiased
by maps or zones or territories. God was talking to the people of Abraham, who would call upon Him as their God. Wherever and whenever
we exist, if He is our God, then we are His people. See what Russell
Moore of the Ethics & Religious Liberty Commission has to say on this
matter:

When God said to them, "If my people who are called by name,"
he was specifically pointing them back to the covenant that he
made with their forefather Abraham. At a specific point in their
history, God had told Abraham about his descendants, saying "I
will be their God" and "They will be my people." That's what

"My people" means. God reminded a people who had been exiled, enslaved, and defeated that a rebuilt temple or a displaced nation cannot change who they were. They were God's people, and would see the future God has for them.[341]

Does this passage apply in today's American politics? It sure can, but the thing that so many people miss is that it applies to *all people whose God is the Lord.* This means that if this concept were properly harnessed and practiced, what we crave in America *could* actually be a worldwide event. Do you want to see a nationwide revival? How about a worldwide revival?

Another mistake often made concerning these verses is that people like to place all of their focus on certain elements, condensing the passage down to something a little more like this: "if my people pray, then I will heal their land." They are leaving out a measurable part of the actual *instructions* God placed within the verse. They are forgetting that in between these orders, we are also told that we are called by His name, we are called to humble ourselves, we are called to seek His face, and we are called to turn from our wicked ways. Only *then* will God hear from Heaven, forgive our sins, and heal our land. Those extra ingredients put a whole different spin on the way that this passage must be interpreted. But before we further explore this text line by line, let's take a look at some very simple words given to us by Christ Himself, and what they within our modern society.

We Are the Salt of the Earth

Exactly what does this phrase mean, anyway? If we explore the verse, "Ye are the salt of the earth: but if the salt have lost his savour, wherewith shall it be salted? It is thenceforth good for nothing, but to be cast out, and to be trodden under foot of men" (Matthew 5:13), we find immediately that it refers to the flavor of salt. Taking a closer look at the properties of salt, we see even further parallels. After all, salt has many effective properties. It can preserve and disinfect, and has even been used as ceremonial offering or currency in some societies throughout history. Salt is a precious commodity that, although useful, also must be used in balance. Both overuse and underuse can lead to damage. When it is diluted, its flavor diminishes, as the Scripture warns. How, as believers, do we become diluted? By losing our focus; our effectiveness. Consider what Daphne Delay of the Christian Broadcasting Network has to say on the matter:

> Why is that? There could be many reasons, but the most common is depression, fatigue, self-doubt, and ultimately reservations about what we believed in to begin with. And we have to clearly understand there is an enemy at work in these cases. If we are the salt of the earth and it's possible to lose our flavoring, then it's no secret the Devil will do his best to make sure our effectiveness (our flavoring) isn't what it used to be. And if he had his way in every case, we'd have no flavoring left at all—returning to transparent grains of sand with no threat to him or his kingdom.[342]

Delay continues later in the same article to explain that although the ocean is full of salt, the way of actually separating it from the water is by boiling; a fiery trial. None of us want to go through trials, but by facing the heat and coming through such events, we become stronger in our faith. This gives us more "flavor."

The salt of the earth have always faced trials for their faith. At times, many have even been martyred. During periods or in cultures where this ultimate sacrifice was not necessary, they have still faced adversity. Modern-day society is certainly no exception, and in some ways it is escalating. The culture crisis American believers face today has placed many of us under attack for merely stating our beliefs. The First Amendment, the right to free speech, has been increasingly placed under threat as those who speak against popular, politically correct opinions are silenced and accused of being hateful. Unsure of how to respond to such attacks, many Christians react by withdrawing or becoming silent.

A problem occurs within our effectiveness, however, when we make the mistake of thinking that being a Christian means that we are powerless in the modern world. Citing Scriptures like, "By this shall all men know that ye are my disciples, if ye have love one to another" (John 13:35), many buy in to the popular modern-day concept that in order to be loving, we must give up power, or flavor. It is a prominent misconception that taking action, speaking out, or trying to otherwise be effective crosses some barrier that means we are not loving. Unfortunately, we live in a society that equates agreeable stances with "love" and contradicting points of view with "hate." Because of this, there is no outlet for balance in a society where only popular views are allowed to be freely spoken. Those who rally their opinions publicly are met with accusatory outcry, leaving many Christians afraid to draw lines, for fear of being considered narrow-minded or mean.

In light of this, believers' responses have often been polarized: One side has stepped back and become all-embracing and all-accepting, while the other has clung desperately to the opposite end of the spectrum by preaching hellfire and condemnation to a society that doesn't want to hear this "outdated" speech. They have either traded their empowered love for a weaker, more silent love, or they have abandoned love altogether. In today's politically correct world where "neutral" seems to be the safe zone to avoid offending someone, many believers begin to foster the concept that "bland" means "loving," while others are so "salty" that people pucker and reject the taste. Salt isn't bland, and just the perfect amount adds an appropriate kick to the right things. Too much, however, is off-putting and thereby ineffective. So, how do we efficiently get involved without losing our witness?

"Action" in and of itself does not have to be some forceful, Bible-thumping, judgmental process that eliminates peace between believers and the outside world. The "us-vs.-them" philosophy that so many begin to feel trapped in only heightens the tension already hovering over the current atmosphere. Believers who feel powerless, outnumbered, or without instruction on how to be effective become inactive or feel defeated. Others go on the offense, giving nonbelievers the opportunity to point a wounded finger and accuse them of being hateful. However, between these two polar opposites is a balance that Jesus Himself actually practiced. His actions show that He held Himself at all times with the utmost integrity, yet we see by the company He kept that He still reached out to those who needed Him most. When He spent time with those who led unsavory lifestyles, it was *their lives* who were changed, and not that of Jesus. He was truly in the world but not of it.

Many of us, unsure of how to achieve this balance, wait backstage for some cosmic cue to tell us when it is time to come out and play our part. Because we lack the courage to take action or we hesitate when we receive direction, we are in danger of giving in to the feeling of defeat and becoming complacent. This means that when the awaited cue does come, we may miss it because we were not ready. We have fallen into the trap of waiting for life to happen to us.

The Danger of Victim Mentality within the Church

Does our society have victim mentality? Does the Church? A person might immediately dismiss this possibility without giving it much thought. But what *exactly* does the phrase even mean? Having a greater understanding of the victim mentality may make a person give the issue further thought.

Huffington Post had the following to say in regard to this question:

The primary source of feeling like a victim is the feeling of powerlessness, and because we don't like feeling that we are powerless, we tend to blame someone or something for causing that feeling. So we feel that we are a victim of circumstances or other people's actions and that we can't do anything about it.... Thus the single most important belief responsible for the feeling of victimization is I'm powerless.... The reason feeling victimized is so debilitating is that it undermines your ability to do anything about your situation. If you are having difficulties in any area of your life...and you experience yourself as powerful and in control of your life, you can devise a strategy to improve your situation. And if one solution doesn't work, you can learn from your experience and try again.

But if you have a victim mentality—in other words, if you feel powerless to affect your circumstances—you are likely to feel that the world is "doing it" to you and that there is nothing you can do about it.... If you have the problem of feeling victimized by life or other people, you are less likely to look for and implement a solution because you feel you can't do anything about your situation.[343]

Contrary to popular belief, not everyone who has a victim mentality is spending his or her days crying out his or her woes to all their friends. Certainly, we have all seen people who make that their habit, but victim mentality describes anyone who feels immobilized in a situation and state of mind. They don't realize there is something they can do about it. They feel, as stated above, *powerless.* Have you ever looked around you at the sin, despair, or unmet needs, and felt outnumbered? We all have. And our modern Church has such insurmountable obstacles facing it that it's easy to fall into this mentality, even as Christians who have the best of intentions. The problem is that we cannot give in to this feeling and allow it to render us incapacitated. If people surrender to the temptation to "freeze," we become ineffective.

The examples of how the world can change during our immobility or complacency are innumerable. Our reluctance to act at times can be because of a desire to please people, hesitancy to offend, lack of leadership, or even pride, just to name a few possibilities. Sometimes our reluctance springs from fear; in other instances, it is because we look around and feel outnumbered. Many who feel incapable have perhaps even grown complacent. It's important that we never surrender to this way of thinking, but unfortunately, people do it all the time, even within the Church. It's vital that we recognize exactly *who we are* in Christ, and understand that God never ordained us as a powerless people.

A Grainy Photograph

Everyone knows that if you copy a photo in a Xerox machine, it loses some of its detail. If you take the copy that you have made and make a copy if *it*, it will likely be grainy and display low quality in the finer detail. Lines begin to blur. Each further reproduction will continue to lose integrity, until finally you are left with a piece of paper that looks very little like the original photograph.

When believers are attending church on Sunday morning and putting no further investment into their Christian walk, the result over time is that we have entire congregations of church members who are grainy, dim, and have no clear lines around them. They may have some idea of what the Bible says, but they know it as it has been reiterated to them through a teacher at church, who likely is reteaching what they learned from someone else, and so on. When people are not exploring and learning God's Word for themselves, His Word is not hidden in their own hearts. They are as blissfully unaware of their spiritual diets as many people are of their physical nutrition. Throw in a little prosperity preaching, a skewed concept of worship, self-indulgent repetition of the sacraments, an added twist in theology here and there, (be it intentional or not), and a generalized growing complacency, and you have a lukewarm, sleepy church.

The Church needs leaders who will stand and give direction to the congregations based on true biblical teachings. As human begins, we are inclined to want a higher power. As Christians, especially in the Church, we are wired to expect a "shepherd" to lead us. People who go to church to be "fed" are usually there with open hearts and minds, awaiting what they believe to be God's message to them. They are seeking leadership. As ministers, it is vital that this position is not taken lightly or for the wrong reasons, but that the message that is delivered be researched through prayer and supplication, and considered somberly before standing before a congregation and representing it as a message from the Lord.

As a church member, we must always bear in mind that in Philippians 2:12, the Bible says to "work out your own salvation with fear and trembling."

Ultimately, we are accountable to take ownership of our relationship with God. It is each individual's responsibility to gain an understanding of God's Word, His will for our lives, and His message to us. He likens us to sheep, but we are not to simply attend a church, lined up at some metaphorical spiritual feeding trough, and expect all things to come to us. *We* must take the initiative to saturate our lives with God. The minister can't do that for us.

When the Church is filled with copies of copies, it is vulnerable. Members' lives are open to compromise and complacency in many areas. A quick study into today's modern Church will reveal the fruits of this scenario everywhere. Sadly, this renders again a picture of a Church that is at times dim, without clarity, and with blurred lines.

Who Are We? If My People...

The turning point in all of this is when we begin to realize exactly who God designed us to be. God never predestined that His people be immobilized by fear, complacency, the feeling of being outnumbered, or the assumption that we have no power over the situation. He ordained that His people be proactive.

Think about how God has always spoken to His people. Since the beginning of time, whenever He has warned His people of impending doom, He then immediately followed with instructions of what *actions* were to be taken. He warned Noah of the need to *build an ark*. He told Joseph to store up food. He sent Jonah to warn Nineveh that *unless their actions changed* that He would destroy the city. God has never once warned His people that something was coming, and then told them to sit and wait for it to happen to them. His messages to man have always had a cause and effect calculated within them. He has always installed some sort of "if/then" exchange that presented those He spoke to with a choice, and a plan of action.

But as a Church, we have often forgotten the second half of these stories. All too often we embrace the warnings and the predictions of doom. We allow our feelings of inadequacy to stall our movement. We freeze when there is a lack of direction or leadership. We are afraid to offend so we hesitate. Frequently, we do indeed have the victim mentality. We fail to remember that He called us His People, and that He is our God, and we lose sight of the power that is embodied in this covenant. We forget that He made us promises centuries before we were even born that we can still access, if we will fulfil the attached actions. It's like having a giant present handed to us that we simply walk away from, because we have forgotten how to unwrap it.

Who Are Called by My Name...

What does it mean to be called by His name? We know that we were made in the image of God. And the Bible is clear that if we are God's people, then we are not called to the spirit of fear, but of power, love and a sound mind (2 Timothy 1:7). The qualities combined in this passage are a declaration that we are to operate with good judgment, behave in a loving manner, and know that we have an ultimate power behind our prayers and actions. You and I are not victims. We are not sitting by waiting for life to happen. We are not to be scared or complacent, hoping that the Church, the government, or any other "they" will protect us or provide for us. We have the power to stand up and begin to make a change.

The very name of Jesus causes forces of evil to flee (James 2:19; Luke 10:17). They recognize Him as the Son of God (Mark 3:11). God's name all by itself is a vital source of command. And we have been called by it. Like an adopted child of a prominent family, we are now given the identity that is recognized as belonging to an authority that we were not born into, but that we have attained full rights to.

What must happen here is for us to finally remember exactly *who* we are in Christ. We are called by His name. The Supreme Creator of the Universe adopts us as His own, and shares His own name with us! He has given us the power to bind or loose in Heaven and on earth, just by our prayers to Him (Matthew 18:18). We are empowered on every level with all the resources of Heaven behind us. This is the authority that God reinforces us with when we are operating within His instructions and His will.

Shall Humble Themselves...

Webster defines humble as "not proud or haughty: not arrogant or assertive...reflecting, expressing, or offered in a spirit of deference or submission"[344] and a Google search will pull up a definition stating that it means to have or show a modest or low estimate of one's own importance. What happens when we remove pride from our Christian behavior?

When we are humble, our energy and focus are not on ourselves. Our own needs are not the biggest things on our minds. Perspective on what really matters in life and in God's eyes can be altered for the better. Materialism declines and ministry becomes more important. People who are humble care more about helping people. They are driven to compassion. Choices are based on values, not on impulses or shallow desires. People who practice this begin to have a higher sense of purpose because their lives are focused on something bigger than they are, and they become service-oriented.

Actions begin to reflect this higher sense of purpose, leading people to feel more fulfilled in life. Because of this, depression is less of an issue. Perspective on what really matters in life comes into place and there is less room to dwell on our own problems. Joy and fulfillment become stronger. This creates an inner light that becomes a beacon to those around us, who see it and want to join in as well. You may have heard this true phrase: "Hurt people hurt people; blessed people bless people."

Because humble people are focused on others, they are more patient and can wait longer periods of time for gratification. They weigh the consequences of their actions more thoroughly, and in so doing, make choices that benefit those around them. This constructive mentality that humble people adopt usually makes them successful when placed in leadership. They applaud those who have done a good job and consider everyone's feedback, while making decisions that are best for the group. Humble people are driven to benevolence. They are ministry-minded, outreach-oriented people who are taking action to reach those around them and make the world a better place. Imagine if this were a more prominent trait among today's Christian population!

Pray, and Seek My Face...

We live in a rat-race lifestyle. Time seems to speed up more and more each day. Does anyone really find the time to pray enough? What does it really, *really* mean to actually seek God's face? Think about the scriptural examples of men who sought God's face. Imagine what that might have looked like as opposed to today's five-minute-prayer-warriors!

The definition for the word "seek" is obvious to most people: "to search for, look for, attempt to find." So when we are *seeking* God's face, we are actually looking for Him. We are attempting to find Him. This phrase inherently describes a depth of prayer that cannot be covered in a three-minute prayer at the beginning of class to pass a test we are about to take, or a lightly spoken "thank you for this food" said before we tear into a meal. These are good times to pray, but attempting to actually find God is a much deeper, soul-level search that many professed Christians are just not making these days.

Are we looking for God because He is lost? No. We are looking for Him because we are lost. Our humanity has separated us from Him and we are trying to find our way out of our sinful nature and into His ways. We are to search for His presence and His righteousness within our lives. This is a constant lifestyle choice. It requires humbling ourselves and realizing that our ways are not best. Our compromises are not justified. Our rationale is not wisdom. Psalm 10:4 says, "The wicked, through the pride of his countenance, will not seek God: God is not in all his thoughts."

In order for us to really seek God's face, we must let go of the pride and esteem that we have in our own thoughts. We have to abandon our human ways and admit that what our nature tells us to do is not the right way to do things. We must stop vindicating and mitigating our sin and realize that we need to be truly changed from the inside out.

Psalm 66:18–20 says:

If I regard iniquity in my heart, the Lord will not hear me: But verily God hath heard me; he hath attended to the voice of my prayer. Blessed be God, which hath not turned away my prayer, nor his mercy from me.

Recall the scenario mentioned before about copies of copies. If we are to seek His face, we have to go back to the very original source. Nothing less than earnestly searching for this will do. Once we set aside our human agendas and really, deeply want God's ways in our very heart and soul, only then will we pave the way for real repentance and make a true and honest turn from our wicked ways.

And Turn from Their Wicked Ways...

When revival sweeps the land and we are really, honestly turning away from our wicked ways as a society, what does that look like? The revolution that would rock the entire country would be undeniable. But this requires action. It requires the end of compromise within the Church. The Church often tolerates so much nonbiblical behavior that it seems in many ways more of a social club than anything.

It appears more and more that people who add Christ to their lives are doing just that, *adding Him*, instead of *surrendering to* Him. Second Corinthians 5:17 says that when we are in Christ we are a new creation. The old is gone and *all things are new.* But many people turn to God as a method of "fire insurance" while clinging to their old lifestyles. Churches who, again, are afraid of offending, have slowly accepted more and more of this behavior until the body of believers in our society has become slowly diluted, losing their saltiness.

See in the following excerpt what Allen Snapp, in a sermon entitled "If My People Will Turn Away from Their Wicked Ways," had to say on this matter:

> Faith in Christ and repenting from our sin are two sides of the same coin. There is no genuine repentance without faith, and no genuine faith without repentance. There is a costless, changeless form of Christianity that not only says "come as you are" but also says "stay as you are". The result is that churches are filled with churchgoers who have little more intention of obeying God than non-churchgoers. At every point that they see sin, they refuse to repent.[345]

We cannot live a life that separates us from God and still call ourselves His people. Many Christians believe that by following the "big-hitters," they are living a holy life. If they are not committing adultery, lying, or committing murder, they feel that they are living an acceptable lifestyle. But think of all the little things that keep us from the will of God in our daily lives, like pride, distraction, or placing idols in the pathway toward our intimacy with God. These are all habits that must be eradicated if we are to call ourselves people who are *turning from our wicked ways*. Snapp, later in the same sermon, went on to say:

> Keeping the Lord's commandments is a product of loving Him with all our heart and soul. Jesus also linked our love with our obedience.... It really comes down to what we love. The things that keep us from loving and obeying the Lord have more of our affections than God. We love God first or we love something else first. It's that simple.... But I have this against you, that you have abandoned the love you had at first. Remember therefore from where you have fallen; repent, and do the works you did at first. If not, I will come to you and remove your lampstand from its place, unless you repent. Revelation 2:4– (ESV). The remedy, according to Jesus, is to repent. Losing our first love (loving Jesus more than anything) is sin...which means we can, by the grace of God, turn away from the sin that is dampening our love and turn towards God and receive a fresh and burning love.[346]

What does it *really mean* to turn from our wicked ways? It means more than going to church or joining a Bible study. These are good activities, but what it really means is to abandon our own urges, leave behind our sinful ways, and truly submit to God's will for our lives by chasing after righteousness, following all of God's laws, and yielding 100 percent to the calling of the Holy Spirit.

Then Will I Hear From Heaven, and Will Forgive Their Sin...

Forgiveness is ours for the asking. It was provided for us when Jesus died on the cross. If we are sincere and not hiding evil in our hearts, God says He will hear our prayers. But while forgiveness is free, it also comes with and "if/then" transfer. We have to recognize that we need it and *ask for it*. We have to surrender our lives to God. We must never forget that when we ask for and receive forgiveness, we are acknowledging that we needed a Savior.

Isaiah 53:5–6 says:

> But he was wounded for our transgressions, he was bruised for our iniquities: the chastisement of our peace was upon him; and with his stripes we are healed. All we like sheep have gone astray; we have turned every one to his own way; and the Lord hath laid on him the iniquity of us all.

We are not enough to make it to Heaven on our own. Our sin was too great and the divide between ourselves and God was too deep a chasm for us to ever bridge. Without His help, we are mere sheep, lost. When we receive His forgiveness, we humble ourselves and acknowledge this. When people quote 2 Chronicles 7:14, this crucial point within the passage is often overlooked. For God to forgive us and heal our land, there must be prayer that includes the acknowledgment that we are not enough on our own and we *need* Him. We turn away from our previous lifestyles, acknowledge our mistakes and our shortcomings, invite Him in, and relinquish control so that He can rearrange our lives and make us new.

When this begins to happen on a regional level, the nation will begin to show signs of revival. Think about it: A population that is corporately acknowledging sin and failure, recognizing the need for a Savior, and chasing God would render the fruits of the Holy Spirit across our country. Under these circumstances, it will be easy for God to heal our land!

Imagine what it would look like if the fruit of the Spirit began cropping up all over our nation. Homeless and hungry would be being fed despite public-assistance programs. Many of the humanitarian things that people work so hard to accomplish would happen naturally, as a mere byproduct of the indwelling of the Holy Spirit. Fear, powerlessness, and complacency would become a thing of the past and an empowered Church would emerge to be a relentless force for good.

And Will Heal Their Land.

Many people like this line the best out of this passage, for obvious reasons. But we cannot forget that God placed the "if/then" contingency in the Scripture. We as His people are offered this as a promise in exchange for prerequisites that God outlined in the earlier part of the passage. Many are tempted to skip to this line and claim the promise, without understanding the series of actions required *before* these results can be attained.

If we were to follow all of the instructions within this passage, it would look like this: We would recognize that we are His people, called to be His own, desired and bought by Him long before we were ever born. We would know that we are given His name, made in His image, and given the mind of Christ. Humanitarian deeds would flow freely as a byproduct of God's Spirit working in us through love and humility. We would realize that we are finite creatures who need a Savior, who are not all-knowing, and who realize that our ways are not best. God would be pronounced the true leader of our lives, and we would journey toward Him with all our hearts, denouncing the ways of sin permanently.

Once we have done that, wholeheartedly, with our whole lives, *then and only then* do we get that last line of the passage to come to fruition.

Understand that this is good news! There is a natural, built-in victory here, because if we are earnestly trying to serve God and giving Him authority over our lives, then we will already be meeting these prerequisites! All we need to do is get on track and stay there! God is waiting for us to begin the process by surrendering our lives to Him and living as He has called us to live.

> If my people, which are called by my name, shall humble themselves, and pray, and seek my face, and turn from their wicked ways; then will I hear from heaven, and will forgive their sin, and will heal their land. (2 Chronicles 7:14)

These are the words that will change this nation. This is what it will take for the land to be healed. And guess what? It is within our power as Christians! We are faced with a choice. Will you obey God's commands or not? Will you be a part of the solution or a tool to propagate the core problem? Will you follow the "if" and receive the "then" within this passage?

God is calling every one of His people...*His People*...to do the very things laid out in this passage. I want to see this country—the entire world—change! Don't you? The promises made so long ago can become a worldwide event if believers will stand together and clean house, starting with our own. It is not a big, unattainable formula that is difficult to decipher. It is already beginning. The signs are everywhere! The undercurrent is swelling and the winds of change are picking up speed. You and I can be a part of this. We can truly begin at this very moment to make the changes that we want to see. It is easy to join the movement. It is as simple as choosing this day whom you will serve. If we will unite and corporately begin in our own lives to make the God of Abraham our God, our *Lord and Master,* and chase Him with all our hearts, our souls, and minds, then He will indeed hear us, forgive our sin, and *heal our land.*

Looking for Security in an Insecure World

Social Justice and Bible Prophecy

By Gary Stearman

hristians watch in dismay as global societies collapse into a series of crises. Revolutionaries around the world march, scream slogans, and set fires to call attention to their dreams of "social justice." The world watched in incredulity as the Women's March assembled in protest groups against the inauguration of the latest US president. Their speeches and outcries were lewd, crude, and insulting. Their pink headgear symbolized the feminist cause...and much, much more! But perhaps unknown to them, the caps also linked them to revolutionaries who marched over two thousand years ago! Their theme: Redemption for women through societal fairness, set in the historical symbolism of oppression.

As belief in a God who is present and active among mankind continues to wane, it is being systematically replaced by various concepts of artificial redistribution and compensation...access to reward and success. Marxism, a nineteenth- and twentieth-century attempt to bring impartiality and justice to society, has been a colossal failure on many levels. Instead of a just society, it brought death tolls that ran into the millions. It resulted in legendary failure to distribute food (millions starved to death in Russia). Its mandatory regulations came at the muzzle of a gun; under Stalin and Mao, millions more were killed.

Everywhere it is tried, it results in social destabilization, driven by attempts at "fairness," followed by the consistent failure to achieve the artificial goals that make up its framework.

From infancy through grade school and beyond, response to the constant cry that "it's not fair" comes in the form of a thousand inadequate excuses.

Students of all ages are told, "Just wait, you'll get your turn." Of course, that may or may not happen. From birth to death, people are differently gifted. Some are smart; some dull…some strong; some weak… some rich; some poor…some sick; some healthy. And on it goes.

Some speak of equity; reward or punishment should be the result of one's productivity. Others speak of equality; everyone gets the same thing. Still others view fairness on the basis of perceived need; the downtrodden, poor, ill or socially deprived must be compensated. Of course, fairness can never be truly achieved, and anyone who has lived a few years into adulthood knows this. Some excel; some decline.

This opens the door to a variety of social theories, all designed to achieve contentment, and all destined to failure! Life isn't fair. Strength, intelligence, wealth, guidance, a stable home and a million other variables are unpredictable, as new generations are born with sin natures… thrust into a world of sin.

Christians who read their Bibles are taught (and in turn, teach) this basic truth.

Scripture doesn't teach equality as the solution to social stability. In fact, fairness, as a concept, is not to be found in the Bible. Instead, it teaches redemption by faith in the finished work of the Lord Jesus Christ.

Christians can offer something better than fairness—that a creator God will bless those who worship Him. We defer to His wisdom and blessing, in the knowledge that this world of sin is not the final disposition of things. The Kingdom—earthly and heavenly—is the real destiny of the believer.

Those privileged by being raised in a Christian culture are not inclined to fall into the trap of believing that any artificial philosophical system can initiate an ideal world. Bible prophecy consistently tells of the inevitable decline and fall of societies, until Jesus returns in glory.

Social Justice

Those who read secular history will realize that in the long social march since Plato wrote a treatise called *The Republic* in the fourth century BC, no one has ever created a system in which everyone is equally fitted into a perfectly designed community. Plato's wonderful utopia failed. A little later, Aristotle's ideas on the matter arrived at an ideal, socially just society. But he was emphatic on one point: His wonderful world would exclude the slave class!

So much for social justice!

The "thirty-somethings" alive today have been steeped in a mixture of educational and philosophical theories, designed to pamper them into productivity. Over the last few decades, a growing segment of these Millennials have been smart enough to become cynical about the nuclear family, obedience to law (either religious or secular), hard work, and idealism of any kind. They are taught to react to that which they find insulting.

They seek "social justice" by displays of vulgarity, rioting, and resistance to established government. As Solomon put it:

There is a generation that curseth their father, and doth not bless their mother. There is a generation that are pure in their own eyes, and yet is not washed from their filthiness. There is a generation, O how lofty are their eyes! and their eyelids are lifted up. There is a generation, whose teeth are as swords, and their jaw teeth as knives, to devour the poor from off the earth, and the needy from among men. (Proverbs 30:11–14)

Like no other writer of Scripture, Solomon wrote with an incisive and pragmatic view of life on planet earth. He called it life *"under the sun,"* (the realm of physical reality). The Lord gave him a particular kind of insight into the twists and turns of life in the realm of an unregenerate world. In the following excerpt from Ecclesiastes, he impassively states a blatant truth. Though one may try to exalt himself and improve his lot in life, he is always subject to random twists of fate that afflict us all. With cool-headed observation, the ancient king writes that one may excel for some unspecified length of time. The strong, skilled, and intellectual may rise to temporary success. In the end, however, every man's work will amount to nothing. He seems to be talking about the unregenerate man, who will be judged when he least expects it:

> Whatsoever thy hand findeth to do, do it with thy might; for there is no work, nor device, nor knowledge, nor wisdom, in the grave, whither thou goest. I returned, and saw under the sun, that the race is not to the swift, nor the battle to the strong, neither yet bread to the wise, nor yet riches to men of understanding, nor yet favour to men of skill; but time and chance happeneth to them all. For man also knoweth not his time: as the fishes that are taken in an evil net, and as the birds that are caught in the snare; so are the sons of men snared in an evil time, when it falleth suddenly upon them. This wisdom have I seen also under the sun, and it seemed great unto me. (Ecclesiastes 9:10–13)

Social Justice and Revolution

What is fair or just about Solomon's view of life? His observations seem dark…indeed, almost cynical. He speaks of a judgment like a net or snare, which falls when one least expects it. What's more, judgment is inexorable.

We must remember that Solomon's viewpoint is focused upon human vanity. He famously opens his discourse by saying, "Vanity of vanities, saith the Preacher, vanity of vanities; all is vanity. What profit hath a man of all his labour which he taketh under the sun?" (Ecclestiastes 1:2, 3).

The vast majority of the world's population is totally ignorant of this truth. It behaves as though the gains and profits of this world are the most important acquisitions that one can realize. Furthermore, it seeks fairness in this life—social justice and equality for all.

This is not always a secular effort. The religions of the world often place their highest emphasis upon bringing sanctity and dignity to the poor. For example, the obligation of performing charity is greatly emphasized within Judaism. The concept of *tzedakah* ("charity"), bringing blessing and equality to the poor, is deeply ingrained in this religion.

Within Catholicism, one finds that the modern concept of "social justice" goes back to the Jesuit Luigi Taparelli. Around 1840, he interpreted the work of Thomas Aquinas in a way that asserted the need to integrate this concept into every society. In fact, many denominations adopted the basic tenets of social reform. Prison reform, health care for the impoverished, and antislavery reforms all came from social justice movements. These movements were badly needed, and accomplished much. Ultimately, however, they have failed to solve endemic social problems. In fact, no society can survive without variability in its population. Lowly work is as vital as exalted capability.

One of the Five Pillars of Islam is the giving of charity and helping the poor...administering social justice. But one has only to look at the Islamic societies of the Middle East to see that wrenching poverty and upper-class rule are prevalent.

Likewise, Hinduism embodies the concept of equality of all beings... human and animal. But in India, low-caste tribes live in grimy poverty, while high-caste tribes enjoy vast social privilege.

Philosophers have long argued that there is no real objective standard for social justice. As it is known today, the concept would not even exist in its present form, except for the vast wealth of Western society, known for its excess, where even the impoverished have cell phones, vehicles, big-screen televisions, and are entitled to free food.

Rather, the present concept of social justice seems to promote jealousy of the wealthy business class. There is the widespread feeling that it should not exist in an unfettered way. Its vast excesses should somehow be harvested for those who don't have as much, and would like to have more.

There is little of moral and ethical worth in this position. Certainly, Christian charity is a large part of our faith, but we never view it in the hope that poverty will be erased. Jesus, in the episode of the women who anointed Him with expensive ointment, spoke on this subject. Judas, the hypocrite, objected to her action, prompting the following response:

> Then saith one of his disciples, Judas Iscariot, Simon's son, which should betray him, Why was not this ointment sold for three hundred pence, and given to the poor? This he said, not that he cared for the poor; but because he was a thief, and had the bag, and bare what was put therein. Then said Jesus, Let her alone: against the day of my burying hath she kept this. 8 For the poor always ye have with you; but me ye have not always. (John 12:4–8)

Jesus noted that there would always be an impoverished underclass. Certainly, He believed in charity. But He also realistically observed that this side of the Kingdom, poverty would always exist in human society.

Social Justice and Revolution

Today, "poverty" has taken on a whole new look. Two recent notorious protest movements illustrate the phenomenon with perfect clarity.

The first, which consumed a great deal of media time, projected a stark and compelling visual message. We remember it as the disgusting and bizarre street display called "Occupy Wall Street." It was the perfect exhibit of class warfare, set in the heart of Manhattan…in New York City's financial district.

The protest movement began in Zucotti Park on September 17, 2011. After a display of lewd behavior, filth, and profanity, protesters were driven from the park only to regather before the world's best-known collection of banks, investment brokerages, and educational institutions. These foolish reprobates were blandly labeled "anti-consumerist" and "pro-environment." World media were enthralled by their obscene behaviors…nudity and drug abuse.

The demonstrators targeted social and economic equality; the greed and corruption in mega-corporations with an excessive influence on government. Their slogan was, "We are the 99%," referring to what they described as the blatantly **unfair** distribution of wealth among the top 1 percent of society. They proudly displayed themselves as the most authentic representatives of humanity. Looking at their motley and degenerate appearance, we can only hope that this is not true.

Of course, they were obsessed with "social justice" and "fairness." In the human march toward an imagined ideal society, cultures around the world are constantly fine-tuning the rules of socioeconomic engagement to create the perfect secular world. And once again, the flames of animosity—the poor against the rich—are being fanned by idealists who feel that in the quest for fairness, any action is justified.

The Women's March and the Phrygian Cap

More recently—on January 21, 2017—we witnessed what was called the Women's March on Washington, DC. Its ostensible purpose was to protest the inauguration of Donald Trump. In their minds, he was the ultimate male chauvinist dictator! But according to the event's organizers, it was only one of six hundred similar marches in the United States.

The media referred to the marchers as a "sea of pink," referring to the knit pink hats worn as an emblem of the protest. Since Thanksgiving Day of 2016…November 24…almost four months earlier, they had formed groups to knit the headgear and plan the direction of their protest.

But those pink knit hats deserve further attention, since there is a long tradition behind them. The knit hats with two "ears" are really a variation of the Phrygian cap, the classic symbol of the revolutionary. They have a colorful history, dating back to fourth-century Greece, where they were usually knitted of wool yarn and topped by a characteristic topknot that flopped to one side. They were worn as a symbol of liberty and emancipation.

In their current manifestation, the pink caps worn by female revolutionaries, they are woven of pink yarn with two "ears," rather than a single topknot. Their "knitters, crocheters and sewers" met in small groups, turning out the caps at top speed, and discussing strategy at the same time. Their intimate meetings formed the communication links of the revolution.

But most likely unknown to them, such crocheting revolutionary groups go all the way back to marching revolutionary groups who knitted and planned their marches in the days of ancient Phrygia.

Down through history, the Phrygian Cap, also known as the "liberty cap," has made numerous appearances. Military groups, "barbarians," and revolutionary groups…including the Trojans…donned the caps at meetings and rallies where they planned strategy and loyalty. Somehow, the tradition persisted through the days of Republican Rome and into the Christian era in the worship of the god Mithra.

As a symbol of liberty in the French Revolution, the caps came to be called the *bonnets rouges,* or "red caps," since they were knitted of red or pinkish yarn. During the period of the "Reign of Terror" in 1793–94, the caps became a blatant symbol of anti-monarchists. They were woven by women called *tricoteuse*. These women became the underground intelligence of the revolution. Charles Dickens' famous narrative on the revolution, *A Tale of Two Cities,* featured the Phrygian Cap as one his central literary devices.

In the early nineteenth century, Phrygian Caps appeared during Napoleon's ascent. In twentieth-century France, the caps were seen again, worn in January, 2013, by women protesting same-sex marriage.

The image of this headgear has even appeared on US political cartoons and coinage. The most famous of these appears on the Morgan Silver Dollar with the head of "Liberty" wearing the Phrygian Cap!

And it's easy to overlook the fact that the classic Mercury dime also features the god of swiftness wearing the Phrygian cap of liberty. Lately, in the name of freedom, marchers for the legalization of marijuana have taken to wearing it.

Somehow, the cap always appears in times of great social upheaval. It is the secular symbol of the quest for "Social Justice"!

The Quest

In the accelerating decline into an agnostic...even atheistic, world, leaders feel an increasing compulsion to assert a variety of rules and regulations based upon the fair and even-handed administration of social power. As God is removed from the public square, secular leaders must become more godlike, distributing both blessings and punishments in ways that they deem most ideal.

One's mind wanders back to the days of Karl Marx, who dreamed of social equitability in his 1848 *Communist Manifesto* and 1867 declaration, *Das Kapital.* He wrestled with the complexities of class struggle and became the leading exponent of sociological equality in politics and economics. He was joined by the man known as the "brutal ideologue," Friederich Engels, Together, they moved the world toward the new ideal of communism, which was to bring all humanity into the beautiful world of social equality. Their dream ended in a nightmare: Bolshevism, Nazism, Communism, and Maoism killed tens of millions of innocent and oppressed citizens and created a world of anguish.

Communism caused the greatest poverty in the history of the world. Still, the quest for utopia rolls on, unabated.

In the media, competing ideologies are mandated to be given equal time. In educational institutions, concepts are to be treated equally, ostensibly allowing students the freedom to make up their own minds about philosophical, political and religious questions. This has led to an endless procession of contesting interest groups, each accusing the other of unfairly influencing young minds.

Political and social utopia has been the dream of idolaters and secularists. Plato's unattainable dream of the perfect society has collapsed again and again, in hundreds of failed and discredited monarchies and governments. But the effort to create human perfection continues to exert itself.

Utopia

Utopian theories range through economics (socialism), ecology (imitating the perfection of nature), politics (living with perfect representation), and religion (imagining a perfected societal godliness). Time and again, religious colonies have attempted this perfection, only to discover that human imperfection always results in social collapse.

But there is the constant urge to tinker with social interaction. Here's a splendid example. Today, we talk electronically. In 1949, the Federal Communications Commission (FCC), ruled that broadcast licensees must present controversial issues in an "honest, equitable and balanced" manner. Matters in the public interest were taken to be of chief importance. It actually required that broadcasters must devote portions of their broadcast day to controversial matters…ideological battlegrounds. And while doing this, they were to remain neutral.

As might be expected, oversight of this doctrine manifested itself as an impossibility. It required government regulators to make subjective judgments on publicly important issues. The FCC found itself in the uncomfortable position of coming into conflict with the Constitution's First Amendment, requiring freedom of speech, religion, and press. In reality, it found itself unqualified to determine what was fair and what was not. Caught in its own web of impossibility, it eliminated the doctrine in 1987.

But today, speech is still monitored in the "political correctness" movement. Those who don't worship God invariably exercise an inner compulsion to set up rules and standards by which society will be made "better." They imagine that they can create a stable and contented world.

There is a compulsion to arrive at a strategy of social betterment that will result in the personal comfort that at least *something* is being done. If you are at all intelligent, you'll soon observe society and see that it needs some sort of control. Someone…or something…must channel man's natural tendency to lie, cheat, steal, and otherwise feather his own nest while despoiling the accumulated wealth of others.

Still, irrational idealism prevails.

Latter-Day False Confidence

Surprisingly, modern Israel gives us an inside view of this sort of idealism. As it achieved statehood, the government of Israel adopted socialism in the hope that it could establish an equitable lifestyle. To this day, its leaders are confident that they can accomplish this. Indeed, confidence is an Israeli hallmark.

This is the Israel of Bible prophecy. We have often read the prophetic account of Gog's invasion of Israel, as given in Ezekiel 38. But perhaps, there is one aspect of this prophecy that isn't examined as closely as it should be. In the following passage, take note of the word "safely," which is used twice:

After many days thou shalt be visited: in the latter years thou shalt come into the land that is brought back from the sword, and is gathered out of many people, against the mountains of Israel, which have been always waste: but it is brought forth out of the nations, and they shall dwell *safely* all of them. Thou shalt ascend and come like a storm, thou shalt be like a cloud to cover the land, thou, and all thy bands, and many people with thee. Thus saith the Lord God; It shall also come to pass, that at the same time shall things come into thy mind, and thou shalt think an evil thought: And thou shalt say, I will go up to the land of unwalled villages; I will go to them that are at rest, that dwell *safely,* all of them dwelling without walls, and having neither bars nor gates. (Ezekiel 38:8–11, emphasis added)

It has often been said that this prophecy portrays Israel exactly as it appears in the present era. Israel has returned and restored the Promised Land. But its depiction of Israel is puzzling, since the tiny nation has already withstood six wars of aggression since its statehood in 1948. How can it then be described as dwelling "safely?"

The key to understanding this seeming paradox lies in the meaning of the word, itself. In fact, modern Israel is much like the rest of the world, in that it is an excellent example of the philosophy that man can create his own world of equality and stability. Modern Israel, seeing itself as God's chosen people, believes itself to be gifted and capable of creating its own peace in the midst of a warring world, despite being surrounded by enemies.

And this is perfectly illustrated by the text, where the two instances that use the word "safely" are a translation of the Hebrew word *betach*, which has the primary meaning of "confidently," but is usually used to describe those living with a false sense of security and without the necessary caution.

In the New Testament, we find exactly the same idea. Only this time, the prophecy applies to the entire world, at the moment when the Tribulation begins:

> But of the times and the seasons, brethren, ye have no need that I write unto you. For yourselves know perfectly that the day of the Lord so cometh as a thief in the night. For when they shall say, Peace and *safety*; then sudden destruction cometh upon them, as travail upon a woman with child; and they shall not escape. But ye, brethren, are not in darkness, that that day should overtake you as a thief. Ye are all the children of light, and the children of the day: we are not of the night, nor of darkness." (1 Thessalonians 5:1–5).

Here, we find exactly the same description of a society living in ignorant confidence at the time of the *Day of the Lord*...the Great Tribulation. In this case, the Greek word translated "safety" is *asphaleia,* the condition of living with a sense of stability and security. Moreover, it describes the mindset of those who ignore the threat of external enemies and dangers.

This portrayal is perfectly descriptive of the mindset of a society preoccupied with finding fairness or social justice. It imagines that because it is solving its own perceived social problems, it will be immune to external threats. Put another way, it ignores global conditions while solving its own difficulties, by creating a "better society."

This is today's world. In spite of all the idealism, it will not change, until the Second Coming, when Jesus arrives to establish the Kingdom Age:

> And I saw heaven opened, and behold a white horse; and he that sat upon him was called Faithful and True, and in righteousness he doth judge and make war. (Revelation 19:11)

Only then will social justice and fairness become a possibility in this world. Until then, we should remember the words of Proverbs 16:11: "A just weight and balance are the LORD's: all the weights of the bag are his work."

The scales of justice are His.

Notes

1. Alinsky, Saul, *Rules for Radicals: A Practical Primer for the Realistic Radical,* p. 4, pub. By Random House, Inc., New York, 1971; text found online via https://archive.org/details/RulesForRadicals (accessed July 20, 2017).

2. Lyrics to *American Pie* found online at Google Play, website: https://play.google.com/music/preview/Tihyertbn7nlthzcum3po5g22d a?lyrics=1&utm_source=google&utm_medium=search&utm_campaign=lyrics&pcampaignid=kp-lyrics (accessed July 20, 2017).

3. Alinsky, Saul, *Rules for Radicals: A Practical Primer for the Realistic Radical,* p. 140, pub. By Random House, Inc., New York, 1971; text found online via https://archive.org/details/RulesForRadicals (accessed July 20, 2017).

4. http://www.washingtontimes.com/news/2014/jul/3/fedewa-bureaucracy-fourth-branch-government/

5. https://www.brainyquote.com/quotes/quotes/a/alankeyes160673.html

6. http://dailycaller.com/2017/05/07/obamas-non-profit-on-same-dubious-path-first-blazed-by-clinton-foundation/

7. https://archive.org/stream/RulesForRadicals/RulesForRadicals_djvu.txt

8. https://en.wikipedia.org/wiki/Saul_Alinsky

9. https://www.washingtonpost.com/news/the-fix/wp/2016/07/20/hillary-clinton-saul-alinsky-and-lucifer-explained/?utm_term=.85ec7ced65cc

10. http://nypost.com/2017/02/11/
    how-obama-is-scheming-to-sabotage-trumps-presidency/

11. http://www.washingtontimes.com/news/2017/feb/15/
    shadow-presidency-against-trump-has-news-media-obs/

12. http://freebeacon.com/issues/
    soros-funded-anti-trump-network-has-acorn-ties/

13. http://freebeacon.com/national-security/
    anti-trump-leak-campaign-damaging-u-s-allied-operations/

14. http://www.wnd.com/2017/06/
    new-warning-resistance-turning-into-american-coup/

15. http://www.rightwingwatch.org/post/e-w-jackson-the-attempted-coup-
    detat-against-trump-is-a-sign-of-the-last-days/

16. http://www.breitbart.com/radio/2017/03/03/robert-barnes-obama-chose-
    dangerous-precarious-path-encouraging-de-facto-coup-attempt-elements-
    deep-state/

17. https://shorensteincenter.org/news-coverage-donald-trumps-first-100-days/

18. http://www.nationalreview.com/article/449594/fifth-american-war-blue-
    state-vs-red-elites-vs-populists-egalitarianism-vs-liberty

19. http://www.newsmax.com/Newsfront/
    war-liberals-resist-Big-Agenda/2017/03/07/id/777516/

20. http://www.thegatewaypundit.com/2017/06/presidential-historian-deep-
    state-attempting-coup-detat-us-administration-video/

21. https://sputniknews.com/analysis/201502021017649839/

22. https://en.wikipedia.org/wiki/Cultural_hegemony

23. http://www.breitbart.com/california/2016/11/28/
    trump-torpedoing-globalism-fall-world-socialism-2-0/

24. http://www.nationalreview.com/article/445882/
    socialism-polls-indicates-its-alarming-rise-public-opinion

25. Mendenhall, Richard A., "Where the Heart is," Realtor Mag, (National
    Association of Realtors), Feb. 2001, http://realtormag.realtor.org/
    news-and-commentary/nar-president/article/2001/02/where-heart.

26. Farah, Joseph, "Meet the Real Walter Cronkite: 'Most trusted' newsman

pushed radical agenda." WND.com, 7-18-2009, http://www.wnd.com/200 9/07/104399/#ybYg7vLB8efQPVrt.99.

27. By Alex Hunt & Brian Wheeler. "Brexit: All you need to know about the UK leaving the EU," BBC News, 30 March 2017, http://www.bbc.com/ news/uk-politics-32810887.

28. Ibid.

29. Ibid.

30. SkyNews. "Supreme Court's Brexit ruling—how day unfolded: The Brexit Secretary faces MPs after the country's top judges rule against the Government over the triggering of Article 50," Jan. 24, 2017, http://news.sky.com/ story/live-pm-must-seek-mps8217-approval-to-trigger-brexit-10740738.

31. Wolf, Stephen. "Republicans now dominate state government, with 32 legislatures and 33 governors," Daily Kos, Nov. 24, 2016, http://www.dai-lykos.com/story/2016/11/14/1598918/-Republicans-now-dominate-state-government-with-32-legislatures-and-33-governors.

32. Unruh, Bob. "Congressional Plan Would Take U.S. Out of U.N.: Proposal cancels any financial support, bans military from serving under its command," WND.com, 1-24-17, http://www.wnd.com/2017/01/ congress-eyes-plan-to-take-u-s-out-of-u-n.

33. Mills, Curt. "EU Holds Emergency Meeting About Trump," U.S. News, Nov. 14, 2016, http://www.usnews.com/news/world/articles/2016-11-14/ europe-holds-emergency-meeting-about-donald-trump.

34. Nastranis, J. "UN to Step Up Implementation of 2030 Development Agenda," In Depth News, http://www.indepthnews.net/index.php/global-governance/un-insider/777-un-to-step-up-implementation-of-2030-devel-opment-agenda.

35. Gallups, Carl, *When the Lion Roars: Understanding the Implications of Ancient Prophecies for our Time,* WND Books—Washington D.C., October 2016, pp. 94–110.

36. Editor, John Mecklin. "2017 Doomsday Clock," Bulletin of the Atomic Scientists, http://thebulletin.org/sites/default/files/Final%202017%20 Clock%20Statement.pdf.

37. Ibid.

38. Mallock, Daniel. "Donald Trump and the Death of Utopianism," American Thinker, Jan. 11, 2017, http://www.americanthinker.com/articles/2017/01/donald_trump_and_the_death_of_utopianism.html

39. Kasssam, Raheem. "Britain's Theresa May in U.S.: Islam is Peaceful, Globalism Good, Climate Change a Priority," Breitbart, Jan. 26, 2017, http://www.breitbart.com/london/2017/01/26/britains-theresa-may-in-u-s-uses-daesh-instead-of-islamic-state-proclaims-belief-in-liberty-despite-expanding-uk-surveillance-state/

40. Dr. Lambert, Rivkah. "Do Putin's Actions in Syria Fulfill the Prophecy of Ezekiel Regarding Gog and Magog?" Breaking News Israel, Oct. 14, 2015, https://www.breakingisraelnews.com/51078/do-putins-actions-in-syria-fulfill-the-prophecy-of-ezekiel-regarding-gog-and-magog-middle-east/#Hoxt6C6XorsLUEOP.97

41. Bert, Didier. "Twenty Signs the Third World War Has Already Begun," MSN.com, 12-17-16, http://www.msn.com/en-gb/news/photos/twenty-signs-the-third-world-war-has-already-begun/ss-BBwdBDR#image=2.

42. "Mikhail Gorbachev: 'It All Looks As if the World Is Preparing for War'," Time.com, 1-26-17, http://time.com/4645442/gorbachev-putin-trump/.

43. Hohmann, Leo, "Stealth Invasion: Muslim Conquest Through Immigration and Resettlement Jihad," WND Books (January 24, 2017).

44. O'Conner, Tom. "Turkey Building New Ottoman Empire? Erdogan Vows to Fight Terrorism at Home And Abroad," International Business Times, 10-19-16, http://www.ibtimes.com/turkey-building-new-ottoman-empire-erdogan-vows-fight-terrorism-home-abroad-2434085.

45. Gallups, Carl, Be Thou Prepared: Equipping the Church for Persecution and Times of Trouble, WND Books (September 29, 2015), pp. 86–87.

46. Richardson, Hayley. "Biological Babies for Same-Sex Parents a Possibility after Stem Cell Breakthrough," Newsweek, 2-25-15, http://www.newsweek.com/biological-babies-same-sex-parents-possibility-after-stem-cell-breakthrough-309453.

47. Brittain, Vera. "Testament of Youth: An Autobiographical Study of the Years 1900-1925," http://www.sjsu.edu/people/julie.sparks/courses/Engl-117B-spr2016/Vera%20Brittain%20selections--reading%20assgt%20week%202.pdf.

48. Elgot, Jessica, "Stephen Hawking: Jeremy Corbyn is a disaster for Labour" The Guardian, March 7, 2107, https://www.theguardian.com/politics/2017/mar/07/stephen-hawking-jeremy-corbyn-disastrous-labour-resign.

49. Hensch, Mark. "Bill Clinton: Nationalism taking us to 'the edge of our destruction'," The Hill, 3-9-17, http://thehill.com/homenews/news/323259-bill-clinton-nationalism-the-edge-of-our-destruction.

50. Donald Trump, Inaugural Address, White House website, January 20, 2017. Accessed January 22, 2017, https://www.whitehouse.gov/inaugural-address

51. Ronald Reagan, Thinkexist.com, accessed January 20, 2017, http://thinkexist.com/quotation/-i_know_it-s_hard_when_you-re_up_to_your_armpits/338218.html

52. Inside GOV by Graphiq. Accessed January 20, 2017. http://us-presidents.insidegov.com/q/13/9699/What-were-President-Ronald-Reagan-s-accomplishments

53. Complete National Film Registry List, Library of Congress, accessed January 20, 2017. https://www.loc.gov/programs/national-film-preservation-board/film-registry/complete-national-film-registry-listing/

54. John Kelly, "What's with all Trump's talk about 'Draining the Swamp'?", Slate, October 26, 2016, http://www.slate.com/blogs/lexicon_valley/2016/10/26/why_do_trump_and_his_supports_keep_talking_about_draining_the_swamp.html

55. "Americans' Confidence in Institutions Stays Low," Gallup, June 13, 2016, accessed January 20, 2017, http://www.google.com/url?sa=t&rct=j&q=&esrc=s&source=web&cd=1&ved=0ahUKEwjqntrw7c7RAhUGbSYKHXW3Cd4QFggaMAA&url=http%3A%2F%2Fwww.gallup.com%2Fpoll%2F192581%2Famericans-confidence-institutions-stays-low.aspx&usg=AFQjCNFq8YbUv9LT4R_MyERl3fxc5rQMiw&bvm=bv.144224172,d.eWE

56. "Rumsfeld: U.S. must 'drain the swamp'", *CNN.Com*, September 19, 2001. Accessed January 20, 2017. http://edition.cnn.com/2001/US/09/18/ret.defense.rumsfeld/

57. "A History of Draining the Swamp," *Roll Call*, January 20, 2017. Accessed January 20, 2017. http://www.rollcall.com/news/politics/history-of-draining-the-swamp

58. Ibid.

59. Ibid.

60. Pierre Charles L'Enfant, Wikipedia, accessed January 20, 2017, https://en.wikipedia.org/wiki/Pierre_Charles_L'Enfant

61. "DC Mythbusting: Built on a Swamp?," WELOVEDC, July 7, 2009, accessed January 20, 2017, http://www.welovedc.com/2009/07/07/dc-mythbusting-built-on-a-swamp/

62. https://www.aoc.gov/facts/capitol-hill

63. https://www.aoc.gov/facts/capitol-hill

64. "Lincoln Memorial Topo Map in District of Columbia County," Topozone.com, accessed January 20, 2017. http://www.topozone.com/district-of-columbia/district-of-columbia-dc/park/lincoln-memorial/

65. "Thomas Jefferson Memorial Topo Map in District of Columbia County," Topozone.com, accessed January 20, 2017, http://www.topozone.com/district-of-columbia/district-of-columbia-dc/park/thomas-jefferson-memorial/

66. Thomas E. Bahl, "Wetlands Loss Since the Revolution," U.S. Fish and Wildlife Service, National Wetlands Newsletter, November-December 1990, pp. 16–17, accessed January 20, 2017. https://www.fws.gov/wetlands/Documents%5CWetlands-Loss-Since-the-Revolution.pdf

67. Linda Qiu, "Yes, Donald Trump donated $100,000 to the Clinton Foundation," PunditFact, August 28, 2016. Accessed January 20, 2016, http://www.politifact.com/punditfact/statements/2016/aug/28/david-plouffe/yes-donald-trump-donated-100000-clinton-foundation/

68. "IRS finally reveals list of tea party groups targeted for extra scrutiny," Washington Times, June 5, 2016. Accessed January 02,

2016, http://www.washingtontimes.com/news/2016/jun/5/ irs-reveals-list-of-tea-party-groups-targeted-for-/

69. Ibid.

70. "Judicial Watch: Justice Department Documents Reveal Widespread Use of Fast and Furious Weapons by Major Mexican Drug Cartels—Linked to at least 69 Killings," Judicial Watch, May 26, 2016. Accessed January 20, 2017, http://www.judicialwatch.org/press-room/press-releases/judicial-watch-justice-department-documents-reveal-widespread-use-fast-furious-weapons-major-mexican-drug-cartels-linked-least-69-killings/

71. Eli Watkins, "Bill Clinton meeting causes headaches for Hillary," *CNN*, June 30, 2016, accessed January 20, 2017, http://www.cnn.com/2016/06/29/politics/bill-clinton-loretta-lynch/

72. Sonali Prasad et al, "Obama's dirty secret: the fossil fuel projects the US littered around the world, *The Guardian*, December 1, 2016. Accessed January 20, 2017. https://www.theguardian.com/environment/2016/dec/01/obama-fossil-fuels-us-export-import-bank-energy-projects

73. Carol Leonnig et al, "Obama's focus on visiting clean-tech companies raises questions," Washington Post, June 25, 2011. Accessed January 20, 2017. https://www.washingtonpost.com/politics/obamas-focus-on-visiting-clean-tech-companies-raises-questions/2011/06/24/AGSFu9kH_story.html?utm_term=.2c38a1b603b0

74. Ashe Schow, "President Obama's Taxpayer-Backed Green Energy Failures," The Daily Signal, October 18, 2012. Accessed January 20, 2016, http://dailysignal.com/2012/10/18/president-obamas-taxpayer-backed-green-energy-failures/

75. As cited in Alan West, "NEW REPORT on Obama corruption has even liberals stunned," August 31, 2016. Accessed January 20, 2016, http://www.allenbwest.com/allen/shake-down

76. As cited in Alan West, "NEW REPORT on Obama corruption has even liberals stunned," August 31, 2016. Accessed January 20, 2016, http://www.allenbwest.com/allen/shake-down

77. Ibid.

78. Top Lobbying Firms, opensecrets.org. Accessed January 20, 2017. https://www.opensecrets.org/lobby/top.php?showYear=2015&indexType=l

79. "Podesta files: Top 10 revelations from leaked Clinton campaign emails," RT, October 13, 2016. Accessed January 20, 2017, https://www.rt.com/usa/362590-podesta-emails-wikileaks-clinton/

80. Paul Watson, "Spirit Cooking": Clinton campaign chairman practices bizarre occult ritual," Infowars, November 4, 2016. Accessed January 20, 2017, http://www.infowars.com/spirit-cooking-clinton-campaign-chairman-invited-to-bizarre-satanic-performance/

81. "Lernaean Hydra," Greek Mythology Accessed January 2017, http://www.greekmythology.com/Myths/Monsters/Lernaean_Hydra/lernaean_hydra.html

82. Frank Ostroff, "Change Management in Government, *Harvard Business Review*, May 2006. Accessed January 20, 2017, https://hbr.org/2006/05/change-management-in-government

83. Paul Bedard, "Boom: Trump eyes 10% spending cuts, 20% slash of federal workers," *Washington Examiner*, accessed January 17, 2017, http://www.washingtonexaminer.com/boom-trump-eyes-10-spending-cuts-20-slash-of-federal-workers/article/2612037

84. Stephen Dinan, "Federal workers hit record number, but growth slows under Obama," Washington Times, February 9, 2016, accessed January 20, 2017, http://www.washingtontimes.com/news/2016/feb/9/federal-workers-hit-record-number-but-growth-slows/

85. "U.S. Federal Government Size, as Measured by Spending, by President / Political Party," Truthful Politics, accessed January 20, 2017, http://www.truthfulpolitics.com/http:/truthfulpolitics.com/comments/u-s-federal-government-size-as-measured-by-spending-by-president-political-party/?utm_source=twitter&utm_medium=friendly%2Blinks&utm_campaign=twitter%2Bfl%2Bplugin

86. "The Spending Outlook," Chapter 3, The Budget and Economic Outlook: 2016 to 2016, Congressional Budget Office, January 2016. Accessed January 20, 2017. https://www.cbo.gov/sites/default/files/114th-congress-2015-2016/reports/51129/51129-Chapter3.pdf

87. "Updated Budget Projections: 2016 to 2026," Congressional Budget Office, March 24, 2016. Accessed January 20, 2016, https://www.cbo.gov/publication/51384

88. Robert Greenstein et al, "Program Spending Historically Low Outside Social Security and Medicare, Projected to Fall Further," Center on Budget and Policy Priorities, February 24, 2016. Accessed January 20, 2017, http://www.cbpp.org/research/federal-budget/program-spending-historically-low-outside-social-security-and-medicare

89. Federal-State Relations Today: Back to States' Rights?, Federalism, American Government, accessed January 20, 2017, http://www.ushistory.org/gov/3c.asp

90. James L. Gattuso and Diane Katz, "Red Tape Rising 2016: Obama Regs Top $100 Billion Annually," Backgrounder 3127, Heritage Foundation, May 23, 2016, accessed January 20, 2017, http://www.heritage.org/research/reports/2016/05/red-tape-rising-2016-obama-regs-top-100-billion-annually

91. Nicolas Loris, "Four Big Problems with the Obama Administration's Climate Change Regulations," Backgrounder 4454, Heritage Foundation, August 14, 2015, accessed January 20, 2017, http://www.heritage.org/research/reports/2015/08/four-big-problems-with-the-obama-administrations-climate-change-regulations.

92. James L. Gattuso and Diane Katz, "Red Tape Rising 2016: Obama Regs Top $100 Billion Annually," Backgrounder 3127, Heritage Foundation, May 23, 2016, accessed January 20, 2017, http://www.heritage.org/research/reports/2016/05/red-tape-rising-2016-obama-regs-top-100-billion-annually

93. James L. Gattuso and Diane Katz, "Red Tape Rising 2016: Obama Regs Top $100 Billion Annually," Backgrounder 3127, Heritage Foundation, May 23, 2016. Accessed January 20, 2017, http://www.heritage.org/research/reports/2016/05/red-tape-rising-2016-obama-regs-top-100-billion-annually

94. Tara O'Neill Hayes, "The Regulatory Burden of the Affordable Care Act," The American Action Forum, January 27, 2016, accessed January 20, 2017, https://www.americanactionforum.org/weekly-checkup/the-regulatory-burden-of-the-affordable-care-act/#ixzz4WJtgFRug

95. James L. Gattuso and Diane Katz, "Red Tape Rising 2016: Obama Regs Top $100 Billion Annually," Backgrounder 3127, Heritage Foundation, May 23, 2016, accessed January 20, 2017, http://www.heritage.org/research/reports/2016/05/red-tape-rising-2016-obama-regs-top-100-billion-annually

96. Dan Mitchell, "A Libertarian Quandary: Should Federal Bureaucracies Be Moved to the Hinterland?," International Liberty, December 12, 2016, accessed January 20, 2016, https://danieljmitchell.wordpress.com/2016/12/09/a-libertarian-quandary-should-federal-bureaucracies-be-moved-to-the-hinterland/

97. Kevin Hassett, "Thinking about the Unthinkable," *National Review*, August 29, 2016, accessed January 20, 2017, http://www.aei.org/publication/thinking-about-the-unthinkable/

98. Steven Price, "Move the federal government out of Washington," CNN, September 6, 2016, accessed January 20, 2017, http://www.cnn.com/2016/09/06/opinions/government-departments-should-be-spread-out-price/

99. Isaac Arnsdorf et al, "Will 'drain the swamp' be Trump's first broken promise?," Politico, December 22, 2016, accessed January 20, 2017, http://www.politico.com/story/2016/12/trump-drain-swamp-promise-232938

100. Ibid.

101. Ibid.

102. Ibid.

103. "Read the Sermon Donald Trump Heard Before Becoming President, Time, January 20, 2017, accessed January 22, 2017, http://time.com/4641208/donald-trump-robert-jeffress-st-john-episcopal-inauguration/?xid=fbshare

104. Psalm 50:15

105. http://www.charismanews.com/politics/issues/62119-curt-landry-donald-trump-and-the-significance-of-5777

106. https://www.breakingisraelnews.com/67748/biblical-numerology-predicts-trump-will-usher-messiah/#YpPoq8q60l05J0SD.97

107. http://www.charismanews.com/politics/elections/61031-rabbi-predicts-trump-will-win-and-usher-in-the-second-coming

108. http://forward.com/news/372256/for-jewish-mystics-trumps-israel-visit-part-of-messianic-process/

109. http://www.israelnationalnews.com/News/News.aspx/220289

110. http://forward.com/news/354530/why-these-jewish-mystics-think-god-helped-trump-win/

111. http://www.rightwingwatch.org/post/end-times-pastor-donald-trump-could-be-the-messiah-or-his-forerunner/

112. https://www.insidescience.org/news/scientists-predict-new-star-will-appear-2022

113. "Islamic 'Messiah' al-Mahdi to Return by 2016, Followed By Jesus? Islamic 'Messiah' al-Mahdi to Return by 2016, Followed By Jesus?" *Israel, Islam and the End Times* May 19, 2015, http://www.israelislamandendtimes.com/islamic-messiah-al-mahdi-to-return-by-2016-followed-by-jesus/, accessed January 3, 2016.

114. http://mychristiandaily.com/mcd/prominent-rabbi-warns-friends-not-to-leave-israel-messiah-is-here-with-us-already/

115. J. R. Church, "The 800-Year-Old Prophecy of Rabbi Judah Ben Samuel," (*Prophecy in the News Magazine*, February 2010), 14.

116. Clarence Goen, "Jonathan Edwards: A New Departure in Eschatology" (*Church History 28*, 1 Mr 1959), 29. 25–40.

117. Jonathan Edwards, *The Works of Jonathan Edwards, Volume 1* (Utgivare; Logos Bible Software), 594.

118 Jonathan Edwards, *The Works of Jonathan Edwards, Volume 1*, PUBLIC DOMAIN, (Utgivare; Logos Bible Software), chapter XV, page c.

119. https://www.irishcentral.com/roots/history/st-malachy-predicted-pope-benedicts-successor-will-be-last-pope-190715001-237789421

120. http://www.catholicnewsagency.com/news/is-francis-the-last-pope-a-rare-interview-with-archbishop-gnswein-46598/

121. Ibid

122. http://www.crossmap.com/news/canon-lawyers-and-theologians-to-hold-conference-on-deposing-the-pope-31709

123. http://www.catholictradition.org/francis-prophecies.htm

124. https://www.lifesitenews.com/news/only-pope-francis-can-end-the-apostasy-his-ambiguous-and-erroneous-words-ha

125. http://www.reuters.com/article/us-pope-mueller-idUSKBN19M3GH?il=0

126. https://colombiareports.com/pope-francis-paving-way-antichrist/

127. https://www.lifesitenews.com/news/pope-benedict-church-is-on-the-verge-of-capsizing

128. http://www.thetablet.co.uk/news/7367/0/vatican-investigates-catholic-group-after-exorcism-claim-that-francis-is-devil-s-man

129. https://www.lifesitenews.com/blogs/the-main-reason-for-the-hate-against-donald-trump

130. https://www.thenewamerican.com/usnews/foreign-policy/item/25256-catholics-ask-trump-to-probe-soros-obama-clinton-conspiracy-at-vatican

131. http://remnantnewspaper.com/web/index.php/articles/item/3001-did-vatican-attempt-to-influence-u-s-election-catholics-ask-trump-administration-to-investigate

132. https://www.thenewamerican.com/culture/faith-and-morals/item/24289-clinton-campaign-s-anti-catholic-emails-will-catholic-voters-react

133. http://catholictruthblog.com/2013/12/30/was-pope-francis-canonically-elected/

134. Rev. Herman Bernard Kramer, The Book of Destiny (Belleville, IL: Buechler Publishing Company, 1955), 277.

135. http://www.huffingtonpost.com/sebastien-maillard/pope-francis-remain-pope_b_9439638.html

136. Sue Bradley, "The Fourth Turning: The Protocols and The Gray Champion," The Sue Bradley Archives, last accessed May 25, 2013, http://suebradleyarchives.com/have-we-entered-the-fourth-turning/.

137. Ibid.

138. Ibid.

139. Ibid.

140. Ibid.

141. Ibid.

142. http://www.independent.co.uk/news/world/americas/steve-bannon-apocalypse-third-world-war-coming-white-house-donald-trump-historian-claim-film-david-a7570631.html

143. http://www.huffingtonpost.com/entry/steve-bannon-apocalypse_us_5898f02ee4b040613138a951?

144. *The Fourth Turning: An American Prophecy—What the Cycles of History Tell Us About America's Next Rendezvous with Destiny*, Broadway Books; Reprint edition (December 29, 1997), 277

145. http://www.telegraph.co.uk/business/2017/06/25/next-global-financial-crisis-hit-vengeance-warns-bis/

146. http://stockboardasset.com/insights-and-research/fourth-turning-s%E2%80%8Bummer-rage-tot%E2%80%8Bal-eclipse-deep-st%E2%80%8Bate/

147. Bruce Lincoln, "The Rhetoric of Bush and Bin Laden," excerpt from Holy Terrors, posted online at University of Chicago Library Digital Collections (http://fathom.lib.uchicago.edu/1/777777190152/).

148. David Ovason, *The Secret Architecture of Our Nation's Capital: The Masons and the Building of Washington DC* (New York: HarperCollins, 2000), 71.

149. Ibid., 361.

150. Julia Duin, "Ergo, We're Virgo," *Questia*, last accessed May 10, 2017, https://www.questia.com/magazine/1G1-66241134/ergo-we-re-virgo.

151. George W. Bush, "President Bush's Acceptance Speech to the Republican National Convention," September 2, 2004, *Washington Post*, last accessed May 10, 2017, http://www.washingtonpost.com/wp-dyn/articles/A57466-2004Sep2.html.

152. H. P. Lovecraft, *Necronomicon: Ye Book of the Laws of the Dead*, translated by Dr. John Dee in 1562. Viewable at the following link, accessed May 10, 2017, https://greyelf.bizland.com/blackletternecro.html.

153. Ibid.; emphasis added.

154. Foster Bailey, *The Spirit of Freemasonry*, Third and Revised Edition (New York: Lucis Press, 1979), 59.

155. https://sonoma-dspace.calstate.edu/bitstream/handle/10211.3/143729/phillips_relative.pdf?sequence=1

156. Spiritual Warfare: The Invisible Invasion, 103.
157. https://books.google.com/books?id=MTQqAQAAMAAJ&pg=PA444&lpg=PA444&dq=The+Secret+Doctrine+%E2%80%9CIt+is+in+America+that+the+transformation+will+take+place&source=bl&ots=7rYBXSmZSv&sig=aWwohFNr1mAAVTx2bYuJLjNebhg&hl=en&sa=X&ved=0ahUKEwightCQ7-jUAhXDx4MKHcVZA9kQ6AEIKjAB#v=onepage&q=The%20Secret%20Doctrine%20%E2%80%9CIt%20is%20in%20America%20that%20the%20transformation%20will%20take%20place&f=false
158. http://www.npr.org/templates/story/story.php?storyId=4460172
159. http://canadafreepress.com/2005/cover062805.htm
160. http://www.breitbart.com/2016-presidential-race/2016/04/18/hillary-clinton-believe-spirits/
161. http://www.cnsnews.com/news/article/bill-eleanor-roosevelt-passed-me-message-through-hillary-week
162. https://www.youtube.com/watch?v=SS7uSmG-R34
163. http://time.com/4308369/hillary-clinton-john-podesta/
164. http://www.dailymail.co.uk/tvshowbiz/article-2380831/Lady-Gaga-nonchalant-as-eats-fake-blood-womans-naked-body-art-show.html
165. https://www.sott.net/article/334002-Progressive-liberal-values-Tony-Podestas-creepy-taste-in-art-the-creepy-people-he-hangs-out-with-and-Pizzagate
166. Ibid.
167. https://www.yahoo.com/news/federal-records-hastert-released-prison-minnesota-125049060.html
168. http://www.npr.org/sections/thetwo-way/2017/03/26/521545788/conspiracy-theorist-alex-jones-apologizes-for-promoting-pizzagate
169. https://www.washingtonpost.com/video/politics/trump-promises-to-solve-human-trafficking-epidemic-in-white-house-meeting/2017/02/23/e6baf42e-fa08-11e6-aa1e-5f735ee31334_video.html
170. http://thefreethoughtproject.com/fmr-congresswoman-child-trafficking-trump-top/
171. https://www.yahoo.com/news/blogs/upshot/pentagon-declined-investigate-hundreds-purchases-child-pornography.html

172. http://www.collective-evolution.com/2017/04/29/dutch-financial-whistle-blower-admits-he-was-forced-to-sacrifice-children-at-elite-parties/

173. http://thefreethoughtproject.com/hollywood-insider-speaks-out-claims-global-pedophile-ring-controls-hollywood/

174. http://weekinweird.com/2016/11/22/adventures-in-demonology-vincent-price-summoning-demons/

175. https://books.google.com/books?id=0-dIAgAAQBAJ&pg=PA2
39&lpg=PA239&dq=I+rejoice+to+see+our+culture+being+tak
en+over+by+joyful+young+messiahs+who+dispel+our+fears+an
d+charm+us+back+into+the+pagan+dance%E2%80%99&sou
rce=bl&ots=039r4vp4_y&sig=ylyM2xottyhv1mQkTMyFK-i_
TuI&hl=en&sa=X&ved=0ahUKEwiK9Y6W4-3UAhVi04MKHbh_
DoAQ6AEIJDAA#v=onepage&q=I%20rejoice%20to%20see%20
our%20culture%20being%20taken%20over%20by%20joyful%20
young%20messiahs%20who%20dispel%20our%20fears%20
and%20charm%20us%20back%20into%20the%20pagan%20
dance%E2%80%99&f=false

176. http://theapologeticsgroup.com/wp-content/uploads/2012/06/HB2-SCRIPT.pdf

177. Graham Hancock, *Supernatural: Meetings with the Ancient Teachers of Mankind*, rev. ed. (New York: Disinformation Co., 2007) 270.

178. Strassman, DMT, xvii.

179. David Deutsch, "Quantum Theory, the Church-Turing Principle and the Universal Quantum Computer," Proceedings of the Royal Society A 400, 1818 (July 1985) 97–117.

180. Graham Hancock, *Supernatural: Meetings with the Ancient Teachers of Mankind*, rev. ed. (New York: Disinformation Co., 2007) 101–2.

181. Strassman, *DMT,* 55.

182. Brad Steiger; Sherry Steiger, Real Encounters, Different Dimensions and Otherworldly Beings (Visible Ink Press, 2013) Kindle Edition, 139–141.

183. John Greer, The New Encyclopedia of the Occult, 9781567183368.

184. "Babalon" in *Thelemapedia,* http://www.thelemapedia.org/index.php/

Babalon#Babalon_as_the_Gateway_to_the_City_of_Pyramids, accessed February 22, 20150.

185. "Babalon as the Gateway to the City of Pyramids," *Thelemapedia* http://www.thelemapedia.org/index.php/Babalon#Babalon_as_the_Gateway_to_the_City_of_Pyramids (accessed February 22, 2015).

186. "City of the Pyramids," Thelemapedia, http://www.thelemapedia.org/index.php/City_of_the_Pyramids (accessed February 22, 2015).

187. "The Scarlet Woman Aspect" in Babalon, Thelemapedia http://www.thelemapedia.org/index.php/Babalon#Individual_Scarlet_Women (accessed February 22, 2015).

188. Hugh B. Urban, *Magia Sexualis: Sex, Magic, and Liberation in Modern Western Esotericism* (Berkeley, CA: University of California Press, 2006) 135–37.

189. George Pendle, Strange Angel: The Otherworldly Life of Rocket Scientist John Whiteside Parsons, 266.

190. Hillary Rodham Clinton (October 26, 1947), a potential 2016 presidential candidate, https://www.readyforhillary.com/splash/hillary.

191. http://www.sacred-texts.com/oto/lib49.htm

192. https://en.wikipedia.org/wiki/Hilary_(name)

193. https://www.nytimes.com/2016/05/11/us/politics/hillary-clinton-aliens.html

194. https://wikileaks.org/podesta-emails/emailid/1802

195. https://en.wikipedia.org/wiki/Xenu

196. Martin Short, *Inside the Brotherhood: Explosive Secrets of the Freemasons* (UK: HarperCollins, 1995), 122.

197. Manly P. Hall, *The Lost Keys of Freemasonry*, 48.

198. Manly P. Hall, *Secret Destiny of America* (Penguin Group, 2008), chapter 18.

199. http://www.charismanews.com/opinion/the-flaming-herald/57571-william-branham-s-7-spectacular-end-times-visions

200. http://www.christianpost.com/news/ted-cruz-pastors-congress-prayer-meeting-cut-satan-power-capitol-172040/

201. http://www.christianpost.com/news/god-delivered-us-from-spirit-of-witch-craft-in-the-oval-office-through-trump-says-christian-leader-174746/

202. http://www.latimes.com/opinion/op-ed/la-oe-wagman-put-a-spell-on-donald-trump-20170523-story.html

203. http://www.pewresearch.org/2017/01/10/how-america-changed-during-barack-obamas-presidency/?utm_source=Pew+Research+Center&utm_campaign=90fcebcb46-EMAIL_CAMPAIGN_2017_01_11&utm

204. http://www.charismanews.com/politics/opinion/62396-fundamentally-transformed-how-atheism-exploded-in-the-obama-era

205. http://www.cnn.com/2017/06/08/politics/donald-trump-under-seige-faith-freedom/index.html

206. http://www.latimes.com/opinion/op-ed/la-oe-wagman-put-a-spell-on-donald-trump-20170523-story.html

207. Lachman, 97–98.

208. https://www.breakingisraelnews.com/88858/rabbi-warns-pagan-arch-end-days-gateway-will-walk/#QYGmpCdvviv2cV0v.97

209. http://www.wnd.com/2016/09/the-harbinger-of-baal-appears-in-nyc/#hgY3VIxzqBoyPWQi.99

210. https://www.breakingisraelnews.com/88858/rabbi-warns-pagan-arch-end-days-gateway-will-walk/

211. https://www.breakingisraelnews.com/83618/mystic-rabbi-warns-black-magic-making-comeback/

212. Thomas Paine, *The Age of Reason; Being an Investigation of True and Fabulous Theology* (Borrois: Paris, 1794), Part 1, Section 1, as quoted by *US History Online*, last accessed April 13, 2017, http://www.ushistory.org/paine/reason/reason1.htm.

213. Thomas Paine, *Age of Reason*, Part 1, Section 5, http://www.ushistory.org/paine/reason/reason5.htm.

214. Thomas Paine, *Age of Reason*, Part 2, Section 20, http://www.ushistory.org/paine/reason/reason36.htm.

215. Thomas Paine, *Age of Reason*, Part 2, Section 14, http://www.ushistory.org/paine/reason/reason30.htm.

216. David L. Holmes, *The Faiths of the Founding Fathers* (Oxford University Press, New York, NY; Kindle Edition: 2006), 41; emphasis added.

217. "Thomas Jefferson to John Adams, 12 October 1813," *National Archives*, last accessed April 17, 2017, https://founders.archives.gov/documents/Jefferson/03-06-02-0431.

218. "From Thomas Jefferson to Alexander Smyth, 17 January 1825," *National Archives*, last accessed April 17, 2017, https://founders.archives.gov/documents/Jefferson/98-01-02-4882.

219. "From Thomas Jefferson to William Short, 31 October 1819," *National Archives*, last accessed April 17, 2017, https://founders.archives.gov/documents/Jefferson/98-01-02-0850.

220. Julius F. Sachse, "The Masonic Chronology of Benjamin Franklin," *Historical Society of Pennsylvania*, last accessed April 17, 2017, https://www.jstor.org/stable/20085334?seq=1#page_scan_tab_contents, 238.

221. Ibid.

222. Ibid., 239.

223. Ibid., 238.

224. Ibid.

225. Ibid., 240.

226. "The Hellfire Club," *Hellfire Caves Online*, last accessed April 18, 2017, http://www.hellfirecaves.co.uk/history/hellfire-club/; emphasis added.

227. Ibid; emphasis added.

228. Daniel P. Mannix, *The Hellfire Club: The Rise and Fall of a Secret Society* (Ballantine: 1959). Quote taken from the 2015 eNet Press edition, 104; emphasis added.

229. "Benjamin Franklin, the Occult, and the Elite," *The Sunday Times*, February 11, 1998.

230. "Benjamin Franklin," *The Encyclopedia Americana*, Vol. XII (Encyclopedia Americana, 1919), 11.

231. Richard Dawkins, *The God Delusion* (New York: Houghton Mifflin Harcourt, 2006), 43.

232. John E. Remsburg, *Six Historic Americans* (New York: Truth Seeker, 1906), 193.

233. Ibid.

234. *The Literary Digest: Volume 24; No. 22* (New York, NY: Funk & Wagnalls, 1902), 746.

235. "House Resolution 33: Recognizing and Honoring Freemasons," *Information Liberation*, January 16, 2007, last accessed April 20, 2017, http://www.informationliberation.com/?id=19540; emphasis added.

236. Manly P. Hall, *The Secret Teachings of All Ages* (Perennial Press: Kindle edition), locations 13114–13116.

237. "The Ancient and Mystical Order Rosae Crucis," *AMORC*, last accessed April 20, 2017, https://www.rosicrucian.org/history.

238. Ibid., emphasis added.

239. Ibid., emphasis added.

240. Ibid., emphasis added.

241. Ian Taylor, during his interview for *Secret Mysteries of America's Beginnings: Volume 1: The New Atlantis*, DVD series, distributed by Total-Content LLC, executive producer David E. Bay, written and directed by Christian J. Pinto, 1:39:38–1:40:24.

242. Ibid., 1:43:26–1:50:00.

243. Albert Pike, *Morals & Dogma: Scottish Rite in Freemasonry* (Jenkins, Inc., Richmond, VA: 1944), 42; emphasis added.

244. preface (Crane, MO: Defender Publishing, 2013), 14–15.

245. Ibid., 15–16.

246. Manly P. Hall, *The Secret Destiny of America* (Kindle Edition, Barvas Books: 2016), Kindle locations 553–565; emphasis added.

247. Chris Pinto, *Zenith 2016*, 15–16; emphasis added.

248. Stanley Monteith, during his interview for *Secret Mysteries*, 40:11–40:56.

249. Charles Finney, *Why I Left Freemasonry*, a work of antiquity as quoted by *Isaiah 54 Online*, last accessed April 26, 2017, http://www.isaiah54.org/finney.htm.

250. Ibid.; italics added, all-caps original.

251. Dr. J. W. S. Mitchell, *History of Free-masonry, and Masonic Digest*, as quoted by: A. P. Bentley, *History of the Abduction of William Morgan, and*

the Anti-Masonic Excitement of 1826–30 (Van Cise & Throop: Mt. Pleasant, Iowa, 1874), 26.

252. Thomas Horn and Steve Quayle, *Unearthing the Lost World of the Cloudeaters* (Defender Publishing: Crane, MO, 2017), 437–438.

253. Azariah T. C. Pierson, *Traditions of Freemasonry and Its Coincidences with the Ancient Mysteries* (Masonic Publishing Company: University of California Press, 1870), 159.

254. Ibid., 240.

255. Daniel Sickels, *The General Ahiman Rezon and the Freemason's Guide* (Masonic Publishing Company: New York, NY, 1871), 195.

256. Ibid., 196.

257. Albert Mackey and Donald Campbell, *A Lexicon of Freemasonry* (C. Griffin, third edition, 1867), 195.

258. Manly P. Hall, *Secret Teachings of All Ages*, locations 6391–6408; emphasis added.

259. Ibid.

260. Ibid.; emphasis added.

261. Arthur Edward Waite, *The Mysteries of Magic* (Kegan Paul, Trench, Trubner & Co.: London, 1897), 68–69; emphasis added.

262. Ibid., 73.

263. Ibid.

264. Ibid., 69; emphasis added.

265. *The Encyclopedia Americana: A Library of Universal Knowledge in Thirty Volumes:* Volume 20, "Obelisk," (Albany, NY: J. B. Lyon Company, 1919), 536–537.

266. "Obelisk," *Online Etymology Dictionary*, last accessed April 27, 2017, http://www.etymonline.com/index.php?allowed_in_frame=0&search=obelisk.

267. Barbara G. Walker, *The Woman's Dictionary of Symbols and Sacred Objects* (San Francisco, CA: Harper & Row Publishers, 1988), 469.

268. Charles G. Berger, *Our Phallic Heritage* (New York: Greenwich Book Publishers, 1966), 60; emphasis added.

269. "Internet," *Dictionary.com*, last accessed November 3, 2016, http://www.dictionary.com/browse/internet?s=t.

270. "Inter-," *Dictionary.com*, last accessed November 3, 2016, http://www.dictionary.com/browse/inter-.

271. "Network," *Dictionary.com*, last accessed November 3, 2016, http://www.dictionary.com/browse/network.

272. Cathy Burns, *Masonic and Occult Symbols Illustrated* (Mt. Carmel, PA: Sharing Publishers, 1998), 341.

273. "Growth of a Young Nation," *U.S. House of Representatives: Office of the Clerk*, last accessed November 4, 2016, http://artandhistory.house.gov/art_artifacts/virtual_tours/splendid_hall/young_nation.aspx.

274. "1964–Present: September 11, 2001, The Capitol Building as a Target," *United States Senate*, last accessed November 4, 2016, http://www.senate.gov/artandhistory/history/minute/Attack.htm.

275. William Henry and Mark Gray, *Freedom's Gate: Lost Symbols in the U.S.* (Hendersonville, TN: Scala Dei, 2009) 3.

276. Ibid., 4.

277. "Sandpit of Royalty," *Extra Bladet* (Copenhagen, January 31, 1999).

278. Manly P. Hall, *Secret Teachings of All Ages*, locations 2215–2217.

279. Arthur Waite, *Mysteries of Magic*, 70–73; emphasis added.

280. Ibid.; emphasis added.

281. William Henry and Mark Gray, *Freedom's Gate*, 3; emphasis added.

282. Manly P. Hall, *Secret Destiny of America*, Kindle locations 553–565.

283. Gary Lachman, *Politics and the Occult: The Left, the Right, and the Radically Unseen* (Wheaton, IL: Theosophical Publishing House, 2008), 39.

284. George W. Bush, "Inaugural Address: January 20, 2005," *The American Presidency Project*, last accessed April 27, 2017, http://www.presidency.ucsb.edu/ws/?pid=58745.

285. http://time.com/4696428/donald-trump-war-state-government/

286. Manly P. Hall, *Secret Teachings of All Ages*, locations 5514–5518; emphasis added.

287. Nicki Scully, Alchemical Healing: A Guide to Spiritual, Physical, and Transformational Medicine (Bear & Company; Rochester: 2003), 321.

288. Ibid., 9–14; emphasis added.

289. "Bald Eagle, US National Emblem," *Bald Eagle Info*, last accessed May 12, 2017, http://www.baldeagleinfo.com/eagle/eagle9.html.

290. Manly P. Hall, *Secret Destiny of America*, Kindle locations 1435–1450.

291. James Davis Carter, *Freemasonry and United States Government: Background, History and Influence to 1846* (The Committee on Masonic Education and Service for the Grand Lodge of Texas A. F. and A. M., Waco, 1955), 119–154. Viewable online at the following link, last accessed May 15, 2017, http://www.mindserpent.com/American_History/organization/mason/freemasonry.html.

292. Manly P. Hall, *Secret Destiny of America*, Kindle locations, 1450–1452.

293. Ibid., 1452–1454.

294. Aleister Crowley, *The Confessions of Aleister Crowley*, 398; book available in full through *Metaphysic Spirit*, last accessed May 15, 2017, http://www.metaphysicspirit.com/books/Confessions%20of%20Aleister%20Crowley.pdf.

295. Manly P. Hall, *Secret Teachings of All Ages*, locations 6391–6408.

296. David Percival, "The All-Seeing Eye: Sacred Origins of a Hijacked Symbol," June 17, 2014, *The Conscious Reporter*, last accessed May 15, 2017, http://consciousreporter.com/conspiracy-against-consciousness/corruption-sacred-symbols-all-seeing-eye/; emphasis added.

297. Manly P. Hall, *Secret Destiny of America*, Kindle locations 1458–1488.

298. Manly P. Hall, *Secret Teachings of All Ages*, Kindle locations 3615–3619.

299. Ibid., 3652–3654; emphasis added.

300. Ibid., 2162–2179; emphasis added.

301. United States Dept. of State, Gaillard Hunt, *The History of the Seal of the United States* (Washington Government Printing Office, 1909), 55.

302. James Davis Carter, *Freemasonry and United States Government*, 119–154. Viewable online at the following link, last accessed May 15, 2017, http://www.mindserpent.com/American_History/organization/mason/freemasonry.html

303. Ethelbert W. Bullinger, *Number in Scripture* (Pleasant Places Press, 2004), 208.

304. Mitch Horowitz, *Occult America: White House Seances, Ouija Circles, Masons, and the Secret Mystic History of Our Nation* (New York, NY: Bantam Books, 2010), 172.

305. John C. Culver and John Hyde, *American Dreamer: The Life and Times of Henry A. Wallace* (W. W. Norton & Company, 2001), 135.

306. Helena Blavatsky, *The Helena Blavatsky Collection: Isis Unveiled, The Secret Doctrine, The Key to Theosophy* (Timeless Wisdom Collection) (Business and Leadership Publishing; Kindle edition), Kindle locations 39444–39467.

307. John C. Culver and John Hyde, *American Dreamer*, 136.

308. Sarah Mimms, "One Is the Loneliest Dollar Bill," January 28, 2014, *The Atlantic*, last accessed May 16, 2017, https://www.theatlantic.com/politics/archive/2014/01/one-is-the-loneliest-dollar-bill/450378/.

309. "How the Great Seal Got on the One Dollar Bill," *GreatSeal.com*, last accessed May 16, 2017, http://www.greatseal.com/dollar/hawfdr.html.

310. "Geoffrey Rush's Left to Right Theory," March 8, 2015, *The Daily Star* last accessed May 16, 2017, http://www.thedailystar.net/geoffrey-rushs-left-to-right-theory-19575.

311. Mitch Horowitz, *Occult America*, 174.

312. Frederick S. Voss, *The Smithsonian Treasury: Presidents* (Random House Value Publishing, 1991), 72.

313. Henry A. Wallace, *Statesmanship and Religion* (New York, NY: Round Table, 1934), 78–79.

314. Chris Pinto, *Zenith 2016*, Introduction.

315. John C. Culver and John Hyde, *American Dreamer*, 134.

316. William Henry, Cloak of the Illuminati: Secrets, Transformations, Crossing the Stargate (Kempton, IL: Adventures Unlimited, 2003), 13.

317. Virgil, *Eclogue IV*, written in 37 BCE. Available online at the following link, last accessed May 17, 2017, http://classics.mit.edu/Virgil/eclogue.4.iv.html.

318. Peter Goodgame, *The Giza Discovery, Part Nine: The Mighty One*, last accessed May 17, 2017, http://www.redmoonrising.com/Giza/Asshur9.htm.

319. *Zenith 2016: Did Something Begin in the Year 2012 that will Reach its Zenith in 2016?* 2013, Defender Publishing, Crane, Missouri, 139–140

320. http://www.prophecynewswatch.com/article.cfm?recent_news_id=1359

321. Jamie Buckingham, *Charisma & Christian Life* (January 1990): 69.

322. Revelation 12:1, 5 (ESV).

323. Ephesians 1:19-23 (ESV), emphasis added.

324. Hebrews 2:7-8 (ESV), emphasis added.

325. 1 Corinthians 15:24-27 (ESV), emphasis added.

326. "The true cost of the bank bailout," PBS.org, September 3, 2010, http://www.pbs.org/wnet/need-to-know/economy/the-true-cost-of-the-bank-bailout/3309/ (accessed 5/29/17).

327. "Tax Reform That Will Make America Great Again," p. 2, https://assets.donaldjtrump.com/trump-tax-reform.pdf (accessed 5/27/17).

328. "Tax Reform That Will Make America Great Again," p. 2, https://assets.donaldjtrump.com/trump-tax-reform.pdf (accessed 5/27/17).

329. Kimberly Amadeo, "Savings and Loans Crisis Explained: How Congress Created the Greatest Bank Collapse Since the Depression," *The Balance*, April 18, 2017, https://www.thebalance.com/savings-and-loans-crisis-causes-cost-3306035 (accessed 5/29/17).

330. "Not Spreading the Wealth," *The Washington Post*, June 18, 2011, http://www.washingtonpost.com/wp-srv/special/business/income-inequality/ (accessed 5/29/17).

331. Martin Neil Baily and Barry P. Bosworth, "US Manufacturing: Understanding Its Past and Its Potential Future," *Journal of Economic Perspectives*, Volume 28, Number 1 (Winter 2014), p. 4.

332. Matt Scully, "U.S. Subprime Auto Loan Losses Reach Highest Level Since the Financial Crisis," March 10, 2017, bloomberg.com, https://www.bloomberg.com/news/articles/2017-03-10/u-s-subprime-auto-loan-losses-reach-highest-level-since-crisis (accessed 5/27/17).

333. Data from Bureau of Labor Statistics, https://data.bls.gov/ (accessed 5/28/17).

334. Data from Bureau of Labor Statistics, https://data.bls.gov/ (accessed 5/28/17).

335. "Reports, Trends & Statistics," American Trucking Association, http://www.trucking.org/News_and_Information_Reports_Industry_Data.aspx (accessed 5/28/17).

336. John Hayward, "Former GAO Chief: True National Debt $65T, Gov't Spending Has 'Lost Touch with Reality'," *Breitbart News*, Nov. 7, 2015, http://www.breitbart.com/big-government/2015/11/07/former-gao-chief-true-national-debt-65t-govt-spending-lost-touch-reality/ (accessed 5/28/17).

337. Ben Casselman, "Trump's Budget Is Built on a Fantasy," *FiveThirtyEight*, May 23, 2017, https://fivethirtyeight.com/features/trumps-budget-is-built-on-a-fantasy/ (accessed 5/28/17).

338. Paul Joseph Watson, "Gingrich: Establishment Scared of Trump Because He 'Didn't Belong to the Secret Society'," *Infowars*, March 4, 2016, https://www.infowars.com/gingrich-establishment-scared-of-trump-because-he-didnt-belong-to-secret-society/ (accessed 5/28/17).

339. Elizabeth Warren, "The Trans-Pacific Partnership clause everyone should oppose," *The Washington Post*, February 25, 2015, https://www.washingtonpost.com/opinions/kill-the-dispute-settlement-language-in-the-trans-pacific-partnership/2015/02/25/ec7705a2-bd1e-11e4-b274-e5209a3bc9a9_story.html (accessed 5/29/17).

340. See chapter 3 of *The Great Inception: Satan's PSYOPs from Eden to Armageddon*.

341. Russell Moore, "2 Chronicles 7:14 Isn't About American Politics," January 14, 2016, *Russell Moore Online*, last accessed April 18, 2017, http://www.russellmoore.com/2016/01/14/2-chronicles-714-isnt-about-american-politics/.

342. Daphne Delay, "Spiritual Life: Salt of the Earth," *CBN Online*, last accessed April 25, 2017, http://www1.cbn.com/devotions/salt-of-the-earth.

343. Morty Lefkoe, "Do You Have 'Victim Mentality'? What To Do About It," November 17, 2011, *Huffington Post Online*, last accessed April 18, 2017, http://www.huffingtonpost.com/morty-lefkoe/victim-mentality_b_794628.html.

344. *Mirriam-Webster Dictionary Online*, Last Accessed April 18, 2017, https://www.merriam-webster.com/dictionary/humble.

345. Allen Snapp, "If My People Turn Away From Their Wicked Ways," January 24, 2010, *Grace Community Church Online,* Last accessed April 26, 2017, http://www.gracecorning.org/sermons/sermon/2010-01-24/if-my-people-turn-away-from-their-wicked-ways.

346. Ibid.